NEW
GOSPEL
PARALLELS

FOUNDATIONS & FACETS
REFERENCE SERIES

NEW GOSPEL PARALLELS

Robert W. Funk

VOL. 1,2 ◆ MARK

THIRD EDITION

Scholars Version Translation

SANTA ROSA, CALIFORNIA
POLEBRIDGE PRESS
1995

Design and composition: Polebridge Press, Santa Rosa, California

Cover design: Helen Melnis Cherullo

Printing and binding: McNaughton & Gunn, Saline, Michigan

Display type: Univers

Text type: Times Roman

Library of Congress Cataloging-in-Publication Data

Bible. N.T. Gospel. English. Scholars. 1990.
    New Gospel parallels / Robert W. Funk. — Rev. ed.
      p. cm. — (Foundations and facets. New Testament)
    Includes bibliographical references and index.
    Contents: — v. 1,2. Mark.
    ISBN 0–944344–12–7 (v. 1,2) : $21.95. — ISBN 0–944344–13–5 (pbk.
: v. 1,2) : $15.95
    1. Bible. N.T. Gospels—Harmonies, English. I. Funk, Robert
Walter, 1926– . II. Title. III. Series.
BS2560.F84   1990
226′.1–dc20
                                                90-44934
                                                CIP

CONTENTS

TABLES

FIGURES AND PHOTOGRAPHS

POLEBRIDGE PRESS

THE SCHOLARS VERSION

EDITOR IN CHIEF

Robert W. Funk
Westar Institute

GENERAL EDITORS

Daryl D. Schmidt
Texas Christian University

Julian V. Hills
Marquette University

EDITORS
APOCRYPHAL GOSPELS

Ron Cameron
Wesleyan University

Karen L. King
Occidental College

TRANSLATION PANEL

Harold Attridge
University of Notre Dame

Edward F. Beutner
Westar Institute

J. Dominic Crossan
DePaul University

Jon B. Daniels
Defiance College

Arthur J. Dewey
Xavier University

Robert T. Fortna
Vassar College

Ronald F. Hock
University of Southern California

Roy W. Hoover
Whitman College

Arland D. Jacobson
Concordia College

John S. Kloppenborg
University of St. Michael's College

Helmut Koester
Harvard University

Lane C. McGaughy
Willamette University

Marvin W. Meyer
Chapman College

Robert J. Miller
Midway College

Stephen J. Patterson
Eden Theological Seminary

Bernard Brandon Scott
Phillips Graduate Seminary

Philip Sellew
University of Minnesota

Chris Shea
Ball State University

Mahlon H. Smith
Rutgers University

PREFACE

The significant enhancement to this third edition of *New Gospel Parallels* is its complete use of the new and most recent edition of the Scholars Version translation of the gospels for primary and parallel texts. The whole of that translation is now available as *The Complete Gospels* (Polebridge Press, revised and expanded edition).

In other respects, this edition builds upon the earlier work. The basic design of the previous edition of *New Gospel Parallels* was inspired by the Directors and Regents of Polebridge Press. John S. Kloppenborg, in particular, urged me to substitute matched cola for the use of bold in the first edition to indicate verbal parallels (in English). This powerful strategy has raised this work to a new level of usefulness.

Directors of the Press were unanimous in their advice to divide old volume one into three volumes, one for each of the Synoptics. This move would accommodate, in smaller volumes, texts made longer by the matching process. At the same time, it becomes possible for the user to have each of the volumes open simultaneously to the same passage in order to compare and contrast the parallels and matches with now one, now another, of the gospels as the primary or lead text.

Mahlon Smith, Daryl Schmidt, and Julian Hills have combed the pages painstakingly to help eliminate errors of every conceivable stripe. This kind of work is pure drudgery. I cannot bring myself to imagine how much poorer this volume would be without their untiring vigilance.

Richard Whitaker created the basic software that made it possible to collect texts and align them by colon. Char Matejovsky enhanced this software and put it to the test in laying out completely new folios. She is also responsible for the book design. Stephanie McFarland is responsible for the Introduction as well as for the many graphics.

As always, I am indebted to colleagues and students too numerous to mention for assistance at many levels and stages.

Santa Rosa, California
August 1995

CATALOGUE OF WRITTEN GOSPELS

Narrative Gospels

Gospel of Matthew An anonymous author compiled the Gospel of Matthew after the fall of Jerusalem in 70 CE and sometime before the Council of Jamnia, 90 CE. This is the period when the Christian community was seeking its own identity over against Judaism, and when Judaism was attempting to recover from the loss of the center of its worship, the temple. Matthew can be dated to about 85 CE, give or take a few years.

Matthew was composed in Greek in dependence on Greek Mark and Greek Q. It is therefore incorrect to identify it with a gospel composed in Hebrew by a disciple of Jesus.

Gospel of Mark An anonymous author composed the Gospel of Mark shortly after the destruction of the temple in 70 CE. Mark may be responsible for forming the first chronological outline of the life of Jesus. He may also be responsible for the first connected account of Jesus' passion (Mark 14–16). He reflects the early Christian view that God was about to bring history to an end in an apocalyptic conflagration.

The Gospel of Mark is attributed to John Mark, a companion of Paul and perhaps an associate of Peter. This attribution, like others in the ancient world, is the product of speculation.

Mark's gospel was widely used in the early Christian community as indicated by the fact that Matthew and Luke made use of his text in creating their gospels a few years later.

Gospel of Luke Luke-Acts, a two-volume work by a single author, depicts the emergence of Christianity on the world stage. It was composed around 85 CE, during the same period as Matthew. Whereas Matthew was concerned with the Jewish reaction to Christianity, Luke is preoccupied with developments among the Gentiles.

The tradition that Luke the physician and companion of Paul was the author of Luke-Acts goes back to the second century CE. It is improbable that the author of Luke-Acts was a physician and it is doubtful that he was a companion of Paul. As in the case of the other canonical gospels, the author is anonymous.

Gospel of John The Gospel of John was allegedly written by John, son of Zebedee, one of an inner group of disciples. According to legend, John lived to a ripe old age in Ephesus where he composed the gospel, three letters, and possibly the Book of Revelation. The legend is highly improbable.

The Gospel of John was probably written towards the close of the first century CE, which makes it a close contemporary of Matthew and Luke. It exhibits evidence of having gone through several editions. Many scholars therefore conclude that John is the product of a "school," which may indeed have been formed by the John of the legend.

Its place of origin is unknown. It was clearly created in a hellenistic city of some magnitude with a strong Jewish community. A city in Asia Minor or Syria, or possibly Alexandria in Egypt, would do.

It is uncertain whether John knew the Synoptics. He almost certainly made use of a "signs" source and possibly a source consisting of lengthy discourses.

Sayings Gospels

Gospel of Thomas The Gospel of Thomas contains 114 sayings of Jesus, consisting of wisdom sayings, parables, proverbs, and prophecies attributed to Jesus. It has virtually no narrative content.

Thomas is extant in complete form only in a Coptic translation found among the fifty-two tractates that make up the Coptic Gnostic Library discovered at Nag Hammadi, Egypt, in 1945. Three fragments of the original Greek version of Thomas were discovered at Oxyrhynchus (1, 654, 655) in Egypt around the turn of the century. The fragments can be dated to around 200 CE. The first edition of Thomas was probably composed around 60 CE.

Thomas is widely regarded as an independent witness to the sayings of Jesus, comparable in form to so-called Q, a sayings collection believed to function as one of two sources utilized by Matthew and Luke in creating their gospels.

Dialogue of the Savior Dialogue of the Savior is a fragmentary and composite document containing dialogues of Jesus with three of his disciples, Judas, Matthew, and Miriam. It was found at Nag Hammadi, Egypt, in 1945.

The earlier portions of the dialogue may be dated to the second half of the first century CE, while the final form of the Dialogue of the Savior is probably to be dated to the second half of the second century CE.

Dialogue of the Savior is closely related to the Gospel of Thomas and the Gospel of John.

Apocryphon of James Apocryphon of James is a Coptic translation of a Greek original containing a dialogue of Jesus with Peter and James. Apocryphon of James was found among the codices of the Nag Hammadi Library in Eygpt in 1945.

Apocryphon of James lacks a narrative framework; like Thomas and Q, it consists entirely of sayings, parables, prophecies, and rules governing the Christian community attributed to Jesus. It is the risen Jesus who speaks. The whole is embedded in a letter purportedly written in Hebrew by James.

Apocryphon of James was probably composed during the course of the second century CE.

Infancy Gospels

Infancy Gospel of Thomas Infancy Gospel of Thomas is a narrative of the miraculous works of the young magician-hero, Jesus, prior to his twelfth birthday. Infancy Gospel of Thomas continues the *divine man* tradition of the ancient world: itinerant miracle workers accredited by their amazing deeds.

Infancy Gospel of Thomas is preserved in a Syriac manuscript of the fourth century CE and in Greek manuscripts of the fourteenth through the sixteenth centuries CE. The gospel is based on oral sources and the Gospel of Luke. In its original form it may be as old as the second century CE.

Infancy Gospel of James Infancy Gospel of James is an infancy gospel containing an account of the birth and dedication of Mary and the birth of Jesus. The traditional title *Protevangelium* indicates that the events recorded precede those narrated in the canonical gospels. Infancy James is dated in the period mid-second century CE to early third century CE.

Passion Gospels

Gospel of Peter The Gospel of Peter is preserved only as a fragment discovered in upper Egypt in 1886–1887; the language is Greek and the fragment dates to the eighth or ninth century CE. However, two Greek papyrus fragments from Oxyrhynchus, dating to late second or early third century CE, may also belong to the Gospel of Peter.

The Gospel of Peter contains a passion narrative, an epiphany story, an account of the empty tomb, and the beginning of a resurrection story.

In its original form, the Gospel of Peter may have arisen in the second half of the first century CE.

Acts of Pilate The Acts of Pilate is an elaborate account of Jesus' trial before Pontius Pilate, his crucifixion and burial, accounts of the empty tomb, and a discussion of his resurrection by a council of Jewish elders. It is an example of early Christian apologetic in narrative form.

The original Acts of Pilate was probably written in Greek sometime during the second or third century CE. The prologue claims that it was written by Nicodemus in Hebrew shortly after Jesus' death. The Acts of Pilate was eventually incorporated into the Gospel of Nicodemus. It is preserved in several medieval Greek manuscripts.

Fragments

Egerton Gospel An unknown gospel is represented by four fragments of Papyrus Egerton 2 and a fifth fragment designated Papyrus Köln 255. The five fragments are from the same papyrus codex, which can be dated to the second century CE, perhaps as early as 125 CE. The Egerton Gospel contains the healing of a leper, a controversy over payment of taxes, a miracle of Jesus by the Jordan, plus two tiny segments closely related to the Gospel of John.

Oxyrhynchus Papyrus 1224 Oxyrhynchus Papyrus 1224 is the remains of a papyrus codex containing fragments of an unknown gospel. It can be dated to the beginning of the fourth century CE.

Oxyrhynchus Papyrus 840 Oxyrhynchus Papyrus 840 is a single leaf of a Greek parchment containing fragments that can be dated to the fourth century CE. It contains the conclusion of a discourse between Jesus and his disciples and a controversy story involving Jesus and a Pharasaic chief priest in the temple court.

Papyrus Cairensis 10 735 Papyrus Cairensis may be a fragment of a noncanonical gospel containing the story of Jesus' birth and flight to Egypt. The fragment is dated to the sixth or seventh century CE. Further identification has not been possible.

Fayyum Fragment Fayyum Fragment is a fragment of the third century CE containing an excerpt from an unknown gospel. The text is too fragmentary to warrant definitive conclusions.

Freer Logion The Freer logion is a variant reading in codex W acquired by Charles L. Freer of Detroit in 1906 and now lodged in the Freer Museum of the Smithsonian Institution in Washington, D.C. (late fourth or early fifth century CE). The variant in question is an insertion in the Gospel of Mark at 16:14.

Secret Gospel of Mark Secret Mark is a fragment of an early edition of the Gospel of Mark containing a story of the raising of a young man from the dead, a rite of initiation, and an encounter of Jesus with three women in Jericho. These stories are presently embedded in a letter of Clement of Alexandria (second century CE), the copy of which dates to the eighteenth century CE. Secret Mark, however, may go back in its original form to the early second century CE.

Gospel of the Ebionites A Jewish-Christian gospel preserved only in quotations by Epiphanius (fourth century CE). The original title is unknown. The Ebionites were Greek-speaking Jewish Christians who flourished in the second and third centuries CE. Their gospel, erroneously called the Hebrew Gospel by Epiphanius, probably dates to the mid-second century CE.

Gospel of the Egyptians The Gospel of the Egyptians consists of sayings of Jesus. The few fragments extant are preserved in Greek by Clement of Alexandria (end of the second century CE). The gospel appears to be oriented to sexual asceticism, to judge by the few remaining fragments. The Gospel of the Egyptians arose in the period 50–150 CE.

Gospel of the Hebrews The Gospel of the Hebrews contains traditions of Jesus' preexistence and coming into the world, his baptism and temptation, a few of his sayings, and an account of his resurrected appearance to James, his brother (1 Cor 15:7). The provenance of the Gospel of the Hebrews is probably Egypt. It was composed sometime between the mid-first century CE and mid-second century CE. The Gospel of the Hebrews has been lost except for quotations and allusions preserved by the Church Fathers.

Gospel of the Nazoreans The Gospel of the Nazoreans is an expanded version of the Gospel of Matthew. It is preserved in quotations and allusions in the Church Fathers and in marginal notations found in a number of medieval manuscripts. These marginal notations appear to go back to a single "Zion Gospel" edition composed prior to 500 CE. The Gospel of the Nazoreans is evidently a translation into Aramaic or Syriac of Greek Matthew, with additions.

The Gospel of the Nazoreans is first quoted by Hegesippus around 180 CE. Its provenance is probably western Syria.

BOOKSHELF OF BASIC WORKS

Titles are listed alphabetically by author within each section

1. The Gospels: Primary Texts

Cameron, Ron, ed. *The Other Gospels: Non-Canonical Gospel Texts.* Philadelphia: The Westminster Press, 1982.

Kloppenborg, John S., et al. *Q–Thomas Reader.* Santa Rosa: Polebridge Press, 1990.

Miller, Robert J., ed. *The Complete Gospels. Annotated Scholars Version.* Santa Rosa: Polebridge Press, 1994.

Schmidt, Daryl D. *The Gospel of Mark.* Santa Rosa: Polebridge Press, 1990.

2. Study of the Gospels

Bultmann, Rudolf. *History of the Synoptic Tradition.* Trans. John Marsh. Rev. ed. San Francisco: Harper & Row, 1963.

Funk, Robert W., Hoover, Roy W. and the Jesus Seminar. *The Five Gospels: The Search for the Authentic Words of Jesus.* New York: Macmillan, 1993.

Kee, Howard C. *Jesus in History. An Approach to the Study of the Gospels.* 2nd ed. New York: Harcourt Brace Jovanovich, Inc., 1977.

Kloppenborg, John S. *The Formation of Q. Trajectories in Ancient Wisdom Collections.* Studies in Antiquity & Christianity. Philadelphia: Fortress Press, 1987.

———. *Q Parallels. Synopsis, Critical Notes & Concordance.* Santa Rosa: Polebridge Press, 1988.

Koester, Helmut. *Introduction to the New Testament.* Vol. 1: *History, Culture, and Religion of the Hellenistic Age;* Vol. 2: *History and Literature of Early Christianity.* Berlin: de Gruyter, 1987.

———. *Ancient Christian Gospels: Their History and Development.* Philadelphia: Trinity Press International, 1990.

Sanders, E. P. and Davies, Margaret. *Studying the Synoptic Gospels.* Philadelphia: Trinity Press International, 1989.

Tatum, W. Barnes. *In Quest of Jesus: A Guidebook.* Louisville: John Knox Press, 1982.

3. Sayings and Parables

Crossan, John Dominic. *In Fragments: The Aphorisms of Jesus.* San Francisco: Harper & Row, 1983.

———. *In Parables: The Challenge of the Historical Jesus.* San Francisco: Harper & Row, 1976; Santa Rosa: Polebridge Press, 1990.

———. *The Dark Interval: Towards a Theology of Story.* Santa Rosa: Polebridge Press, 1988.

Dodd, C. H. *The Parables of the Kingdom.* London: Nisbet & Co., 1935. 3rd ed., 1936. Rev. ed., 1961.

Funk, Robert W., et al. *The Parables of Jesus: Red Letter Edition.* Santa Rosa: Polebridge Press, 1988.

Jeremias, Joachim. *The Parables of Jesus.* Rev. ed., trans. S.H. Hooke. New York: Charles Scribner's Sons, 1963.

Scott, Bernard Brandon. *Hear Then the Parable. A Commentary on the Parables.* Philadelphia: Fortress Press, 1988.

4. Pronouncement Stories

Butts, James R. "The Chreia in the Synoptic Gospels." *Biblical Theology Bulletin* 16 (1986) 132–38.

Mack, Burton L. and Robbins, Vernon K. *Patterns of Persuasion in the Gospels.* Foundations & Facets. Santa Rosa: Polebridge Press, 1989.

Robbins, Vernon K., ed. *Ancient Quotes & Anecdotes. From Crib to Crypt.* Foundations & Facets. Santa Rosa: Polebridge Press, 1989.

Tannehill, Robert, ed. *Pronouncement Stories. Semeia: A Experimental Journal for Biblical Criticism.* Vol. 20 (1981).

5. Miracle Stories

Achtemeier, Paul J. "Toward the Isolation of Pre-Markan Miracle Catenae." *Journal of Biblical Literature* 89 (1970) 265–91.

———. "The Origin and Function of the Pre-Marcan Miracle Catenae." *Journal of Biblical Literature* 91 (1972) 198–221.

Funk, Robert W. "The Form of the New Testament Healing Miracle Story." *Semeia* 12 (1978), ed. William A. Beardslee: *The Poetics of Faith. Essays Offered to Amos Niven Wilder.*

Mack, Burton L. *A Myth of Innocence* (see 7).

Theissen, Gerd. *The Miracle Stories of the Early Christian Tradition.* Trans. Francis McDonagh. Philadelphia: Fortress Press, 1983.

6. The Passion Narrative

Brown, Raymond E. *The Death of the Messiah.* New York: Doubleday, 1994.

Crossan, John Dominic. *The Cross That Spoke. Origins of the Passion Narrative.* San Francisco: Harper & Row, 1988. (Available from Polebridge Press.)

———. *Who Killed Jesus?* San Francisco: HarperSanFrancisco, 1995.

Kelber, Werner H., ed. *The Passion in Mark: Studies on Mark 14–16.* Philadelphia: Fortress Press, 1976.

Mack, Burton L. *A Myth of Innocence* (see 7).

Nickelsburg, George W. E. "The Genre and Function of the Markan Passion Narrative." *Harvard Theological Review* 73 (1980) 153–84.

7. The Gospel of Mark

Funk, Robert W., et al. *The Sayings of Jesus in Mark: Red Letter Edition.* Santa Rosa: Polebridge Press, 1990.

Haenchen, Ernst. *Der Weg Jesu. Eine Erklärung des Markus-Evangeliums und der kanonischen Parallelen.* Berlin: Alfred Töpelmann, 1966.

Kee, Howard C. *Community of the New Age. Studies in Mark's Gospel.* Philadelphia: The Westminster Press, 1977.

Kelber, Werner H. *The Oral and the Written Gospel. The Hermeneutics of Speaking and Writing in the Synoptic Tradition, Mark, Paul, and Q.* Philadelphia: Fortress Press, 1983.

Mack, Burton L. *A Myth of Innocence. Mark and Christian Origins.* Philadelphia: Fortress Press, 1988.

Rhoads, David and Michie, Donald. *Mark As Story. An Introduction to the Narrative of a Gospel.* Philadelphia: Fortress Press, 1982.

Schmidt, Daryl D. *The Gospel of Mark* (see 1).

Sellew, Philip. "Composition of Didactic Scenes in Mark's Gospel." *Journal of Biblical Literature* 108 (1989) 234–67.

———. "Oral and Written Sources in Mark 4.1–34." *New Testament Studies* 36 (1990) 234–67.

Taylor, Vincent. *The Gospel According to St. Mark.* London: Macmillan & Co. Ltd., 1953; 2nd ed., 1966.

8. The Scholars Version

Schmidt, Daryl D. *The Gospel of Mark* (see 1).

9. New Gospel Parallels

Funk, Robert W. *The Poetics of Biblical Narrative.* Foundations & Facets. Santa Rosa: Polebridge Press, 1988.

ABBREVIATIONS

Gospels

AcPil	Acts of Pilate
ApJas	Apocryphon of James
DialSav	Dialogue of the Savior
GEger	Egerton Gospel
GEgy	Gospel of the Egyptians
GEbi	Gospel of the Ebionites
GHeb	Gospel of the Hebrews
GNaz	Gospel of the Nazoreans
GPet	Gospel of Peter
InThom	Infancy Thomas
InJas	Infancy James
John	John
Luke	Luke
Mark	Mark
Matt	Matthew
PEger2	Papyrus Egerton 2
PKöln255	Papyrus Köln 255
POxy1	Papyrus Oxyrhychus 1
POxy654	Papyrus Oxyrhychus 654
POxy655	Papyrus Oxyrhychus 655
POxy840	Papyrus Oxyrhychus 840
POxy1224	Papyrus Oxyrhychus 1224
Q	Synoptic Sayings Source
SecMk	Secret Gospel of Mark
Thom	Gospel of Thomas

New Testament

Acts	Acts
Rom	Romans
1 Cor	1 Corinthians
Gal	Galatians
Phil	Philippians
1 Thess	1 Thessalonians
1 Tim	1 Timothy
Jas	James
1 Pet	1 Peter
Rev	Revelation

Old Testament, Apocrypha and Pseudepigrapha

Gen	Genesis
Exod	Exodus
Lev	Leviticus
Num	Numbers
Deut	Deuteronomy
Josh	Joshua
Judg	Judges
1 Sam	1 Samuel
2 Sam	2 Samuel
1 Kgs	1 Kings
2 Kgs	2 Kings
Isa	Isaiah
Jer	Jeremiah
Ezek	Ezekiel
Hos	Hosea
Joel	Joel
Amos	Amos
Jonah	Jonah
Mic	Micah
Hab	Habakkuk
Zech	Zechariah
Mal	Malachi
Ps	Psalms
Job	Job
Prov	Proverbs
Esth	Esther
Dan	Daniel
2 Chr	2 Chronicles
1 Macc	1 Maccabees
Sir	Sirach
Tob	Tobit
4 Ezra	4 Ezra
1 Enoch	1 Enoch

Church Fathers and Jewish Authors

Barn	Barnabas
1 Clem	1 Clement, a letter from Clement of Rome to the church at Corinth, ca. 95 CE
2 Clem	2 Clement, a sermon attributed to Clement of Rome, dating ca. 150 CE

Clement (of Alexandria), II/III CE
Stromateis
Excerpta ex Theodoto

Did	Didache, a compendium of teachings or catechetical work attributed to the twelve apostles; early II CE

Epiphanius (of Salamis), IV CE
Adv. Haer. *Adversus Haereses*

Eusebius (of Caesarea), III/IV CE
Theophania

Ign	Ignatius (bishop of Antioch in Syria), early II CE
Smyr	*Smyrnaeans,* a letter to the church at Smyrna

Irenaeus (of Lyons), II CE
Adv. Haer. *Adversus Haereses*

Josephus, I CE
Against Apion

Jerome (of Jerusalem), IV/V CE
Adversus Pelagianos
Commentary on Matthew
Commentary on Isaiah
De viris inlustribus
Epistulae

Justin (Martyr), II CE
Apology (1)
Dialogue

Origen (of Alexandria and Caesarea), III CE
Commentary on Matthew
Commentary on John

Philo (of Alexandria), I CE
On the Life of Moses

Zion Gospel — an edition of Matthew dating from about 500 CE reflected in a group of thirty-six medieval manuscripts of the text of Matthew

General Abbreviations and Sigla

BCE	Before the common era
CE	The common era
MT	Massoretic (Hebrew) Bible
LXX	The Septuagint or Greek translation of the Hebrew Bible
⟨ ⟩	subject, object, or other element implied by the original language and supplied by the translator
[ ]	a doubtful textual reading
[[ ]]	a textual reading almost certainly secondary
†	a primary parallel lacking substantial verbal or narrative agreement, yet which serves the same narrative function
‡	a parallel exhibiting some agreement, but which serves a different narrative function
•	a doublet: the repetition in the same gospel of a narrative segment or sayings cluster
△	a similar narrative incident that appears in a different context
☆	a parallel with a comparable theme or motif
a,b,c	bold indicates cola that are out of order

Textual Notes

The Greek text on which Scholars Version is based was edited by Daryl Schmidt with the assistance of the editor.

The evidence cited in the textual notes is based on the third edition of *The Greek New Testament,* edited by Aland, Black, Martini, Metzger, and Wikgren (1975), and on Bruce Metzger's *A Textual Commentary on the Greek New Testament* (corrected edition, 1975).

Witnesses are cited in the customary categories, with papyri coming first, followed by the uncials and then the minuscules. The ancient versions are also cited where appropriate. The evidence is normally abbreviated; for full citations the reader is referred to the UBS *Greek New Testament* or to Nestle-Aland, *Novum Testamentum Graece.*

The Papyri

Number	Content	Location	Date
$\mathfrak{P}^1$	Matthew	Philadelphia	III
$\mathfrak{P}^{25}$	Matthew	Berlin	late IV
$\mathfrak{P}^{37}$	Matthew	Ann Arbor	III/IV
$\mathfrak{P}^{39}$	John	Chester, PA	III
$\mathfrak{P}^{45}$	gospels, acts	Dublin & Vienna	200–250
$\mathfrak{P}^{64,67}$	Matthew	Oxford, Barcelona	ca. 200
$\mathfrak{P}^{66}$	John	Geneva	ca. 200
$\mathfrak{P}^{75}$	gospels	Geneva	early III
$\mathfrak{P}^{77}$	Matthew	Oxford	III/IV
$\mathfrak{P}^{88}$	Mark	Milan	IV

The Letter Uncials

Designation/Name	Content	Location	Date
ℵ, Sinaiticus	NT	London	IV
A, Alexandrinus	NT	London	V
B, Vaticanus	gospels, acts, epistles	Rome	IV
C, Ephraemi Rescriptus	NT	Paris	V
D, Bezae Cantabrigiensis	gospels, acts	Cambridge	V/VI
K	gospels	Paris	IX
L, Regius	gospels	Paris	VIII
N, Purpureus Petropolitanus	gospels	Leningrad etc.	V
P, Porphyrianus	gospels	Wölfenbüttel	VI
T, Borgianus	gospels	Rome	V
W, Freerianus	gospels	Washington, D.C.	V
X	gospels	Munich	X
Y	gospels	Cambridge	IX
Γ	gospels	Leningrad & Oxford	X
Δ	gospels	St. Gall	IX
Θ, Koridethi	gospels	Tiflis	IX
Ξ, Zacynthius	gospels	London	VIII
Π	gospels	Leningrad	IX
Ψ	gospels, acts, epistles	Athos	VIII/IX

Abbreviations

The Numbered Uncials

050	IX
063	IX
073	VI
074	VI
084	VI
090	VI
0106	VII
0107	VII
0119	VII
0124	VI
0138	IX
0133	IX
0135	IX
0148	VIII
0170	V/VI
0196	IX
0212	III
0250	VIII

The Greek Minuscules

28	XI
33	IX
157	XII
304	XII
565	IX
700	XI
892	IX
1009	XIII
1010	XII
1195	1123
1216	XI
1230	1124
1241	XII
2148	1337
2174	XIV

The Ancient Versions

arm	Armenian version
cop	Coptic version
cop^{bo}	Bohairic dialect
cop^{sa}	Sahidic dialect
eth	Ethiopic version
geo	Georgian version
goth	Gothic version
it	Itala or Old Latin version
syr	Syriac version
syr^c	Curetonian Syriac version
syr^s	Sinaitic Syriac version
vg	Vulgate version

The Latin Manuscripts

b	V
d	V
ff²	V
k	IV/V
q	VI/VII
r¹	VII

Other Abbreviations and Symbols

f^1	"Family 1": manuscripts 1, 118, 131, 209
f^{13}	"Family 13": manuscripts 13, 69, 124, 174, 230 (174 and 230 not used in Mark), 346, 543, 788, 826, 828, 983, 1689
*	The reading of the original hand of a manuscript
c	The corrector of a manuscript
c,2,3	The successive correctors of a manuscript
a,b,c	The successive correctors of a manuscript in ℵ D
comm	The commentary section of a manuscript
mg	Textual evidence found in the margin of a manuscript
gr	The Greek text of a bilingual manuscript
supp	A portion of a manuscript supplied by a later hand to fill in a blank in the original
( )	Means that the witness reads something trivially different but in general conforms to what is cited; or, the reading of the witness is uncertain
pc	pauci: a few (other witnesses)
al	alii: other (witnesses; more than pc)
pm	permulti: a great many (witnesses)

INTRODUCTION

§§1–6: The Study of the Gospels

§1. The Gospels

The word **gospel** is derived from an Old English term *godspel*. *Gospel* is a translation of the Greek term, εὐαγγέλιον, which means *good news*. Mark's work is the first to refer to itself as a gospel: *Here begins the good news of Jesus the Anointed.*

Most of the information we have about Jesus of Nazareth is preserved in a group of documents known as **gospels**. The gospels of which copies or fragments survive fall into five categories, generally speaking. They are: (1) narrative gospels, (2) sayings gospels, (3) infancy gospels, (4) passion gospels, and (5) fragments of known and unknown gospels. A complete inventory of these gospels, together with a brief description of each, is provided in the *Catalogue of Written Gospels* (pp. x–xi).

Canon: an authoritative list or collection of gospels (and other books) accepted as holy scripture by the Christian community or church.

The four narrative gospels, Matthew, Mark, Luke, and John, belong to the New Testament **canon**. Fragmentary gospels have not been accorded canonical status. Nevertheless, scholars take all surviving texts seriously, whether canonical or non-canonical, complete or fragmentary, evaluate them independently, and examine them closely for any information pertinent to the rise and development of the gospel tradition.

CE stands for the Common Era, used out of deference to those who do not reference chronology by Christian events.

The gospels that contain significant data about Jesus were composed between 50 CE and 300 CE. The time line of gospel composition, insofar as scholars have been able to reconstruct it, is summarized in the *Time Line of the Gospels and Manuscripts* (p. 25).

Apostolic Fathers designates a modern collection of works ascribed to authors who were associated with apostles or disciples of apostles. **Fathers** is a title given to theologians of the ancient church.

Sources of information about Jesus outside the gospels include the letters of Paul, the **Apostolic Fathers**, and other **Fathers** of the early church. Indeed, information about some lost gospels is provided only by the Fathers. This information, however, is fragmentary and incidental. Information in secular sources is unfortunately limited.

§2. Surviving Records

The original copies (autographs) of gospels have completely disappeared. In fact, the oldest fragment of any portion of a gospel now in existence dates from the early second century CE, about one hundred years after Jesus' death. It is a tiny fragment of the Gospel of John. $\mathfrak{P}^{52}$, as it is numbered in inventories of **papyri**, can be dated to about 125 CE.

Papyrus is the predecessor to modern paper. Ancient books and records were written either on the skins of animals, called parchment, or on papyrus, a kind of paper made from Egyptian reeds.

Papyrus Egerton 2, along with Papyrus Köln 255, are fragments of an unknown gospel, now called the Egerton Gospel. These fragments may actually be older than the fragment of John, although scholars usually date them to the same period.

The earliest extensive surviving fragments of Matthew, Luke, and John date to about 200 CE, those of the Gospel of Mark only slightly later (225 CE). Unfortunately, most of the surviving copies of the gospels are fragmentary. Codex Sinaiticus, discovered by Count Tischendorf in 1844 at the monastery of St. Catharine at the foot of Mt. Sinai, is exceptional: it contains the whole of the Greek New Testament; it is dated to the fourth century CE. Most of the great **uncials** have gaps or lacunae where pages have been lost or have decayed in places. A select list of surviving Greek manuscripts and fragments is found in Table 1 (p. 43).

To put matters in perspective, three centuries separate Jesus from the earliest complete surviving copy of the gospels. One full century separates him from the earliest surviving fragments. To make matters worse, no two copies or fragments are exactly alike, since they were all made by hand. It was only with the invention of printing from movable type in 1454 CE that identical copies of the biblical text could be reproduced.

About 5,000 Greek manuscripts and fragments survive from the period prior to Johannes Gutenberg's printing press. That is a greater number by far than the surviving records of any other ancient book, including Homer's *Iliad*, the *McGuffey's Reader* of the hellenistic world. Of course, the Fathers also cite the gospels frequently, often from memory, which provides another kind of textual evidence. Surviving manuscripts of the gospels have been carefully collated and the results summarized in a shorthand code in **critical editions** of the Greek New Testament.

Papyrus fragments are dated by internal reference (if any) and by the style of writing. Since most written texts were made by professional scribes, the style of writing, whether in all capital letters (**uncials**) or in cursive script (minuscules), remains fairly consistent and evolves slowly. Specialists (palaeographers) can usually date manuscripts to within a decade or two of their transcription, partly because so many surviving legal and business texts include internal dates.

Modern **critical editions** of the gospels are composites: editors select what they think are the best readings sentence by sentence, word by word, from a variety of ancient manuscripts, in creating a critical text. Accordingly, modern editions do not correspond to any particular manuscript, but represent an educated selection of the oldest known readings.

§3. From the Gospels to Jesus

Jesus was a Galilean peasant who wrote nothing, so far as we know. His native tongue was Aramaic, although he also undoubtedly spoke Greek, as a consequence of the strong Greek presence at Sepphoris, a hellenistic city just a few miles from Nazareth. Surviving records exist solely in Greek, with a few gospel texts preserved only in secondary translation: Latin, Coptic, or other ancient language. The gospel tradition has preserved a few Aramaic words attributed to Jesus.

Scholars believe that written records about Jesus can be traced well back into the first century CE, perhaps even to a date as early as 50 CE, a mere two decades after Jesus' death, although neither copies nor fragments from those early years have been discovered. However, before the gospels were written, . and even after they were written, the lore about Jesus circulated primarily in oral form. Oral reminiscence rather than written record was the principal vehicle of creation and transmission. The cultures and communities in which Christianity arose were essentially oral—all cultures were oral prior to the invention of writing, and most cultures, particularly those of the lower classes, continued to be oral until the invention of the printing press. In oral cultures and communities, traditional lore is not fixed in writing, but is passed on as talk, and, as common experience demonstrates, talk is more liquid, so to speak, than writing. The fluidity of talk is restrained by two factors. One is the formal structure given to stories or sayings; the other is the use of fixed phrases or clichés. Otherwise, in oral communities purveyors of the Jesus tradition freely invented, modified, omitted, expanded, and abbreviated.

The oral transmission of the Jesus tradition did not end when the first written records appeared. Indeed, the primacy of the oral transmission continued well into the second century. The living testimony of disciples and disciples of disciples remained more highly esteemed than the relatively rare and suspicious written text. Moreover, very few persons were wealthy enough to enjoy the possession and use of written copies of books. The gospel tradition thus remained fluid for more than a century.

We no longer have direct access to the oral tradition that was alive in the first hundred years or so after Jesus' death. But we do have immediate access to the written deposit left by that tradition. We must therefore begin with the written records and work backwards. Working backwards requires that we search the written gospels for clues of what transpired in their formation, of what took place during the oral period preceding and paralleling the first written gospels, and, finally, what changes the written texts must have suffered in being copied and recopied by hand prior to the first surviving fragments and documents.

Tracing the tradition backwards is a complex process. In general, scholars carry out their work in two basic steps: (a) they collect factual data of every sort; (b) they construct theories to account for as many of those data as possible. Then, as a way of reviewing and testing the first two steps, they add other phases to the process. In order to discipline speculation, (c) scholars must know the history of critical scholarship. In other words, they make themselves responsible to a body of data and theory, on which they build, much in the same way that lawyers examine precedent in analyzing legal problems, and much in the same way that the practice of medicine is governed by established data, theory, and practice.

When scholars collect new data or construct new or modified theories, (d) they must submit their work to the critical review of other scholars by publishing it in learned journals and books. The sifting process is continuous and arduous. Eventually, (e) a new scholarly consensus is formed on this or that point and the critical process begins all over again.

§4. Basic Facts and Critical Theory

The basic facts and critical theories currently accepted by the majority of scholars include the following:

4.1 Critical Greek text. The critical Greek text of the gospels from which scholars work is a composite of surviving fragments and documents. Since no autographs, no original copies, exist, textual critics have had to reconstruct what they take to be the best text.

4.2 Original Greek text. The original Greek texts may have differed, at least at some points, from the present reconstructed Greek text. Scholars speak of a proto-Mark, a proto-Luke, earlier editions of Matthew, and different editions of Thomas. These proposals, which seem to proliferate endlessly, are actually attempts to account for some particular set of data not covered by other theories.

4.3 Earliest gospels. The earliest gospels were sayings gospels, in the judgment of most scholars. Many of the sayings recorded by Matthew and Luke probably came from a common source, now lost, known as the synoptic sayings source or **Q**. Thomas is also a sayings gospel, and an early edition of Thomas may be among our earliest sources of the Jesus tradition. Q and the earliest strata of Thomas may be dated to the period 50–70 CE.

Mark is thought to have been composed around 70 CE, just before or just after the destruction of Jerusalem by the Romans. Matthew and Luke belong

Q is a hypothetical document believed to have contained an extensive compilation of the sayings of Jesus, like the Gospel of Thomas. It was used by Matthew and Luke in creating their gospels. Q stands for *Quelle*, a German word meaning *source*. Q is now often referred to as the synoptic sayings gospel.

to the decade of the 80s or perhaps the 90s of the first century CE. The Gospels of John and Peter and the Egerton Gospel were also almost certainly composed before the end of the first century. The matter of dates is presented more fully in the *Catalogue of Written Gospels* (pp. x–xi) and summarized in the *Time Line of Gospels and Manuscripts* (p. 25).

4.4 Names of the gospels. The names attached to the several gospels are the product of pious imaginations in the second century. None of the gospels was composed by an immediate disciple of Jesus, although some gospels may reflect the reminiscences of one or the other of Jesus' immediate companions.

How the Gospels Got Their Names is summarized on page 10.

4.5 Sources of the gospels. Scholars are all but certain that Matthew and Luke made use of Mark in composing their gospels. They also believe that Matthew and Luke shared a second source, so-called Q. Whether John knew the other canonical gospels is debated; it is certain that the author of John knew some of the same traditions as the synoptic writers knew. Many John specialists believe that the Fourth Gospel went through several editions and that the author made use of written sources for both discourses and miracles. The theory has recently been advanced that an earlier version of the Gospel of Peter is the first draft of the passion narrative on which Mark drew. And, of course, it has been proposed that Mark also went through two or more editions before reaching the stage in which we know it.

4.6 Gospels not biographies. The gospels are not biographies or histories of Jesus in the modern sense. The gospels actually provide very little personal information about Jesus. They do not develop his character or the character of those around him, and, as we shall see, they record virtually nothing of the chronology of events. The gospels are what their title suggests: the announcement of the good news—Jesus is the messiah, the son of Adam, the son of God. As a consequence, the modern historian must sort and sift the data in the gospels in order to isolate the facts.

4.7 Jesus' Bible. It is easily forgotten that the Hebrew scriptures had not yet taken final shape in Jesus' day. Jesus' Bible consisted of the Torah (the five books of Moses or the Pentateuch), the Prophets, and the Psalms. It was not until the Council of Jamnia in 90 CE that the rabbis formed their definitive list of sacred books.

The **Septuagint** (LXX) is the oldest Greek version of the Hebrew scriptures. According to legend, it was made by seventy (LXX) elders, or by seventy-two elders, working in seclusion for seventy-two days. Actually, the LXX is a collection of translations made by various anonymous translators over an extended period of time.

Another forgotten fact is that the version of the Hebrew scriptures commonly used by the early Christian community was the Greek version known as the **Septuagint**, or LXX for short. The LXX differs at many points from the Hebrew Bible.

§5. The Synoptic Gospels

5.1 Triple tradition: verbal agreement. Matthew, Mark, and Luke are commonly called synoptic gospels. Synoptic means that they share a common view of the deeds and words of Jesus. When laid out in parallel columns with matched **pericopes** or **cola**, the similarities between and among them are striking. What they have in common is so striking, in fact, that scholars have concluded that direct literary dependence is involved: they must have copied from one another, from a common source, or from a combination of the two.

Many of the same passages or pericopes appear in all three Synoptics:

A **pericope** (literally, *something cut out*) is a discrete unit of discourse, much like a paragraph in a well-ordered story.

Cola (singular: **colon**) are short pieces of discourse, formally consisting of a verb and its modifiers (a predicate). Texts are sometimes broken into short lines or cola for close comparison.

triple tradition: material the three synoptic gospels have in common.

such material is called the **triple tradition**. Mark is shortest of the three, so comparisons begin with the relation of Matthew and Luke to Mark. Approximately 90% of Mark is duplicated in Matthew; more than half of Mark also appears in Luke. Very few pericopes in Mark are not paralleled in some form or another in either Matthew or Luke. The three major Markan segments that do not appear in either Matthew or Luke are:

Mark 4:26–29	Seed and Harvest
7:31–37	Jesus Cures a Deaf Mute
8:22–26	Jesus Cures a Blind Man

In addition, three short texts have no parallels:

Mark 3:20–21	Jesus' relatives think him mad
9:49	Salted by fire
14:51–52	Young man fleeing in Gethsemane

In common passages, the **verbatim agreement** averages around fifty percent.

By one count, 600 of 661 verses in Mark also appear in Matthew. In another set of statistics, the Greek text of Mark contains 11,078 words, of which 8,555 appear in Matthew, about 6,737 in Luke. Of Mark's 855 sentences, 709 show up in Matthew, 565 are shared with Luke.

Statistics are no substitute, however, for the perusal of a gospel parallels: even where verbatim agreement is not close, the structural similarities or the outline of an incident or narrative summary are often close or identical.

5.2 Triple tradition: order. Similarities extend beyond verbatim and near verbatim parallels. Incidents and sayings in the triple tradition most often appear in the same order or context. Where there is variation in order, Mark's order is supported by either Matthew or Luke.

In the triple tradition, there are frequent agreements between Matthew and Mark against Luke, and between Luke and Mark against Matthew, but there are relatively few between Luke and Matthew against Mark.

It is noteworthy that agreements in the triple tradition begin where Mark begins (with the appearance of John the Baptist) and end where Mark ends (the empty tomb). Agreements begin and end also in individual pericopes or passages where Mark begins and ends.

These facts strongly suggest that Mark is the middle term of the three: either Mark is first and Matthew and Luke are dependent on him, or Mark is last and dependent on the other two directly or indirectly. The scholarly consensus that has emerged after one hundred and twenty years of debate is that Mark is prior, and that Matthew and Luke have copied from, and revised and expanded, Mark.

5.3 Synoptic sayings gospel. In addition to the triple tradition Matthew and Luke have in common with Mark, they have in common another two hundred verses, give or take a few, for which Mark offers no parallels. This material is known as the **double tradition**.

double tradition: material that Matthew and Luke have in common.

The double tradition consists largely of sayings material. Agreement between Matthew and Luke varies from absolute verbatim agreement to similar texts with very little verbatim agreement. Matthew and Luke have distributed the double tradition in each of their gospels quite differently.

In the judgment of most scholars, the double tradition points to the existence of a document, now lost, that contained an extensive compilation of the sayings of Jesus. That hypothetical document came to be known as Q. Q is sometimes referred to as the synoptic sayings gospel.

Matthew and Luke are thus dependent on two prior written sources,

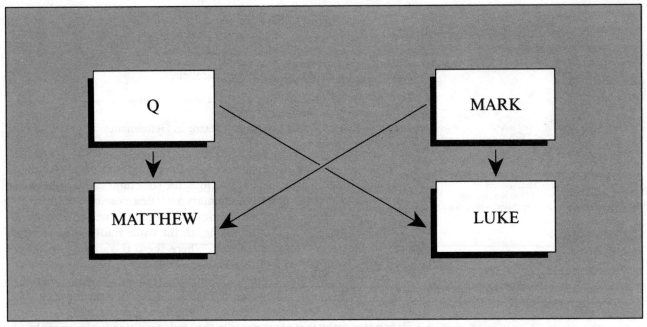

The Two Source Theory is the view that Matthew and Luke made use of two written sources—Mark and the Sayings Gospel Q—in composing their gospels.

Mark and Q. This view of synoptic relationships is called the two source theory (above).

5.4 Special Matthew and Luke. To be sure, Matthew and Luke have knowledge of still other traditions that do not derive from either Mark or Q. This is suggested by the fact that Matthew and Luke each contains material unique to it alone. Either Matthew and Luke knew of other written documents that contained these materials, or they learned of them from the oral tradition. Scholars are divided on whether these special sources, known as M and L, respectively, were oral or written. Those who propose additional sources speak loosely of the four source theory (p. 7). In any case, Matthew and Luke each have two sources in common, plus a third special source unique to each, out of which they fashioned their gospels. Their third sources have virtually nothing in common. Particularly striking are the strong divergences in the Matthean and Lukan birth and childhood stories and in the their accounts of the resurrection appearances.

5.5 Chronology of Jesus' life. Matthew and Luke used Mark as their first source, and it was from Mark that they derived their outline of the life of

THE FOUR SOURCE THEORY

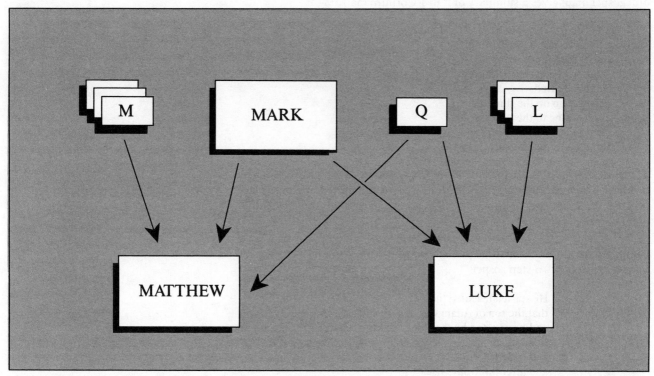

The Four Source Theory is a common explanation of the relationships found among the Synoptic Gospels. Matthew used Mark, Q, and his own special source called M. Luke also used Mark and Q, but had another source called L, that Matthew did not have. The material in M and L probably comes from oral tradition.

Q material may be observed in K2: A Voice in the Wilderness (Matt 3:7–12//Luke 3:7–20).

Jesus. Into that outline they integrated materials from the Q-source and from their individual special sources. No other explanation seems to fit all the facts equally well.

Since both Matthew and Luke are dependent on the chronological outline of Mark, Mark is responsible for the synoptic chronology of the life of Jesus. Matthew and Luke have no independent knowledge of that chronology. This is demonstrated by the fact that when they draw on Q, they do not agree about where items should be placed in the Markan outline.

The **Q-source** lacks any chronology. Q is a collection of wisdom material attributed to Jesus (and John the Baptist). It contains very little biographical data; it has no birth or childhood stories and no passion narrative. It has virtually no narrative connectives. It is a sayings gospel, much like the Gospel of Thomas.

§6. The Oral Gospel

6.1 Paul's "gospel." The earliest version of the "gospel" preserved for us in written records is the "gospel" of Paul. Paul's gospel was not, of course, a narrative or sayings gospel like those included in *New Gospel Parallels,* but an oral gospel. Paul gives a summary of it in 1 Corinthians 15:3–5:

> I handed on to you among the very first things
> what I also received as tradition:
> > Christ died for our sins
> > > according to the scriptures,
> > and was buried,
> > and rose up on the third day
> > > according to the scriptures.
> > He then appeared to Cephas,
> > and then to the eleven.

There are two steps in this formulation: Christ died; Christ was raised. The death of Christ, but not his resurrection, was *for us*. Both steps take place because the scriptures said they would. The two events are thus the fulfillment of prophecies.

6.2 Mark's "gospel." Paul's gospel was in general circulation when Mark composed his story. In the three predictions of the passion Mark betrays his knowledge of the two-step gospel:

8:31a	He started teaching them
b	that the son of Adam was destined to suffer a great deal,
c	and be rejected by the elders and the ranking priests and the scholars,
d	and be killed,
e	and after three days rise.
9:31c	The son of Adam is being turned over to his enemies,
d	and they will end up killing him.
e	And three days after he is killed
f	he will rise!
10:33b	The son of Adam will be turned over to the ranking priests and the scholars,
c	and they will sentence him to death,
d	and turn him over to foreigners,
34a	and they will make fun of him,
b	and spit on him,
c	and flog him,
d	and put ⟨him⟩ to death.
e	Yet after three days he will rise!

These Markan predictions indicate that the author knew the two-step gospel quoted by Paul and was aware that each step was in accordance with the scriptures. Accordingly, the author of Mark developed a narrative gospel that climaxed in the death of Jesus, with the promise of the resurrection. However, Mark does not emphasize the saving efficacy of Jesus' death (but note 10:45); rather, Mark interprets Jesus' death as the result of a conspiracy against him.

Mark 10:45 "After all, the son of Adam didn't come to be served, but to serve, even to give his life as a ransom for many."

Unlike Paul, Mark wanted to incorporate into his gospel other kinds of materials: Jesus as miracle worker; Jesus as aphorist, parabler, sage; and other legends about Jesus. He therefore had to create a number of framing stories, including the three predictions of the passion, to serve as his outline, and into that outline he inserted various kinds of stories he knew from the older tradition.

§§7–11: The Gospel of Mark

§7. The Composition of Mark

The Gospel of Mark was composed by an anonymous author (see *How the Gospels Got Their Names,* p. 10) shortly after 70 CE. In the preceding section, we have already indicated how he went about his task (§6). As an introduction to Mark, we will spell out the process: What kinds of oral materials did Mark use in the composition of his gospel? What aspects of Mark betray its oral origins? What are the features of Mark as a written gospel?

§8. Types of Oral Material in Mark

8.1 Units of oral discourse. The materials out of which Mark and other authors crafted narrative gospels include, as a major component, units of discourse that had circulated orally—in unwritten form—prior to their inclusion in written gospels. Such units had a more or less independent existence in their oral form, although they were soon gathered into clusters and complexes, arranged by topic, form, or catchword to aid the memory. Yet because the same or similar units often appear in different clusters and complexes, we can be certain that particular units took more than one path in the unfolding tradition.

Oral units of discourse may be anything from a short, pithy saying—an aphorism—to a more extended account of a miraculous cure, from a parable without context to an elaborate narrative setting for a wise saying or pronouncement. Scholars have endeavored to isolate and classify such units as they have been preserved in the extant written gospels. Authors of gospels have of course adapted oral materials to the contexts in which they have placed them, so it is sometimes difficult or even impossible to determine the oral shape of specific units. Nevertheless, the basic types of oral units are clearly discernible and may readily be compared with similar forms appearing elsewhere in hellenistic literature.

The basic oral forms include sayings and saying clusters, parables and parable clusters, pronouncement stories (also called *chreiai*, singular: *chreia*), and stories of exorcisms and miraculous cures. Form critics, who specialize in the history of oral tradition, have described the formal patterning of each type and have endeavored to trace the history of individual units. In the brief sketch to follow, we will describe the principal types and provide catalogues of occurrences in the Gospel of Mark.

8.2 Sayings and parables. Two forms of speech appear to have been characteristic of Jesus: the *saying* (epigram, maxim, proverb, aphorism—all names for the same form) and the *parable.*

MARK

The Gospel of Mark is attributed to John Mark, a companion of Paul (Acts 12:12, 25, 13:5, 15:36–41, Phlm 24, Col 4:10, 2 Tim 4:11), a cousin of Barnabas (Col 4:10), and perhaps an associate of Peter (1 Pet 5:13). The suggestion was first made by Papias (ca. 130 CE), as reported by Eusebius (d. 310), both Fathers of the ancient church. In this, as in other matters, Papias is unreliable, because he is interested in the guarantees of an eye-witness rather than in the oral process that produced Mark.

MATTHEW

It is Papias again, as reported by Eusebius, who names Matthew (Matt 10:3) as the author of the first gospel. Matthew may have another name, Levi, which is the name given to the tax-collector in Mark 2:14 and Luke 5:27, but who is called Matthew in the parallel passage, Matt 9:9. We cannot account for the differences in name. Papias' assertion that canonical Matthew was composed in Hebrew is patently false; Matthew was composed in Greek in dependence on Q and Mark, also written in Greek by unknown authors.

LUKE

The tradition that Luke the physician and companion of Paul was the author of Luke-Acts goes back to the second century CE. The Luke in question is referred to in Col 4:14, Phlm 24, 2 Tim 4:11, where he is identified as a physician. It is improbable that the author of Luke-Acts was a physician; it is doubtful that he was a companion of Paul. Like the other attributions, this one, too, is fanciful.

THOMAS

The Gospel of Thomas is attributed to Didymus Judas Thomas, who was revered in the Syrian church as an apostle (Matt 10:3, Mark 3:18, Luke 6:15, Acts 1:13; cf. John 11:16, 20:24, 21:2) and as the twin brother of Jesus (so claimed by the Acts of Thomas, a third-century CE work). The attribution to Thomas may indicate where this gospel was written, but it tells us nothing about the author.

JOHN

The Fourth Gospel was composed by an anonymous author in the last decade of the first century. About 180 CE Irenaeus reports the tradition that ascribes the book to John, son of Zebedee, while others ascribed it to John the elder who lived at Ephesus, and still others to the beloved disciple (John 13:23–25, 19:25–27, 20:2–10, 21:7, 20–23). The Fourth Gospel was opposed as heretical in the early church, and it knows none of the stories associated with John, son of Zebedee. In the judgment of many scholars, it was produced by a "school" of disciples, probably in Syria.

PETER

Gospel of Peter 14:3 identifies Simon Peter as the author of the Gospel of Peter: "But I, Simon Peter, and Andrew, my brother, took our fishing nets and went away to the sea." Like other authorial attributions, this one, too, is fanciful, even though the ascription is given in the Gospel of Peter itself. The Gospel of Peter was probably composed originally in the late first century CE. Surprisingly, it is the only known gospel attributed to Simon Peter.

All the gospels originally circulated anonymously. Authoritative names were later assigned to them by unknown figures in the early church. In most cases, the names are guesses or perhaps the result of pious hopes.

An aphorism is a prose miniature: a concise, pithy, pointed formulation that sticks in the memory. The proverb is formally identical with the aphorism, but is sometimes distinguished from it in content: the proverb represents collective wisdom or ancestral authority; it reflects what is accepted, tried and true. The aphorism, on the other hand, embodies personal insight or individual authority; it represents counter wisdom, a vision of a different order of things. Many of the aphorisms (and aphoristic parables) of Jesus concern the coming of God's imperial rule or God's domain, which he apparently took to be a different order of things.

Proverbs are also attributed to Jesus. In Mark 2:17 Jesus is reported to have repeated a well-known dictum:

Since when do the able-bodied need a doctor?
It's the sick who do.

An aphorism of Jesus is preserved in Mark 10:31:

Many of the first will be last,
and of the last many will be first.

A catalogue of proverbs and aphorisms preserved in the Gospel of Mark is found in Table 2 (p. 59). The catalogue is relatively brief compared with Matthew and Luke, since Mark is less interested in the teachings of Jesus than in his activities.

C. H. Dodd, whose work on the parables is still highly regarded, gave this classic definition of a parable as Jesus employs it:

At its simplest the parable is a metaphor or simile drawn from nature or the common life, arresting the hearer by its vividness or strangeness, and leaving the mind in sufficient doubt about its precise application to tease it into active thought.   —*The Parables of the Kingdom,* 16, rev. ed., 5

Mark records relatively few parables: only five are preserved (Table 2, p. 59). The great narrative parables of Jesus are found for the most part in Matthew, Luke, and Thomas.

8.3 Pronouncement stories. The Gospel of Mark is rich in pronouncement stories—the author records thirty-two of them (catalogue in Table 3, p. 69). Consequently, they are a major component in the composition of Mark's gospel. Such stories are very close to the sayings tradition and are therefore among the earliest stories told about Jesus.

A pronouncement story is a short narrative describing a situation to which a sage or prominent person gives a response, usually in the form of an astute observation or aphorism or proverb. The story depicts a challenge, or inquiry, or statement, which sets the stage for the response. The hellenistic rhetoricians called pronouncement stories chreiai. Vernon K. Robbins and his colleagues have collected hundreds of chreiai from hellenistic literature under the title, *Ancient Quotes and Anecdotes:* the designation aptly characterizes the pronouncement story as a combination of anecdote and quotation.

Mark employs a chain of pronouncement stories in 2:1–3:6 to depict Jesus' activity at the outset of his ministry. Two stories in the group are modified miracle tales. Mark uses another sequence of pronouncement stories in 11:27–33, 12:13–37 to underscore Jesus' confrontation with officials after his arrival in Jerusalem.

8.4 Miracle stories. The Gospel of Mark, like other narrative gospels, contains a number of miracle stories. These are of several broad types: healing stories, including exorcisms (it is sometimes impossible to segregate the two); nature wonders; **epiphanies**. A catalogue of miracle stories is to be found in Table 4 (p. 99). This catalogue does not include stories of the resurrection and ascension of Jesus.

An **epiphany** is a manifestation of a divine being or God: Yahweh appearing to Moses in the burning bush; Jesus being transformed on the mountain.

Form critics have developed formal paradigms for the healing story. The healing story, like other narrative segments, consists of an introduction, a narrative nucleus, and a conclusion. The nucleus normally has two parts: a dialogue and the healing proper. The patient is introduced with some minimal description of his or her affliction. A request is put to the healer, either by the patient or by a representative, and in response the healer effects the cure. The part of the story that treats the healing may consist of as many as four discrete parts: a healing word or pronouncement ("Be opened"); some indication of the healing technique (he put his fingers in his ears); an affirmation that the cure has been effected (ears were opened, tongue released); and a demonstration that the patient is cured (he spoke plainly). The illustrations in parentheses are taken from *The Man with the Mute Spirit,* Mark 7:31–37.

In exorcisms, an exchange between the demon and the exorcist takes the place of the request. And some healing stories are mixed with controversy stories, in which case the dialogue involves a dispute with opponents.

Several scholars have argued that Mark made use of two chains of miracle stories. Each chain consisted of five stories, beginning with a miracle connected with a sea crossing and concluding with a miraculous feeding of a huge crowd in an isolated place. Interpreters of Mark had always been puzzled by duplicate stories, and the use of a pre-Markan collection of stories seems to account for the repetition. Between the opening and closing stories, the chains contained an account of an exorcism and two miraculous cures. Mark has of course slightly rearranged the sequence, as indicated by Table 5 (p. 111).

Other scholars have proposed a second pre-Markan collection of miracle stories reflected in both Mark and the Fourth Gospel. The series begins with the healing of an infirm man and concludes with a resurrection. A miraculous feeding in the wilderness, Jesus walking on the sea, and the cure of a blind man come between. It is striking that the two chains occur in the same order in Mark and John (Table 5, p. 111).

§9. Compounds, Clusters, Collections, and Complexes

9.1 Building blocks of the gospel. Out of the oral materials catalogued in §8, the author of Mark began to fashion a gospel. However, some fashioning had already taken place: single sayings of Jesus had been turned into compounds (two sayings joined) and clusters (three or more sayings). Healing stories were joined, pronouncement and miracle stories were collected into chains, and rhetorical complexes began to take shape. Some of this compositional activity clearly belongs to the oral period and thus antedates the creation of Mark. In other cases, we can be reasonably certain the author of Mark is responsible. But in many instances, it is difficult to tell whether the compositional process precedes or belongs to the author of Mark.

In the following, we shall catalogue some of the various compounds, clusters, collections, and complexes that have been identified in Mark. This catalogue will provide the student of Mark with some sense of the building blocks out of which the gospel was constructed.

9.2 Aphoristic compounds and clusters. A detailed analysis of one aphoristic compound, following the pioneering work of J. Dominic Crossan, will serve as a general introduction to the complexities involved in most compounds, clusters, collections, and complexes.

Mark 2:18–20 is a pronouncement story that climaxes with the sayings in 19–20. To this pronouncement story has been appended two additional aphorisms, one concerning the impropriety of combining shrunk with unshrunk cloth, the other the folly of putting young wine into old wineskins (2:21–22). The two metaphors appear in Thom 47:4–5 but in reverse order. Although the order is not fixed, the two sayings seem to have been combined already at the earliest stage of the tradition known to us, one that antedates both Mark and Thomas. Mark 2:21–22 therefore constitutes an aphoristic compound.

Mark 2:20, the saying about the incompatibility of combining a wedding and fasting, has a counterpart in Thom 104:3. This suggests (a) that 2:20 was not always a part of a pronouncement story, and (b) that 2:20 and 2:21–22 once circulated separately. It was thus Mark who probably first combined them. If so, Mark has created a new cluster.

The situation is even more complex. Both Luke and Thomas attach a third saying to the cluster: no one wants to drink young wine after drinking aged wine (Luke 5:39, Thom 47:3). In Luke the additional saying comes after the compound just identified, in Thomas it comes before. Once again there is disagreement in order. However, the clustering of the same three aphorisms in both Luke and Thomas indicates that these two gospels may have known a different combination of sayings than did Mark. This suggestion is supported by differences in Luke's version of the saying concerning cloth: Luke advises against patching an old garment with a piece of cloth from a new garment, since the two won't match—quite a different matter than combining unshrunk with shrunk cloth. Luke and Thomas, then, may reflect a cluster of sayings that has a history different from that of the compound known to Mark.

The series of sayings in Mark 2:20–22 has a common theme: the impossibility of combining certain things. This may be Mark's basis for joining them: wedding and fasting do not go together, nor do shrunk/unshrunk cloth and young wine/old wineskins. However, in Luke and Thomas the third saying exhibits a catchword link: that catchword is *wine.* We thus have one cluster that is combined on the principle of theme or topic, another that joins that principle to a second: catchword association. Two other principles are employed in creating compounds and clusters: similarity in form (for example, beatitudes, parables), and an external framing device.

A catalogue of aphoristic compounds and clusters is found in Table 6 (p. 143).

9.3 Sequence in Capernaum. The sequence in Mark 1:21–39 covers a period of twenty-four hours and is located in Capernaum. The sequence opens in the synagogue at Capernaum with an exorcism, moves to Simon's house for a miraculous cure, after which Jesus steals away to an isolated place. It concludes with the notice of a speaking tour in Galilee. Editorial observations are provided in 1:28, 32–34, 39. In the judgment of many scholars, this complex was created by Mark, largely but not entirely out of traditional materials.

9.4 A sequence of controversy stories. A series of controversy stories has been collected into Mark 2:1–3:6. Five stories are involved. All five are pronouncement stories (Table 3, p. 69). The first and last are combinations of miraculous cures and a controversy dialogue. The only passage not integral to this collection is 2:13–15, which concerns the call of Levi to discipleship. The collection was probably put together by Mark, although some scholars have argued that it came to Mark already assembled.

There is a second series of pronouncement stories in Mark 11:27–12:37. Again, five stories are involved. Into the group Mark has inserted the parable of the leased vineyard, 12:1–12. As in the first collection, these stories are also controversy stories.

9.5 Jesus' relatives and the Beelzebul controversy. Another complex Mark seems to have assembled is found in 3:20–35. The literary envelope for the complex is formed by the account of Jesus' relatives coming to get him because they think him out of his mind (3:20–21, 31–35). Sandwiched between is an accusation on the part of some scribes that Jesus is in league with the prince of demons (3:22), to which Jesus responds with rhetorical questions and aphorisms (3:23–26). Mark then appends the metaphor of the powerful man (3:27) and sayings about blasphemy (3:28–30), on the grounds that Jesus' accusers are blaspheming the spirit. The entire complex consists, then, of two pronouncement stories (3:22–26, 3:31–35) and various sayings arranged in a thematic complex.

9.6 Teaching in parables. The complex Mark 4:1–34 is almost certainly a Markan creation as it now stands, although it may incorporate smaller older complexes. The introduction is found in 4:1–2, the conclusion in 4:33–34. The conclusion refers to 4:1–2 and also to 4:10–12. The three passages form a strong framing device.

The complex contains three of the five parables preserved by Mark, as well as sayings clusters, and an explanation of the parable of the sower, seeds, soils. In the judgment of Burton Mack, the complex is an elaboration of the chreia containing the parable, that opens the complex. This complex and the one found in 13:3–37 are the only two teaching complexes of any length in the Gospel of Mark. In Mark, Jesus is more of a doer than a teacher.

9.7 Didactic scenes. Philip Sellew has recently identified five complexes in Mark as didactic scenes. In a didactic scene, Jesus teaches in public, after which he is interrogated privately by his closest followers, who have not understood his public remarks. Two of these didactic scenes probably took shape before Mark composed his gospel: 4:3–20 (now incorporated into an even larger complex, 4:1–34: see §9.5) and 7:14–23. Three of them seem to have been created by the author of the Gospel: 8:11–21, 9:14–29, and 10:1–

Didactic refers to something (treatise, method, scene) designed to teach or instruct. The Didache is an early Christian compendium of instruction or a catechism.

12. Mark 9:14–29 is of course a healing story, to which a private explanation has been attached. And the core of 10:1–12 is a pronouncement story.

Didactic scenes are made up of five elements: public pronouncement, withdrawal to a private place, query by disciples, rebuke of disciples for being dim-witted, and explanation of the pronouncement or saying.

Didactic scenes are another illustration of the multilayered nature of the tradition: smaller units embedded in long sequences, longer sequences turned into still larger complexes.

9.8 Intercalations in Mark. There are eight instances where the author of Mark appears to insert one block of material into the midst of another block. Scholars have come to call this phenomenon *intercalation,* which can refer either to the practice of inserting one thing into the midst of other things, or to the inserted material itself.

The story of the paralytic (2:1–12) is basically a healing story in which Jesus cures a paralytic. Into that story Mark seems to have inserted a controversy over whether Jesus has the authority to forgive sins: 2:5b–10b. It should be noted that the phrase, *he says to the paralytic,* is repeated in 2:10c. The intervening controversy can thus be omitted without affecting the integrity of the surrounding healing story.

Intercalations in Mark are not all of this type. Some have to do with the interruption of one story to tell another, others with the insertion of further sayings material. A catalogue of Markan intercalations is found in Table 7 (p. 157).

9.9 Chains of miracle stories. It was suggested earlier (§8.4) that Mark incorporated two chains of miracle stories into his gospel. These chains may well have been put together before Mark made use of them. Mark may also have shared a chain of miracle stories with the Gospel of John. A catalogue of chains of miracle stories in Mark is found in Table 5 (p. 111).

9.10 The death of John the Baptist. The pericope reporting the death of John the Baptist (6:14–29) is unique among the materials incorporated into the Gospel of Mark. The language of the story lacks characteristic Markan stylistic features, it makes use of more elevated language than is customary for Mark, and it records several words unique in Mark's vocabulary. Composers of narratives in the hellenistic world frequently copied materials out of earlier documents in composing their own. We know that Josephus made frequent use of sources, as did Matthew and Luke. It would not be surprising if the pericope on the death of John were a report Mark copied from some unknown document.

9.11 The passion narrative. It was once thought that the passion narrative (chaps. 14–15) was put together in something like its present form prior to the creation of Mark. Many scholars now take the view that Mark is the creator of the passion narrative. However, some hold the view that an earlier version of the Gospel of Peter (see the *Catalogue of Written Gospels,* p. x, for a description) is the basis for Mark's account. This looks like a return to the earlier view, in which the Gospel of Mark was described as a traditional passion narrative with a long introduction.

It is evident, in any case, that the passion narrative—the narrative of the events leading up to the death of Jesus—differs from the first thirteen chap-

The **passion narrative**, strictly speaking, refers to the sufferings of Jesus on the cross, or to the period immediately before and including his death. Scholars use the term more loosely to refer to the narrative of events surrounding his arrest, trial, and crucifixion.

ters of the gospel. The passion story exhibits a higher degree of narrative coherence than do the earlier chapters. Except for the story of the anointing of Jesus (14:3–9), there are no pronouncement stories in the passion account. Sayings and parables end with chapter 13. Miracle stories also disappear with the transition. Markan summaries and transitions are also lacking. In sum, it seems that the oral units and pre-Markan complexes out of which Mark built the first thirteen chapters were not used to create the passion narrative. The passion narrative exhibits a somewhat more cohesive cast. This may be accounted for in large part by Mark's use of scriptural quotations from the Greek Old Testament around which he formed the story. The large number of quotations and allusions suggests that Mark, or perhaps the primitive Christian community, molded the story of the death of Jesus to fit the details of various scriptural prophecies and assertions. This practice may be the reason the passion narrative exhibits a higher degree of cohesiveness and draws less on material formed in the oral period.

§10. Mark as Spoken Gospel

10.1 Oral and print cultures. Members of modern, industrialized societies view a text like the Gospel of Mark from the perspective of a print culture. In a print culture, books and treatises are read silently for the most part, which means that the reader can read and reread passages, flip back and forth in the book, and study specific aspects closely. By contrast, members of an oral culture are permitted only to hear the text recited: books were not commonly available, were clumsy to use, especially in scroll but also in codex form, and not many persons could read, even when written texts were more readily available, as in Alexandria.

Oral texts tend to be brief and concise, although longer narratives can be created by stringing together patterned episodes on a travel narrative or some other narrative thread. Oral narratives lack the overarching narrative connectiveness of the mystery story or the modern novel. The hero of the oral narrative is a simplified figure, whose actions and values contrast sharply with those of his or her opponents: there are only good guys and bad guys, none that are ambiguous. The oral story majors in stereotyped participants rather than in individualized character. It prefers action over reflection, the unusual rather than the ordinary, polarization rather than bland harmony. In sum, the oral narrative must consist of memorable and relevant speech.

10.2 Marks of orality in Mark. Mark's gospel bears the marks of its oral origins and social context (cf. §3). It has mostly oral material at its base. It consists of patterned episodes of three or four basic types. And its content is largely relevant to the Markan community: oral communities do not retain what is not memorable. They tend to preserve segments and sequences that are formally patterned (mnemonically arranged), and thus easy to recall, and to retain material that is applicable to the community's life. Mark was designed for public reading or recitation, and not silent reading.

The signs of Mark's orality can be divided into two categories: microfeatures and macrofeatures. The smaller features include the oral connectives in the gospel that abound everywhere: Mark strings sentences together with *and* (καί), rather than create complex sentences with subordinate clauses. Mark employs a Greek word εὐθύς so often that the translators of the

The conception of **Scholars Version** is sketched in §12.

Scholars Version had to think of alternative translations to avoid distracting redundancy: among them are *right away, right then (and there), right now, just then, just as;* they also endeavored to reduce the occurrences of *and* by substituting other, less obvious connectives. *Again* (πάλιν) is one of the author's favorite words. Mark prefers direct speech to indirect discourse, a preference that is characteristic of folk stories generally. The author frequently arranges items in twos and threes, also typical of folk literature. There are two identical call stories in Mark 1:16–18 and 19–20, each of which concerns two brothers, to cite one striking example of duality. In the narrative of the leper (Mark 1:40–45), there are numerous double lines, a few of which may be cited here:

> 1:42a And right away the leprosy left him,
> b and he was made clean.
> 1:43a And Jesus snapped at him,
> b and dismissed him curtly
> 1:45b he started telling everyone
> c and spreading the story
> 1:45d so that Jesus could no longer enter a city openly,
> e but had to stay out in the country.

Although brevity and conciseness are the soul of oral discourse, nevertheless, in order to slow down the flow of information for the sake of the memory, repetitions are necessary. There are often groups of three: three disciples form the inner circle (Peter, James, and John), just as three women do (two Marys and Salome). Jesus finds the three disciples sleeping three times in Gethsemane, Peter disowns Jesus three times, and Jesus predicts his death on three different occasions. These are all mnemonic devices useful to the oral raconteur, and all conform to the law of three in folk narrative: only three participants on the story stage at one time.

10.3 Macrofeatures. Mark's gospel also exhibits other signs of orality that can be called macrofeatures. Like the so-called interlace of medieval romances, where episodes are strung together indefinitely in the quest story, Mark strings episodes together on a thin narrative thread consisting largely of brief journeys. As we have already observed, Mark makes use of collections and complexes arranged in matching pairs or strings. His tale is breathless as it moves from one episode to another without major pause. The only long discourses in Mark are the string of parables in 4:1–34 and the little apocalypse in 13:3–37. Otherwise, the movement is steady. The author is empathetic, emotionally involved in the story, rather than objectively distanced. The gospel is not the work of the historian gathering and arranging hard data; there is no discernible nostalgia for a Jesus of the past (cf. §4.6). Rather, the author is creating narrative proclamation—a sermon in story form.

10.4 Narrative asides. Mark has interspersed his narrative with numerous asides. He translates Aramaic words for the benefit of his readers (5:41, 7:11, 34, 14:36, 15:34). He explains unfamiliar customs (7:3–4). Once he addresses his readers directly: he alerts them to a critical point (13:14). Most narrative asides are *analepses*: something necessary to understanding the sequence of events is narrated belatedly. Put in other words, the analepsis allows the author to pause and give the reader a piece of information required to comprehend what is going on. At 3:21, for example, we are told that Jesus'

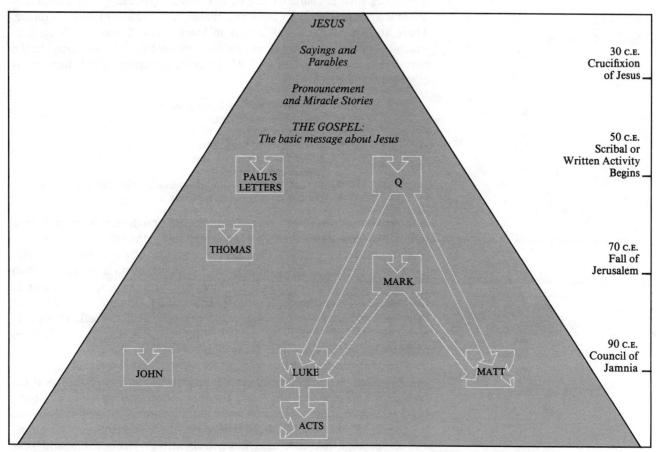

JESUS

*Sayings and
Parables*

*Pronouncement
and Miracle Stories*

*THE GOSPEL:
The basic message about Jesus*

PAUL'S
LETTERS

Q

THOMAS

MARK

JOHN

LUKE

MATT

ACTS

30 C.E.
Crucifixion
of Jesus

50 C.E.
Scribal or
Written Activity
Begins

70 C.E.
Fall of
Jerusalem

90 C.E.
Council of
Jamnia

The written documents produced by early Christian writers emerged from the stream of oral tradition—represented by the pyramid—and drew from that stream—represented by internal arrows. In addition, some authors made use of earlier written sources—represented by connecting arrows. Possibility not represented: John may have known and used one or more of the Synoptic Gospels.

relatives have come to get him. Then, in an aside, the narrator explains that they thought Jesus was out of his mind. This aside provides the motivation for their action.

The large number of asides in Mark suggest that the author was attempting to make the story reader-friendly by explaining an unusual turn of events, dispelling a mystery or puzzle, or just providing necessary information for readers removed from the original context. Such asides are characteristic of oral narration. But they are also found in written discourse.

A catalogue of narrative asides in Mark is found in Table 8 (p. 167).

§11. Mark as Written Gospel

11.1 Mark as author. When Mark undertook the composition of his gospel, he had at his disposal several kinds of material, some of which was in oral form, some perhaps already in written form: sayings, clusters of sayings, pronouncement stories, miracle stories of two or three types, and undoubtedly partially formed legends about Jesus. In all probability he had also some sequences or chains of stories. What he did not have was an overall pattern for his gospel. The precise pattern for what was to become a (narrative) gospel had not yet been created.

The author found it necessary to make a choice among the materials available and to arrange selected materials in some kind of sequence. He also had the option of creating additional stories about Jesus and of designing additional clusters and complexes. He may have edited traditional materials and modified and rearranged the sequences and complexes he adopted. It is not easy to determine, especially not in detail, what the author has taken over and what he has created himself, nor is it possible to determine in every instance when he has modified an existing tradition.

Finally, the author had to decide on some plan to weave these materials into one continuous narrative.

11.2 Framework stories. Several stories found in Mark are conspicuously absent from the catalogues of traditional materials referred to above. These stories may be termed framework stories since they appear at the beginning, in the middle, and at the end of the gospel. These stories appear to have been composed by the author specifically to provide a narrative frame for the gospel. They narrate Jesus' relation to John the Baptist, Jesus' baptism, his wilderness test, and summarize the message Jesus announced at the outset (1:1–15). This first group forms an introduction to the gospel.

A second group forms the turning point of the story and narrates the three predictions of Jesus' death (8:31–33, 9:30–32, 10:32–34) and the epiphany on the mount of transfiguration (9:2–8).

The third group comprises the bulk of the stories in the passion account proper (14:1–15:47) and the account of the empty tomb (16:1–8). The use of oral forms and pre-Markan segments and sequences ceases at the beginning of the passion story. Most of the materials making up the last section of the gospel are therefore of Markan inspiration, in all probability, although at many points he may be drawing upon oral legends about Jesus.

These framework stories are catalogued in Table 9 (p. 229).

11.3 Transitions and narrative summaries. Scholars have also identified numerous transitions and narrative summaries that the author of the gospel almost certainly supplied. These devices provide connective glue that the author employed to join segments and sequences. As in the case of materials the author had taken over from the tradition, these connectives cease before the passion story begins. These transitions and summaries are catalogued Table 10 (p. 239).

11.4 Participants, setting, plot. Interpreters of Mark differ on how the Gospel of Mark is to be read as a written narrative. That should come as no surprise since the work was composed of a variety of materials in an oral and thus relatively fluid environment. Nevertheless, certain elements—those that belong to the structure of any story—are readily identifiable: participants or characters; setting, including both time and place; and plot.

(a) Participants. The **continuity participant** is of course Jesus, who is represented as endowed with the power to perform miracles, to best his opponents in controversy, to attract followers, and, initially at least, to inspire public trust. Jesus is also represented as the anointed one who must die although innocent. The reader is led to be sympathetic with Jesus.

The **continuity participant** furnishes the narrative thread that gives the story continuity.

Jesus' opponents—the scribes, Pharisees, priests, Sadducees, and civil authorities—are cast in a consistently negative light. They are pictured as self-serving and obstinate. They plot against Jesus because they hate him. The reader is prompted to be hostile to them.

The disciples—the circle around Jesus, the twelve, but especially the inner circle of three (Peter, James, John)—are quick to respond to Jesus' call, profess loyalty, but turn out to be dim-witted, fearful, and unreliable. They misunderstand Jesus and resist his determination to go to Jerusalem. Gradually, the reader is made to feel ambivalent towards the disciples.

The general public—*hoi polloi*, to use the Greek phrase—function as a chorus in the story: they all act and speak in unison. They are initially impressed with Jesus and rush to follow him about. But they, too, misunderstand him and eventually forsake him. They are depicted as sheep without a shepherd.

There are numerous minor participants in Mark, each of which occupies the stage for a brief time and then disappears.

(b) Setting. Locales in the gospel include: the road, the desert or wilderness, the river Jordan, the lake and the sea, and the mountains. These are all important spatial settings in the story of Israel, especially from the exodus from Egypt to the crossing of the Jordan. Mark employs them because they resonate for his audience.

The temporal setting of the story is the time when God's imperial rule is closing in (1:14–15). The little apocalypse in chapter 13 indicates that the final agonies are near. It is a time of crisis. Jesus is acutely aware of the time, but the other participants in the story seem not to know what time it is.

(c) Plot. The story turns on the conflict of Jesus with three parties: the cosmic powers, as represented by the demons and by "natural" forces such as the sea; the religious authorities, represented by the scribes, Pharisees, priests, and Sadducees; and the civil authorities, represented by Herod, Pilate, and the Roman soldiers.

This conflict is resolved by Jesus' death, in which his opponents win an ironic victory. It is ironic because it actually produces precisely what it was not supposed to produce: salvation for humankind.

The disciples are caught in the conflict between Jesus and the authorities. They are victims because they seem not to understand, are afraid, and in the end flee from the scene. However, Joseph of Arimathea and the small group of women who had followed Jesus are there to witness the promise of the future.

In all of this, the reader is made party to the true course and meaning of events and so is an insider with special knowledge and genuine understanding.

§12: The Scholars Version

The Scholars Version is a new translation of the Bible. The first division of the Scholars Version consists of fresh translations of all gospel texts that provide independent information about Jesus of Nazareth. The Scholars Version of the gospels has been utilized as the basis of *New Gospel Parallels.*

12.1 A scholars canon. The Scholars Version—SV for short—is free of ecclesiastical and religious control, unlike other major translations into English, including the King James version and its descendants (Protestant) and the Douay-Rheims version and its progeny (Catholic). Since SV is not bound by ecclesiastical considerations, it will include among biblical books many that are not found in traditional bibles. SV will incorporate all texts related to the origins of Judaism and Christianity, without respect to theological orientation.

12.2 Translation from original languages. The Scholars Version is a translation from the ancient biblical languages: Hebrew, Aramaic, Greek, Coptic, Latin, and other languages. In some instances, the only primary source is a translation into a secondary language. The Gospel of Thomas, for example, has survived in full form only in Coptic. In other cases, derivative versions are the means of checking the understanding of the original language. The Greek translation of the Old Testament, for example, known as the Septuagint (LXX for short) is an aid for understanding the Hebrew text in many passages. Indeed, the LXX was the primary version for the early Christian movement.

12.3 Translation into American English. The scholars who serve on the translation panel for SV have adopted certain guidelines for themselves. SV is a translation into American English as it is spoken and written in North America. American English is not to be understood as "standard" English: the translators want to avoid stilted, wooden, flat, and insipid English, yet they have not adopted, nor do they recommend, substandard English, in spite of an occasional substandard original. On the contrary, they have attempted to select sparkling, intriguing, flavorful, lucid, incisive diction wherever possible, so long as that diction is consonant with the style and level of the original, and so long as that diction does not violate the canons of good English usage. However, they have only rarely elected literary language where more colloquial speech would do, except when the original requires the former. The Gospel of Luke—to cite one example—will sound more literary to the American ear than the Gospel of Mark, which will read more like colloquial English, since the Greek originals reflect a correlative difference.

12.4 A new experience for the reader. The translators have taken as their motto this dictum: A translation is artful to the extent that one can forget, while reading it, that it is a translation at all. Accordingly, rather than attempt to make SV a **pony** to the original language, they worked diligently to produce in the American reader an experience comparable to that of the first readers—or hearers—of the original.

A **pony** is a literal line-by-line translation often used as an aid in learning a foreign language.

12.5 Biblical language and euphemisms. In pursuit of this goal, the translators have been guided by several additional principles.

They have sought to avoid "biblical" English. Biblical language is phraseology that has become faded, trite, empty, or simply misleading by virtue of long usage and over-interpretation. They have also eliminated heavily freighted theological terms—especially those that call to mind particular schools of thought or parochial perspectives. After all, composers and the first readers of biblical texts had not yet formed fixed notions of theological orthodoxy associated with later church councils and the first English translations.

For similar reasons, the translators have refused to perpetuate pietisms and euphemisms dictated by liturgical interests and putative good taste. They have endeavored to represent colloquialisms and rough language in the original by comparable English terms, in other words, to call a spade, a spade. For example, when Jesus swears an oath, the translators let him swear, or when Paul refers to his inherited and acquired merits as "a pile of crap," they let him say so in English, without indulging the merely vulgar.

The panel has assiduously avoided translating words or even phrases in the style of the King James version and its descendants. The translators have attempted to agree on what the original sentence, or phrase, or word meant in its own context and then to state that meaning in American English, as though they were composing (better: hearing or reading) that text for the first time.

12.6 Readability. The translators have made readability the final test of every sentence, every paragraph, every book. They have read the text silently to themselves, aloud to each other, and have had it read silently and aloud by others. Every expression that did not strike the ear as native was reviewed and revised, not once but many times. Nevertheless, the translators are aware that many facets of these ancient texts are unfamiliar to speakers of American English: we could not find a single wheat farmer who could tell us what a winnowing shovel was. At the same time, scholars of the Bible have ears accustomed to traditional English translations, so that many archaic phrases and terms would not sound odd to them. Faced with this dilemma, they have had to retrain their own ears and then go in search of responses from those who were less familiar with both ancient custom and older translation.

12.7 The archaic and the offensive. Translation is always a compromise, some say even a betrayal. If translators strive to make the Greek of the Gospel of Mark sound as familiar to the modern American ear as the original did to its first readers, will they not have translated out much that was there in the text? Will they not have eliminated the archaic in the interests of readability?

The panel agreed at the outset not to translate out the social and cultural features of the text that are unfamiliar—worse yet, distasteful—to the modern reader. That would be to deny the contemporary reader any direct experience of the world, the social context, of the original. On the contrary, they have tried to put those features, as alien and as distasteful as they sometimes are, into plain English. So there are still slaves in the text, the Pharisees and the Jews are often turned into uncomplimentary stereotypes, Jesus gets angry and exasperated, the disciples are dim-witted, and the society of the Mediterranean world is male-dominated, to mention only a few features.

At the same time, the translators have avoided sexist language where not required by the original. Male singulars are occasionally turned into genderless plurals. The language of SV is inclusive wherever possible, without violating the text and its social context. In the New Testament, the translators are following the lead of Jesus, who included a number of women in his inner circle, and of Paul, who quoted, although he did not put into full practice, the adage, "In Christ there is neither male nor female."

The SV version of the gospel texts that appear in *New Gospel Parallels* is a translation in process: improvements and emendations will be made from time to time as scholars make use of SV in their publications.

§§13–18: New Gospel Parallels

§13. Revised Edition

New Gospel Parallels is a newly conceived instrument for the study of the gospels. The entire work consists of two parts: Part I covers the Synoptic Gospels; Part II includes the Gospels of John and Thomas, together with other sayings gospels, infancy gospels, passion gospels, as well as fragments of known and unknown gospels.

In this second, thoroughly revised edition, the Synoptic Gospels have been segregated into three independent volumes, in accordance with user preference. This arrangement makes it possible to have each of the Synoptics open to the same passage simultaneously, without having to flip back and forth.

In addition, the texts of the gospels have been broken into short lines known as cola (singular: colon) and the cola matched wherever possible to facilitate close comparison. Matched cola reveal at a glance what the gospels have in common and what is peculiar to each.

Other features of the first edition have been retained and will be discussed below.

§14. Matched Segments and Cola

The gospels, like other written texts, are composed of units of discourse. Words, phrases, clauses, sentences, paragraphs, and groups of paragraphs make up the composition. As the preceding list indicates, the units are of ascending size, with the larger units encompassing the smaller units, in a pyramidal or hierarchal structure.

It is not possible to compose an extended text without conceiving it in blocks marked by openings, closings, and transitions. In the study of the gospels, the unit most scholars work with in their analytic operations is the pericope. Pericopes (literally, "something cut out") are thought to be self-contained units, partly on the grounds that they are segments of discourse, and partly because many of them were thought to have circulated orally as independent units of discourse before they became an ingredient in a more extended gospel.

Units of discourse may be termed segments, and groups of units will be referred to as sequences. A segment may be represented graphically as an oval: O. Sequences would then consist of a series of ovals enclosed by brackets to indicate the beginning and end of the sequence: [OOO]. A complex document, such a gospel, would consist of many such sequences. Sequences, in turn, would be organized into sequences of sequences in a hierarchal structure embracing the whole. A sequence of sequences could be represented as two sequences enclosed in square brackets: [[OOO][OOO]].

The gospel texts collected in *New Gospel Parallels* have been analyzed into segments and sequences in accordance with their internal markers as developed in *The Poetics of Biblical Narrative*. The segments and sequences are numbered and identified for convenience of reference.

Identification of segments and sequences employs the following codes: M=Matthew, K=Mark, L=Luke, J=John, T=Thomas. Segments and sequences are numbered consecutively. Mark, for example, is divided into 17 sequences (S1–S17) and 72 segments (K1–K72).

Where verbal similarities permit, the text of the gospels has been broken into short lines, known as cola, in order to facilitate close comparison. A colon normally consists of one verb plus modifiers. However, the requirements of matched cola frequently override this principle of division. When a verse consists of several cola, they are assigned letters (a, b, c, etc.) to facilitate ease and accuracy of comparison and reference.

§15. Kinds of Comparative Study

The study of the gospel tradition involves two basic types of comparison, the paradigmatic and the syntagmatic.

The comparison of segments recording the same or similar materials (stories, sayings, summaries) is the **paradigmatic** study of the tradition. By comparing the different versions of the parable of the sower found in Matthew, Mark, Luke, and Thomas, one may discover a common pattern or paradigm, of which each of four versions is an expression or performance. In paradigmatic comparison, one compares segments without reference to the sequence in which they appear.

A **paradigm** is a model or pattern. In linguistics, a paradigm is a model of a noun or verb in which all of its inflectional forms are displayed. In literary criticism, a paradigm is a story pattern: common plot, common participants, common setting.

The comparative study of the order of events and the contexts in which certain events occur is **syntagmatic** study of the tradition. The account of Jesus driving merchants out of the temple appears in all three Synoptics and the Gospel of John. A syntagmatic study of this story would reveal that in John it takes place almost at the beginning of the public activities of Jesus, while in Matthew, Mark, and Luke it occurs at the outset of the final week in Jerusalem, just prior to the crucifixion.

The word **syntax** in Greek means *ordering together*, which is what one does in creating words, phrases, clauses, sentences, paragraphs. The 'syntax' of extended discourse of any kind is how the various segments are ordered in the string that constitutes that text.

New Gospel Parallels is designed and laid out to keep both the paradigmatic and syntagmatic dimensions of the gospel narratives steadily in view, without sacrificing one to the other. That is an exceedingly complex task, and it must be achieved without creating an unduly complicated page.

TIME LINE OF THE GOSPELS AND MANUSCRIPTS

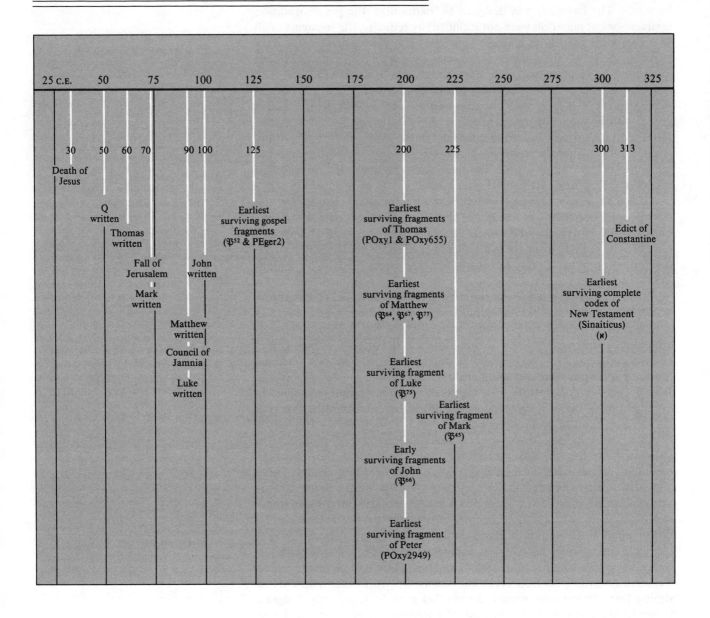

| 25 C.E. | 50 | 75 | 100 | 125 | 150 | 175 | 200 | 225 | 250 | 275 | 300 | 325 |

30   50   60   70   90 100   125   200   225   300   313

Death of
Jesus

Q
written

Thomas
written

Fall of
Jerusalem

Mark
written

John
written

Matthew
written

Council of
Jamnia

Luke
written

Earliest
surviving gospel
fragments
($\mathfrak{P}^{52}$ & PEger2)

Earliest
surviving fragments
of Thomas
(POxy1 & POxy655)

Earliest
surviving fragments
of Matthew
($\mathfrak{P}^{64}$, $\mathfrak{P}^{67}$, $\mathfrak{P}^{77}$)

Earliest
surviving fragment
of Luke
($\mathfrak{P}^{75}$)

Earliest
surviving fragment
of Mark
($\mathfrak{P}^{45}$)

Early
surviving fragments
of John
($\mathfrak{P}^{66}$)

Earliest
surviving fragment
of Peter
(POxy2949)

Edict of
Constantine

Earliest
surviving complete
codex of
New Testament
(Sinaiticus)
($\aleph$)

§16. Synopses and Harmonies

16.1 The gospel harmony. The older study instrument in which the canonical gospels were presented in parallel columns is called the gospel harmony. The harmony was designed to 'harmonize' the gospel tradition (extracanonical materials were not included) by reducing the segments of all four canonical gospels to a single sequence. The gospel harmony lacks a genuine interest in the differences revealed by paradigmatic analysis; it is more concerned to smooth out the versions into a single sequence. The resulting sequence in each harmony was of course arbitrary: there were as many sequences as there were harmony editors, and none of them was congruent with the sequence presented by any one of the evangelists. It cannot be said that the harmony was really interested in the syntagmatic study of the gospels either, since in creating its own sequence, it merely ignored the sequences of the various gospels. For these and other reasons, critical scholars no longer use or create gospel harmonies.

16.2 The gospel synopsis. Synopses were originally created for the microscopic comparison of words and phrases in parallel texts. To be of the most use, of course, they had to be constructed in the original language, Greek. In its original form, the synopsis was oriented to source criticism: the determination of the literary relation of the gospels, particularly the Synoptics, to each other.

The synopsis oriented to source criticism was concerned to determine which of the gospels was chronologically prior and was therefore employed as a source by the other two synoptic writers. Once the consensus formed around the two source hypothesis (that Mark was the original written gospel and was copied and revised by Matthew and Luke in creating their versions; Matthew and Luke were dependent on a second written source, dubbed Q), John dropped out of contention for high historical honors, and consequently dropped out of many synopses as well. Almost by definition the synopsis became a synopsis of the synoptic gospels.

16.3 Form criticism. Under the tutelage of Karl Ludwig Schmidt, Martin Dibelius, and Rudolf Bultmann, form criticism became the dominant method of gospel study during the first half of the twentieth century. These and other scholars had demonstrated how the written sources of the canonical gospels were preceded by a significant period of oral creativity and transmission of the Jesus tradition. The form critics held that the gospels may be broken apart at their editorial seams, in which case clearly demarcated oral segments emerge from the editorial framework created by the evangelists to weave the pieces together into weak narratives. These oral segments can be classified according to their form and compared with other segments of similar form, in the same gospel and in other gospels. A properly designed synopsis can assist with this process of paradigmatic comparison. Form criticism was and remains the preeminent form of paradigmatic research.

16.4 Redaction criticism. The form-critical use of synopses took the oral segments to be relatively stable and reliable in relation to the editorial framework. The sequential framework, consequently, was regarded as secondary and of little or no value in establishing the historical sequences of events. But as the flower of form criticism faded, a new type of gospel study emerged under the aegis of literary criticism. This type, called redaction criticism, turned its attention precisely to the editorial framework and asked how each evangelist took oral segments and reshaped them to suit their own perspectives. The redaction critics also inquired after the narrative framework each evangelist created in the process of forming a new version of the gospel. It was discovered that the synopsis could serve the purposes of redaction criticism as well as it could serve source criticism or form criticism.

The shift from form criticism to redaction criticism after the second world war signaled a shift from the paradigmatic to the syntagmatic mode of analysis.

16.5 Gospel criticism in transition. Today, gospel criticism appears to be in transition: the balance between the paradigmatic and the syntagmatic is being restored. At the same time, interests in both the paradigmatic and syntagmatic aspects of the gospels has broadened to include miracle stories, anecdotes (chreiai), parables, and aphorisms drawn from all over the hellenistic world. The new aim is to discover how these particular units of discourse came to be employed as building blocks of the gospels, rather than some other types of discourse.

The new shape of literary criticism has bequeathed to biblical scholars an interest in the gospel narratives in and of themselves. Narrative is a form of discourse with its own grammar. As such narrative discourse is a linguistic screen through which the story of Jesus must pass to be understood. By examining that screen closely, we can learn why the first raconteurs elected to narrate the things they did the way they did. This sort of analysis, called narratology, is thus emerging as an important new approach to the study of the gospels.

Other literary critics are interested in the way the gospels were read in antiquity and how they are read by the modern reader. Readers, too, function as a screen through which the written text must pass on its way to understanding. Reader response criticism examines the way the codes in the text and the social codes governing the reader compete and converge in the reading process. For we know that alien social codes block, or interfere with, signals in the text.

Finally, the interest in who Jesus really was continues to fuel the study of the gospels as it has for centuries. While the harmony is a discredited instrument, the well-conceived synopsis, or gospel parallels, is indispensable to historical aims, as it is to the other goals of gospel study.

§17. Primary Features

17.1 Basic features. Many of the gospels are narrative in form. Even in those cases in which the gospels are made up predominantly of some other form of discourse, sequence is extremely important. In order to respect the sequential integrity of each gospel, three things are required:

(a) Each gospel is taken in turn as the primary or lead text.

(b) The sequence of the primary text is to be strictly observed.

(c) Each gospel is to be divided into segments in accordance with its own discourse markers, and those segments are to be utilized wherever discourse units are being compared.

17.2 Sequential integrity. New Gospel Parallels presents each of the gospels, in turn, in its own narrative or sequential integrity. There are no exceptions to this rule. As a consequence, *New Gospel Parallels* will have as many parts as there are gospels, since each gospel serves as a primary text. In accordance with this principle and the design sketched in §13, Volume I is divided into three volumes: I,1 Matthew, I,2 Mark, and I,3 Luke. Volume II contains John, Thomas, and the balance of the gospels known to us.

By following this more elaborate design, *New Gospel Parallels* avoids the artificial chronology of the old gospel harmony. But it also avoids the impression left by most synopses, in spite of themselves, that the Synoptics, or the Synoptics and John, constitute a single narrative. In the traditional synopsis, pericopes from each gospel are interwoven in a single strand, so that the last pericope, or the next, from a particular gospel may be one or several pages away. In *New Gospel Parallels*, what precedes and what follows in the lead gospel will never be more than one page away.

Moreover, since only one gospel at a time functions as the primary text, parallels are selected to go with that gospel and that gospel alone. In traditional synopses, parallels relative to all the gospels are intermingled on the same page or folio, so that it impossible to tell what goes with what.

Finally, *New Gospel Parallels* avoids a canonical bias insofar as it puts all gospels, intracanonical and extracanonical, on the same footing. A full range of parallels is arrayed for each pericope in the primary text.

17.3 Lead gospel on left. The primary or lead text is always presented in the left-hand column of the folio. This arrangement permits the reader to follow the primary text, forwards or backwards, without difficulty, without gap, without confusion.

The pericopes of the primary text are numbered consecutively (K1, K2, K3, etc.) and provided with headings, the language of which is derived from the text itself.

17.4 Segmentation. It was not possible, until recently, to divide narratives and other forms of discourse into segments on the basis of a grammar of discourse. Editors divided the gospel texts into units for a variety of reasons, often inconsistent within a single synopsis or harmony, and sometimes for no apparent reason at all. The emergence of a grammar of narrative discourse makes it possible to segment narratives on the basis of formal properties. Those properties and the grammar into which they are organized is presented in *The Poetics of Biblical Narrative.*

The conclusion of one narrative segment may also function as the introduction to the following segment. Where this occurs, the sentence is repeated in order to indicate the double function.

§18. Design of the Folio

18.1 Primary text. The primary text is always presented in the left-hand column of the folio.

18.2 Matched cola. Matched cola are presented in columns to the right, in the order Matthew, Luke, doublets, John, Thomas.

18.3 Order of matched cola. Matched cola are always presented in the order of the lead text. Cola may be presented out of order in parallels in order to effect the match, particularly if the lines in question occur in close proximity; cola given out of order are indicated by bold letters (a, b, c).

18.4 Secondary parallels. Secondary parallels are printed in columns four through six in a block format. Occasional matched lines are set off in cola and the lines in the primary text with which they are matched indicated by an arrow (◊).

18.5 Sigla of secondary parallels. The various kinds of secondary parallels are distinguished by sigla. These sigla will assist the reader in determining why particular parallels have been included on the folio.

Unmarked block parallels are primary parallels, without matching cola, because verbal agreement or parallel sentence structure was lacking.

A daggar (†) designates primary parallels that lack substantial verbal agreement or agreement in narrative content, yet serve the same narrative function (e.g., † Luke 5:4–11//Mark 1:16–20; Matt 4:18–22).

A double dagger (‡) indicates a parallel with some agreement in diction or narrative content, or both, but which serves a different narrative function (e.g., ‡ Luke 4:16–30//Mark 6:1–6; Matt 13:53–58).

A bullet (•) denotes doublets: the repetition in the same gospel of what appears to be the same narrative segment or cluster of sayings (e.g., • Mark 8:1–9//Mark 6:35–44: miraculous feeding of a crowd).

A triangle (△) indicates a similar narrative incident or a segment with comparable subject matter, but which appears in a different context (e.g., △ Acts 1:12–14//Mark 3:16–19: the formation of a group of twelve).

A star (☆) denotes a parallel with a comparable theme or motif (e.g., ☆ Luke 5:1–3//Mark 4:1, Matt 13:1–2: teaching from a boat). The possibilities of thematic parallels are virtually unlimited.

18.6 Parallels by complete segment. As a rule, parallels are presented by complete segment. However, when fragments are being compared, the parallel fragment alone is presented and the verse or line in the primary text to which the fragment is related is indicated by an arrow.

18.7 References and allusions. References and allusions to the Hebrew scriptures are presented on the right, after all other parallels have been presented. The verse in the primary text to which they are related is always indicated by an arrow (◊). Since the early Christian community utilized the Greek translation of the Hebrew scriptures, known as the Septuagint (LXX), references and allusions are to the LXX, and translations are based on the Greek text.

18.8 Notes. Notes are of two types: textual notes and notes on the translation.

Textual notes are presented in conventional form. Abbreviations are found in the Table of Abbreviations (pp. xiv–xvi).

Translation notes explain the choices adopted by the translators of the Scholars Version. An account of this translation is given in §12.

MARK

K1: Title

Mark 1:1

1 1 Here begins the good news of Jesus the Anointed

† Luke 1:1–4

[1]Since so many have undertaken to compile an orderly narrative of the events that have run their course among us, [2]just as the original eyewitnesses and ministers of the word transmitted them to us, [3]it seemed good that I, too, after thoroughly researching everything from the beginning, should set them systematically in writing for you, Theophilus, [4]so that Your Excellency may realize the reliability of the teachings in which you have been instructed.

† Acts 1:1–5

[1]In the first book, O Theophilus, I treated all that Jesus began to do and to teach, [2]until the day he was taken up, after he had given instructions, under the influence of holy spirit, to the apostles whom he had chosen. [3]To them he presented himself alive after his passion by many proofs, appearing to them during a period of forty days, and speaking of God's imperial rule. [4]And while staying with them he enjoined them not to depart from Jerusalem, but to wait for the promise of the Father, which, he said, "you heard from me, [5]for John baptized with water, but before many days you shall be baptized with holy spirit."

Thom Title

These are the secret sayings that the living Jesus spoke and Didymos Judas Thomas recorded.

InThom Title, 1:1

Boyhood deeds of our Lord Jesus Christ.
[1]I, Thomas the Israelite, am reporting to you, all my non-Jewish brothers and sisters, to make known the extraordinary childhood deeds of our Lord Jesus Christ—what he did after his birth in my region. This is how it all started:

☆ John 15:27

[27]And you are going to testify because you were with me from the beginning.

1:1 Verse 1 of the Gospel of Mark is here interpreted as the title of the book. In the next segment it is interpreted as part of the first sentence.

Scholars are divided as to which interpretation is original.
Some mss add: *son of God* (B D W *al*); the phrase is not found in ℵ Θ 28ᶜ *al*.

The word χριστός (*christ*) literally means *the anointed one* and the translators have so rendered it, partly to avoid misunderstanding *Christ* as a proper name.

INTRODUCTION

K2: A Voice in the Wilderness

Mark 1:1–8	Matt 3:1–12, 11:10	Luke 3:1–20, 7:27
1 1 The good news of Jesus the Anointed begins		
	3 3a No doubt this is the person described	**3** 4a As is written
		b in the book of the sayings
2a with something Isaiah the prophet wrote:	b by Isaiah the prophet.	c of Isaiah the prophet,
	11 10a This is the one about whom it was written:	**7** 27a This is the one about whom it is written,
b "Here is my messenger,	b "Here is my messenger,	b 'Here is my messenger,
c whom I send on ahead of you	c whom I send on ahead of you	c whom I send on ahead of you
d to prepare your way!	d to prepare your way before you!"	d to prepare your way before you.'
3a A voice of someone shouting in the wilderness:	**3** 3c "A voice of someone shouting in the wilderness:	**3** 4d "The voice of someone shouting in the wilderness:
b 'Make ready the way of the Lord,	d 'Make ready the way of the Lord;	e 'Make ready the way of the Lord,
c make his paths straight.'"	e make his paths straight.'"	f make his paths straight.
		5a Every valley will be filled,
		b and every mountain and hill leveled.
		c What is crooked will be made straight,
		d and the rough ways smooth.
		6 Then the whole human race will see the salvation of God.'"
	1a In due course	1a In the fifteenth year of the rule of Emperor Tiberius,
		b when Pontius Pilate was governor of Judea,
		c Herod tetrarch of Galilee,
		d his brother Philip tetrarch of the district of Iturea and Trachonitis,
		e and Lysanias tetrarch of Abilene,
		2a during the high-priesthood of Annas and Caiaphas,
		b the word of God came to John, son of Zechariah,
4a So, John the Baptizer appeared	b John the Baptist appears	c in the wilderness.
b in the wilderness	c in the wilderness of Judea,	3a And he went into the whole region around the Jordan,
c calling for	2a calling out:	b calling for
d baptism and a change of heart that lead to forgiveness of sins.		c baptism and a change of heart that lead to forgiveness of sins.

1:1 Some mss add: *son of God* (B D W *al*); the phrase is not found in ℵ Θ 28c *al*.

1:2a Some mss read: *the prophets:* A K P W Π *f*¹ 28 *al*.

1:4a–b Some mss read: *John was baptizing in the wilderness and* (A K P W Π *f*¹ *f*¹³ *al*).

K2: A Voice in the Wilderness

† John 1:19–28

[19]This is what John had to say when the Judeans sent priests and Levites from Jerusalem to ask him, "Who are you?" [20]He made it clear—he wouldn't deny it— "I'm not the Anointed." [21]And they asked him, "Then what are you? Are you Elijah?" And he replies, "I am not." "Are you the Prophet?" He answered, "No." [22]So they said to him, "Tell us who you are so we can report to those who sent us. What have you got to say for yourself?" [23]He replied, "I am the voice of someone shouting in the wilderness, 'Make the way of the Lord straight'— that's how Isaiah the prophet put it." [24](It was the Pharisees who had sent them.) [25]"So," they persisted, "why are you baptizing if you're not the Anointed, not Elijah, and not the Prophet?" [26]John answered them, "I baptize, yes, but only with water. Right there with you is someone you don't recognize; [27]He's the one who is to be my successor. I don't even deserve to untie his sandal straps." [28]All this took place in Bethlehem on the far side of the Jordan, where John was baptizing.

John 1:31–32 ◊ Mark 1:2–3

[31]"I didn't know who he was, although I came baptizing with water so he would be revealed to Israel." [32]And John continued to testify: "I have seen the spirit coming down like a dove out of the sky, and it hovered over him."

Acts 13:24–25 ◊ Mark 1:4

[24]Prior to his arrival, John announced a baptism of repentance to Israel as a people. [25]As John was completing his course, he would say, "What do you take me to be? I am not the one! But look here, another one comes after me, whose sandal thong I am not good enough to untie."

△ Acts 19:1–7

[1]It so happened, during the time Apollos was at Corinth, that Paul traveled through the interior and came to Ephesus. There he found some disciples. [2]He asked them, "When you came to have faith, did you receive holy spirit?" They ⟨responded⟩ to him: "Of course not. We didn't even know there was such a thing as holy spirit." [3]He continued, "What, then, was the point of your baptism?" They replied, "The point of John's baptism." [4]Paul said, "The baptism John practiced was a baptism of repentance; he told the people to trust in the one who was to come after him, namely, Jesus." [5]When they heard this, they were baptized in the name of the Lord Jesus. [6]When Paul laid his hands on them, the holy spirit came upon them. And they would speak in tongues and prophesy. [7]There were about a dozen of them altogether.

GEbi 1a ◊ Mark 1:4, 7

Now the beginning of their gospel goes like this: [1]In the days of Herod, king of Judea, John appeared in the Jordan river baptizing with a baptism that changed people's hearts. [2]He was said to be a descendant of Aaron the priest, a son of Zachariah and Elizabeth. [3]And everybody went out to him.

Epiphanius, *Haer.* 30.16.6

Mal 3:1a (LXX) ◊ Mark 1:2

[1]"Here is my messenger whom I send to prepare the way before me . . ."

Isa 40:3 (LXX) ◊ Mark 1:3

[3]A voice of one shouting in the desert: "Make ready the way of the Lord, make straight the paths of our God."

Mark   **Luke**

3 2b "Change your ways
      c because Heaven's imperial rule is
        closing in."
   5b and all of Judea,

1 5a And everyone from the Judean
      countryside
      b and all the residents of Jerusalem

      a Then Jerusalem,
      c and all the region around the Jordan
      c streamed out to him   d streamed out to him,
      d and got baptized by him in the   6a and got baptized in the Jordan river
        Jordan river,   by him,
      e admitting their sins.   b admitting their sins.
                                     7a When he saw that many of the
                                        Pharisees and Sadducees were
                                        coming for baptism,   3 7b that came out to get baptized by him,
                                      b ⟨John⟩ said to them,
                                                                        a So ⟨John⟩ would say to the crowds
                                      c "You spawn of Satan!   c "You spawn of Satan!
                                      d Who warned you to flee from the   d Who warned you to flee from the
                                        impending doom?   impending doom?
                                     8 Well then, start producing fruit   8a Well then, start producing fruits
                                        suitable for a change of heart,   suitable for a change of heart,
                                     9a and don't even think of saying to   b and don't even start saying to
                                        yourselves,   yourselves,
                                      b 'We have Abraham for our father.' c 'We have Abraham for our father.'
                                      c Let me tell you,   d Let me tell you,
                                      d God can raise up children for   e God can raise up children for
                                        Abraham right out of these rocks. Abraham right out of these rocks.
                                    10a Even now the axe is aimed at the   9a And already the axe is aimed at the
                                        root of the trees.   root of the trees.
                                      b So every tree not producing choice b So every tree not producing choice
                                        fruit gets cut down   fruit gets cut down
                                      c and tossed into the fire."   c and tossed into the fire."
                                                                       10a The crowds would ask him,
                                                                          b "So what should we do?"
                                                                       11a And he would answer them,
                                                                          b "Whoever has two shirts should
                                                                            share with someone who has none;
                                                                          c whoever has food should do the
                                                                            same."
                                                                       12a Toll-collectors also came to get
                                                                            baptized,
                                                                          b and they would ask him,
                                                                          c "Teacher, what should we do?"
                                                                       13a He told them,
                                                                          b "Charge nothing above the official
                                                                            rates."
                                                                       14a Soldiers also asked him,
                                                                          b "And what about us?"
                                                                          c And he said to them,
                                                                          d "No more shakedowns!
                                                                          e No more frame-ups either!
                                                                          f And be satisfied with your pay."

The Dead Sea Scroll of Isaiah found near Qumran antedates the Gospel of Mark and Jesus. The scroll is open to columns 32–33: Isaiah 38:8–40:28. Mark cites Isa 40:3 in the opening of his gospel. Photo courtesy of John C. Trever.

Mark		**Luke**

Mark

1 6a And John wore a mantel made of camel hair
   b and had a leather belt around his waist
   c and lived on locusts and raw honey.

  7a And he began his proclamation

   b by saying:
   c "Someone more powerful than I
   d will succeed me,
   e whose sandal straps I am not fit to bend down and untie.
  8a I have been baptizing you with water,

   b but he'll baptize you with holy spirit."

3 4a Now this same John wore clothes made from camel hair
   b and had a leather belt around his waist;
   c his diet consisted of locusts and raw honey.

  11c but someone more powerful than I
   d will succeed me.
   e I am not fit to carry his sandals.

   a "I baptize you with water

   b to signal a change of heart,
   f He'll baptize you with holy spirit

   g and fire.
  12a His pitchfork is in his hand
   b and he'll make a clean sweep of his threshing floor
   c and gather his wheat into the granary,
   d but the chaff he'll burn in a fire that can't be put out."

Luke

3 15a People were filled with expectation
   b and everyone was trying to figure out whether John might be the Anointed.
  16a John's answer was the same to everyone:

   c "but someone more powerful than I
   d is coming.
   e I am not fit to untie his sandal straps.

   b "I baptize you with water;

   f He'll baptize you with holy spirit

   g and fire.
  17a His pitchfork is in his hand,
   b to make a clean sweep of his threshing floor
   c and to gather his wheat into the granary,
   d but the chaff he'll burn in a fire that can't be put out."
  18a And so, with many other exhortations
   b he preached to the people.
  19a But Herod the tetrarch,
   b who had been denounced by John
   c over the matter of Herodias,
  20a topped off all his other crimes
   b by shutting John up in prison.

K3: John Baptizes Jesus

Mark 1:9–11	**Matt 3:13–17**	**Luke 3:21–22**

Mark 1:9–11

1 9a During that same period
   b Jesus came from Nazareth, Galilee,

   c and was baptized in the Jordan by John.

Matt 3:13–17

3 13a Then
   b Jesus comes from Galilee
   c to John at the Jordan
   d to get baptized by him.

1:6a Or: *wore a camel skin* (D a).
1:6b 1:6b is omitted by D it (its inclusion may be a harmonizing addition inspired by Matthew).

GEbi 3 ◊ Mark 1:5–6

And [1]It so happened that John was baptizing, and Pharisees and all Jerusalem went out to him and got baptized. [2]And John wore clothes made of camel hair and had a leather belt around his waist. [3]His food, it says, consisted of raw honey that tasted like manna, like a pancake cooked with oil.

Thus they change the word of truth into a lie and instead of "locusts" they put "pancake cooked with honey." [◊ GEbi 1].

Epiphanius, *Haer.* 30.13.4–5

△ **John 1:15** ◊ Mark 1:7

[15]John testifies on his behalf and has called out, "This is the one I was talking about when I said, 'He who is to come after me is actually my superior, because he was there before me.'"

☆ **Acts 1:5** ◊ Mark 1:8

[5]"for John baptized with water, but before many days you shall be baptized with holy spirit."

☆ **Acts 11:16** ◊ Mark 1:8

[16]Then I recalled the words of the Lord Jesus, who used to say, "John baptized with water, but you were baptized with holy spirit."

Justin, *Dialogue* **88.7** ◊ Mark 1:4, 6

[7]When John was encamped at the Jordan and would call for baptism and a change of heart, he wore only a leather belt and a garment made from camel hair, and ate nothing but locusts and raw honey . . .

2 Kgs 1:8 (LXX) ◊ Mark 1:6

[8]They answered him: "He wore a garment made of hair, with a leather belt around his waist." And he said: "It is Elijah the Tishbite."

† **John 1:29–34**

[29]The next day John sees Jesus approaching and says, "Look, the lamb of God, who does away with the sin of the world. [30]This is the one I was talking about when I said, 'Someone is coming after me who is actually my superior, because he was there before me.' [31]I didn't know who he was, although I came baptizing with water so he would be revealed to Israel." [32]And John continued to testify: "I have seen the spirit coming down like a dove out of the sky, and it hovered over him. [33]I wouldn't have recognized him, but the very one who sent me to baptize with water told me, 'When you see the spirit come down and hover over someone, that's the one who baptizes with holy spirit.' [34]I have seen this and I have certified: this is God's son."

K3: John Baptizes Jesus

GNaz 2 ◊ Mark 1:9

In the Gospel of the Hebrews . . . the following story is told:
[1]The mother of the Lord and his brothers said to him, "John the Baptist baptized for the forgiveness of sins. Let's go and get baptized by him." [2]But he said to them, "How have I sinned? So why should I go and get baptized by him? Only if I don't know what I'm talking about."

Jerome, *Adversus Pelagianos*, 3.2

Mark	Matt	Luke
	3 14a And John tried to stop him	
	b with these words:	
	c "I'm the one who needs to get baptized by you,	
	d yet you come to me?"	
	15a In response,	
	b Jesus said to him,	
	c "Let it go for now.	
	d After all, in this way we are doing what is fit and right."	
	e Then John deferred to him.	
		3 21a And it so happened, when all the people were baptized,
		b and after Jesus had been baptized
		c and while he was praying,
	16a After Jesus had been baptized,	
1 10a And just as he got up out of the water,	b he got right up out of the water,	
b he saw the skies torn open	c and—amazingly—the skies opened up,	d that the sky opened up,
c and the spirit coming down toward him	d and he saw God's spirit coming down on him	22a and the holy spirit came down on him
		b in bodily form
d like a dove.	e like a dove, perching on him,	c like a dove,
11a There was also a voice from the skies:	17a and—listen!—there was a voice from the skies,	d and a voice came from the sky,
	b which said,	
b "You are my favored son	c "This is my favored son	e "You are my son;
c —I fully approve of you."	d —I fully approve of him!"	f today I have become your father."

K4: Jesus Is Put to the Test

Mark 1:12–13	**Matt 4:1–11**	**Luke 4:1–13**
		4 1a Jesus departed from the Jordan,
		b full of the holy spirit,
1 12 And right away the spirit drives him out into the wilderness,	4 1a Then Jesus was guided into the wilderness by the spirit	c and was led by the spirit into the wilderness,
13a where he remained for forty days,	2a And after he had fasted 'forty days and forty nights,'	2b for forty days.
	1b to be put to the test by the devil.	a where he was put to the test by the devil
b being put to the test by Satan.		c He ate nothing that whole time;
		d and when it was all over,
	2b he was famished.	e he was famished.
	3a And the tester confronted him	
	b and said,	3a The devil said to him,
	c "To prove you're God's son,	b "To prove you're God's son,
	d order these stones to turn into bread."	c order this stone to turn into bread."

40

GEbi 4

After saying many things, it adds:

[1]When the people were baptized, Jesus also came and got baptized by John. [2]As he came up out of the water, the skies opened and he saw the holy spirit in the form of a dove coming down and entering him. [3]And there was a voice from the sky that said, "You are my favored son—I fully approve of you." [4]And again, "Today I have become your father."

[5]And right away a bright light illuminated the place. When John saw this, it says, he said to him, "Who are you?" [6]And again a voice from the sky said to him, "This is my favored son—I fully approve of him."

[7]And then, it says, John knelt down in front of him and said, "Please, Lord, you baptize me."

[8]But he stopped him and said, "It's all right. This is the way everything is supposed to be fulfilled."

Epiphanius, *Haer.* 30.13.7–8

☆ **Mark 9:7** ◊ Mark 1:10–11

[7]And a cloud moved in and cast a shadow over them, and a voice came out of the cloud: "This is my favored son, listen to him!"

☆ **Matt 17:5** ◊ Mark 1:10–11

[5]While he was still speaking, there was a bright cloud that cast a shadow over them. And just then a voice spoke from the cloud: "This is my favored son of whom I fully approve. Listen to him!"

☆ **Luke 9:34–35** ◊ Mark 1:10–11

[34]While he was still speaking, a cloud moved in and cast a shadow over them. And their fear increased as they entered the cloud. [35]And out of the cloud a voice spoke: "This is my son, my chosen one. Listen to him!"

John 1:32 ◊ Mark 1:10

[32]And John continued to testify: "I have seen the spirit coming down like a dove out of the sky, and it hovered over him."

John 12:28–30 ◊ Mark 1:10–11

[28]"Father, glorify your name!" Then a voice spoke out of the sky: "I have glorified it and I will glorify it further."

[29]The crowd there heard this, and some people remarked that it had thundered, others that a heavenly messenger had spoken to him.

[30]"That voice did not come for me but for you," Jesus rejoined.

GHeb 3 ◊ Mark 1:10–11

Later on, in the same gospel, we find the following:

[2]And it happened that when the Lord came up out of the water, the whole fountain of the holy spirit came down on him and rested on him. [3]It said to him, "My Son, I was waiting for you in all the prophets, waiting for you to come so I could rest in you. [4]For you are my rest; you are my first-begotten Son who rules forever."

Jerome, *Comm. In Esaiam* 4 on Isa 11:2

Isa 42:1 (LXX) ◊ Mark 1:11

[1]Here is my servant, whom I uphold,
    my chosen, in whom my soul delights;
I have put my spirit on him,
    he will produce justice for the nations.

Isa 44:2 (LXX) ◊ Mark 1:11

[2]"Thus says the Lord who made you, who formed you from the womb and will help you: favored Israel, whom I have chosen."

Ps 2:7 (LXX) ◊ Mark 1:11

[7]I will tell of the decree of the Lord: He said to me, "You are my son, today have I conceived you."

K4: Jesus Is Put to the Test

Mark	**Matt**	**Luke**

Matt

4 4a He responded,
  b "It is written,
  c 'Human beings are not to live on bread alone,
  d but by every word that comes out of God's mouth.'"
5a Then the devil conducts him to the holy city
  b sets him on the pinnacle of the temple,
6a and says to him,
  b "To prove you're God's son,
  c jump off;
  d remember, it is written,
  e 'To his heavenly messengers he will give orders about you,'

  f and 'with their hands they will catch you,
  g so you won't even stub your toe on a stone.'"
7a Jesus said to him,
  b "Elsewhere it is written,
  c 'You are not to put the Lord your God to the test.'"
8a Again the devil takes him to a very high mountain

  b and shows him all the empires of the world
  c and their splendour,
9a and says to him,
  b "I'll give you all these,

cf. Matt 4:8c

  c if you will kneel down and pay homage to me."
cf. Matt 4:9b
10a Finally, Jesus says to him,
  b "Get out of here, Satan,
  c Remember, it is written,
  d 'You are to pay homage to the Lord your God,
  e and you are to revere him alone.'"

11a Then the devil leaves him,
  b and heavenly messengers arrive out of nowhere
  c and look after him.

Luke

4 4a Jesus responded to him,
  b "It is written,
  c 'Human beings are not to live on bread alone.'"

9a Then he took him to Jerusalem,

  b set him on the pinnacle of the temple,
  c and said to him,
  d "To prove you're God's son,
  e jump off from here;
10a remember, it is written,
  b 'To his heavenly messengers he will give orders about you,
  c to protect you,'
11a and 'with their hands they will catch you,
  b so you won't even stub your toe on a stone.'"
12a And in response Jesus said to him,
  b "It is said,
  c 'You are not to put the Lord your God to the test.'"
5a Then he took Jesus up,

  b and in an instant of time
  c showed him all the empires of the civilized world.
cf. Luke 6:6c
6a The devil said to him,
  b "I will bestow on you authority over all this
  c and the glory that comes with it;
  d understand, it has been handed over to me,
  e and I can give it to anyone I want.
7a So, if you will pay homage to me,

  b it will all be yours."
8a Jesus responded,

  b "It is written,
  c 'You are to pay homage to the Lord your God,
  d and are to revere him alone.'"

13a So when the devil had tried every kind of test,
  b he let him alone for the time being.

Mark

1 13c While he was living there among the wild animals,

  d the heavenly messengers looked after him.

☆ **John 1:51** ◊ Mark 1:13d

51Then he adds, "As God is my witness before you all: You'll see the sky split open and God's messengers traveling to and from the son of Adam."

☆ **InJas 1:9–11** ◊ Mark 1:12–13

9And so he continued to be very upset and did not see his wife but banished himself to the wilderness and pitched his tent there. 10And Joachim fasted 'forty days and forty nights.' 11He would say to himself, "I will not go back for food or drink until the Lord my God visits me. Prayer will be my food and drink."

Table 1

Catalogue of Select Greek Manuscripts

Listed in Chronological Order

Designation	Date	Contents	Location/Notes
Greek Papyri			
PEgerton 2	100–150	Unknown gospel frags.	London
PKöln 255	100–150	Unknown gospel frags.	Cologne
$\mathfrak{P}^{52}$	ca. 125	John frag.	Manchester
$\mathfrak{P}^{75}$	175–225	Luke & John frags.	Cologny
POxy 2949	ca. 200	Peter frags.	Oxford
POxy 1	ca. 200	Thom frag.	Oxford
POxy 655	ca. 200	Thom frag.	Cambridge, Mass.
$\mathfrak{P}^{64}$ & P^{67}	ca. 200	Matt frag.	Oxford; Barcelona
$\mathfrak{P}^{66}$	ca. 200	John frags.	Cologny; Dublin
$\mathfrak{P}^{77}$	II/III	Matt 23:30–39	Oxford
$\mathfrak{P}^{1}$	III	Matt frags.	Philadelphia
$\mathfrak{P}^{4}$	III	Luke frags.	Paris
$\mathfrak{P}^{45}$	200–250	Gospels & Acts	Dublin
$\mathfrak{P}^{53}$	III	Matt & Acts frags.	Ann Arbor, Mich.
$\mathfrak{P}^{69}$	III	Luke frags.	Oxford
$\mathfrak{P}^{70}$	III	Matt frags.	Oxford
$\mathfrak{P}^{37}$	III/IV	Matt 26:19–52	Ann Arbor, Mich.
$\mathfrak{P}^{88}$	IV	Mark 2:1–26	Milan
Greek Uncials			
ℵ	IV	e, a, p, r	British Museum; only complete copy of Greek New Testament in unical script.
B	IV	e, a, p	Vatican Library
A	V	e, a, p, r	British Museum
C	V	e, a, p, r	Paris
D	V	e, a	Cambridge
W	V	e	Washington, D.C.
Θ	IX	e	Tiflis, Georgia, USSR
0212	III	e	New Haven, Conn.

Definitions: All dates are CE. Roman numerals indicate centuries. Papyrus is a writing material made from Egyptian reeds. Parchment is a writing material made from animal skins. Uncials is a form of writing using all capital letters. *Codes:* e=gospels; a=Acts; p=letters; r=Revelation.

K5: Jesus Proclaims the Good News

Mark 1:14–15	Matt 4:12–17	Luke
1 14a After John was locked up,	**4** 12a When Jesus heard that John had been locked up,	
b Jesus came to Galilee	b he headed for Galilee.	
	13a He took leave of Nazareth	
cf. Mark 1:21a	b to go	
	c and settle down in Capernaum-by-the-sea,	
	d in the territory of Zebulun and Naphtali,	
	14 so that the word spoken through Isaiah the prophet would come true:	
	15a "Land of Zebulun and of Naphtali,	
	b the way to the sea,	
	c across the Jordan,	
	d Galilee of the pagans!	
	16a You who languished in darkness have seen a great light,	
	b you who have wasted away in the shadow of death,	
	c for you a light has risen."	
c proclaiming God's good news.	17a From that time on Jesus began to proclaim	
	b in these words:	
15a His message went:		
b "The time is up:		
c God's imperial rule is closing in.	**d** because Heaven's imperial rule is closing in."	
d Change your ways,	c "Change your ways,	
e and put your trust in the good news!"		

1:14c Some mss read: *the good news of God's imperial rule* (A D W 074 0133 0135 *pm*).

1:15c Greek ἡ βασιλεία τοῦ θεοῦ: *the kingdom of God* was a suitable translation under the political auspices of King James (1611); it is now something of an anachronism. Since the phrase both refers to divine activity (*rule, reign*) and

sometimes has the sense of a place, the translators have elected to translate it variously as *God's imperial rule* and *God's domain*, depending on the context. Matthew avoids the term *God*; in Matthew, accordingly, the phrase is *Heaven's imperial rule* and *Heaven's domain*.

1:15c *closing in* (Greek: ἤγγικεν) suggests more of the foreboding and threatening character of *God's imperial rule* than do traditional translations (e.g., *at hand*), yet without any loss of the apocalyptic horizon characteristic of Mark.

1:15d Traditional translation: *repent.*

K5: Jesus Proclaims the Good News

† Luke 4:14–15

[14]Then Jesus returned in the power of the spirit to Galilee. News about him spread throughout all the surrounding area. [15]He used to teach in their synagogues, and was acclaimed by everyone.

† Luke 4:16–30

[16]When he came to Nazareth, where he had been brought up, he went to the synagogue on the sabbath day, as was his custom. He stood up to do the reading [17]and was handed the scroll of the prophet Isaiah. He unrolled the scroll and found the place where it was written: [18]"The spirit of the Lord is upon me, because he has anointed me to bring good news to the poor. He has sent me to announce pardon for prisoners and recovery of sight to the blind; to set free the oppressed, [19]to proclaim the year of the Lord's amnesty." [20]After rolling up the scroll, he gave it back to the attendant, and sat down; and the attention of everyone in the synagogue was riveted on him.

[21]He began by saying to them, "Today this scripture has come true as you listen."

[22]And they began voicing approval of him, and marveling at the pleasing speech that he delivered; and would remark, "Isn't this Joseph's son?" [23]And he said to them, "No doub you will quote me that proverb, 'Doctor, cure yourself,' and you'll tell me, 'Do here in your hometown what we've heard you've done in Capernaum.'"

[24]Then he said, "The truth is, no prophet is welcome on his home turf. [25]I can assure you, there were many widows in Israel in Elijah's time, when the sky was dammed up for three and a half years, and a severe famine swept through the land. [26]Yet Elijah was not sent to any of them, but instead to a widow in Zarephath near Sidon. [27]In addition, there were many lepers in Israel in the prophet Elisha's time; yet none of them was made clean, except Naaman the Syrian."

[28]Everyone in the synagogue was filled with rage when they heard this. [29]They rose up, ran him out of town, and led him to the brow of the hill on which their town was built, intending to hurl him over it. [30]But he slipped away through the throng and went on his way.

Mark 6:17 ◊ Mark 1:14

[17]Earlier Herod himself had sent someone to arrest John and put him in chains in a dungeon, on account of Herodias, his brother Philip's wife, because he had married her.

Matt 14:3 ◊ Mark 1:14

[3]Herod, remember, had arrested John, put him in chains, and thrown him in prison, on account of Herodias, his brother Philip's wife.

Luke 3:19–20, 23a ◊ Mark 1:14

[19]But Herod the tetrarch, who had been denounced by John over the matter of Herodias, his brother's wife, [20]topped off all his other crimes by shutting John up in prison.

[23]Jesus was about thirty years old when he began his work.

☆ John 1:43 ◊ Mark 1:14

[43]The next day Jesus decided to leave for Galilee. He finds Philip and says to him, "Follow me."

☆ John 4:1–3 ◊ Mark 1:14

[1]Jesus was aware of the rumor that had reached the Pharisees: Jesus is recruiting and baptizing more disciples than John. ([2]Actually, Jesus himself didn't baptize anyone; his disciples did the baptizing.) [3]So he left Judea again for Galilee.

☆ John 4:43 ◊ Mark 1:14

[43]Two days later Jesus left for Galilee.

† Luke 5:1–3

Matt 3:1–2 ◊ Mark 1:15

[1]In due course John the Baptist appears in the wilderness of Judea, [2]calling out: "Change your ways because Heaven's imperial rule is closing in."

K6: Simon and Andrew Become Followers

Mark 1:16–18	**Matt 4:18–20**	Luke
1 16 a As he was walking along by the Sea of Galilee,	4 18 a As he was walking by the Sea of Galilee,	
b he spotted	b he spotted two brothers,	
c Simon	c Simon, also known as Peter,	
d and Andrew, Simon's brother,	d and Andrew his brother,	
e casting ⟨their nets⟩ into the sea—	e throwing their net in the sea,	
f since they were fishermen—	f since they were fishermen.	
17 a and Jesus said to them:	19 a And Jesus says to them,	
b "Become my followers	b "Become my followers	
c and I'll have you fishing for people!"	c and I'll have you fishing for people!"	
18 a And right then and there they abandoned their nets	20 a So right then and there they abandoned their nets	
b and followed him.	b and followed him.	

K7: James and John Become Followers

Mark 1:19–20	**Matt 4:21–22**	Luke
1 19 a When he had gone a little farther,	4 21 a When he had gone a little farther,	
b he caught sight of	b he caught sight of two other brothers,	
c James, Zebedee's son,	c James, Zebedee's son,	
d and his brother John	d and his brother John,	
	e in the boat with Zebedee their father,	
e mending their nets in the boat.	f mending their nets,	
20 a Right then and there he called out to them as well,	g and he also called out to them.	
b and they left their father Zebedee behind in the boat with the hired hands	22 a They abandoned their boat and their father right then and there	
c and accompanied him.	b and followed him.	

K6: Simon and Andrew Become Followers

K7: James and John Become Followers

† Luke 5:1–3

[1]On one occasion, when the crowd pressed him to hear the word of God, he was standing by the lake of Gennesaret. [2]He noticed two boats moored there at the shore; the fishermen had left them and were washing their nets. [3]He got into one of the boats, the one belonging to Simon, and asked him to put out a little from the shore. Then he sat down and began to teach the crowds from the boat.

† Luke 5:4–11

[4]When he had finished speaking, he said to Simon, "Put out into deep water and lower your nets for a catch."

[5]But Simon replied, "Master, we've been hard at it all night and haven't caught a thing. But if you insist, I'll lower the nets."

[6]So they did and netted such a huge number of fish that their nets began to tear apart. [7]They signaled to their partners in the other boat to come and lend a hand. They came and loaded both boats until they nearly sank. [8]At the sight of this, Simon Peter fell to his knees in front of Jesus and said, "Have nothing to do with me, Master, heathen that I am." [9]For he and his companions were stunned at the catch of fish they had taken, [10]as were James and John, sons of Zebedee and partners of Simon.

Jesus said to Simon, "Don't be afraid; from now on you'll be catching people." [11]They then brought their boats to shore, abandoned everything, and followed him.

△ GPet 14:1–3

[1]Now it was the last day of Unleavened Bread, and many began to return to their homes since the feast was over. [2]But we, the twelve disciples of the Lord, continued to weep and mourn, and each one, still grieving on account of what had happened, left for his own home. [3]But I, Simon Peter, and Andrew, my brother, took our fishing nets and went away to the sea. And with us was Levi, the son of Alphaeus, whom the Lord . . .

† John 1:35–42

[35]The next day John was standing there again with two of his disciples. [36]When he noticed Jesus walking by, he says, "Look, the lamb of God."

[37]His two disciples heard him ⟨say this⟩, and they followed Jesus. [38]Jesus turned around, saw them following, and says to them, "What are you looking for?"

They said to him, "Rabbi" (which means Teacher), "where are you staying?"

[39]He says to them, "Come and see."

They went and saw where he was staying and spent the day with him. It was about four in the afternoon.

[40]Andrew, Simon Peter's brother, was one of the two who followed Jesus after hearing John ⟨speak about him⟩. [41]First he goes and finds his brother Simon and tells him, "We have found the Messiah" (which is translated, Anointed), [42]and he took him to Jesus.

When Jesus laid eyes on him, he said "You're Simon, John's son; you're going to be called Kephas" (which means Peter ⟨or Rock⟩).

† John 1:43–51

[43]The next day Jesus decided to leave for Galilee. He finds Philip and says to him, "Follow me."

[44]Philip was from Bethsaida, the hometown of Andrew and Peter. [45]Philip finds Nathanael and tells him, "We've found the one Moses wrote about in the Law, and the prophets mentioned too: Jesus, Joseph's son, from Nazareth."

[46]"From Nazareth?" Nathanael said to him. "Can anything good come from that place?"

Philip replies to him, "Come and see."

[47]Jesus saw Nathanael coming toward him, and he remarks about him: "There's a genuine Israelite—not a trace of deceit in him."

[48]Where do you know me from?" Nathanael asks him.

Jesus replied, "I saw you under the fig tree before Philip invited you ⟨to join us⟩."

[49]Nathanael responded to him, "Rabbi, you are God's son! You are King of Israel!"

[50]Jesus replied, "Do you believe just because I told you I saw you under the fig tree? You're going to see far more than that."

[51]Then he adds, "As God is my witness before you all: you'll see the sky split open and God's messengers traveling to and from the son of Adam."

△ GEbi 2

At any rate, in the gospel that they call "According to Matthew," which is not complete but adulterated and mutilated—they call it the "Hebrew" gospel—is found the following:

[1]There was this man named Jesus, who was about thirty years old, who chose us. [2]And when he came to Capernaum, he entered the house of Simon, who was nicknamed Peter. He then began to speak as follows:

[3]"As I was walking along by the lake of Tiberias, I chose John and James, sons of Zebedee, and Simon and Andrew, and Thaddeus and Simon the Zealot and Judas the Iscariot. [4]Then I summoned you, Matthew, while you were sitting at the toll booth, and you followed me. [5]Therefore, I want you to be twelve apostles, to symbolize Israel."

Epiphanius, *Haer.* 30.13.2

† John 21:1–14

[1]Some time after these events, Jesus again appeared to his disciples by the Sea of Tiberias. This is how he did it: [2]When Simon Peter and Thomas, the one known as "the Twin," were together, along with Nathaniel from Cana, Galilee, the sons of Zebedee, and two other disciples, [3]Simon Peter says to them, "I'm going to go fishing."

"We're coming with you," they reply.

They went down and got into the boat, but that night they didn't catch a thing.

[4]It was already getting light when Jesus appeared on the shore, but his disciples didn't recognize that it was Jesus.

[5]"Lads, you haven't caught any fish, have you?" Jesus asks them.

"No," they replied.

[6]He tells them, "Cast your net on the right side of the boat and you'll have better luck."

They do as he instructs them and now they can't haul it in for the huge number of fish. [7]The disciple Jesus loved most exclaims to Peter, "It's the Master!"

When Simon Peter heard "It's the Master," he tied his cloak around himself, since he was stripped for work, and threw himself into the water. [8]The rest of them came in the boat, dragging the net full of fish. They were not far from land, only about a hundred yards offshore.

[11]Then Simon Peter went aboard and hauled the net full of large fish ashore—one hundred fifty-three of them. Even though there were so many of them, the net still didn't tear.

[12]Jesus says to them, "Come and eat."

None of the disciples dared ask, "Who are you?" They knew it was the Master. [13]Jesus comes, takes the bread and gives it to them, and passes the fish around as well.

[14]This was now the third time after he had been raised from the dead that Jesus appeared to his disciples.

K8: Jesus Gives Orders to an Unclean Spirit

Mark 1:21–28	**Matt 7:28–29**	**Luke 4:31–37**
1 21a Then they come to Capernaum,	*cf. Matt 4:13*	**4** 31a He went down to Capernaum,
b and on the sabbath day		b a town in Galilee,
c he went right to the synagogue		c and he would teach them on the sabbath day.
d and started teaching.		
	7 28a And so,	
	b when Jesus had finished this discourse,	
22a They were astonished at his teaching,	c the crowds were astonished at his teaching,	32a They were astonished at his teaching
b since he would teach them on his own authority,	29a since he had been teaching them on his own authority,	b because his message carried authority.
c unlike the scholars.	b unlike their ⟨own⟩ scholars.	
23a Now right there in their synagogue		33a Now in the synagogue
b was a person possessed by an unclean spirit,		b there was a person who had an unclean demon,
c which shouted,		c which screamed at the top of his voice,
24a "Jesus! What do you want with us,		34a "Hey, Jesus! What do you want with us,
b you Nazarene?		b you Nazarene?
c Have you come to get rid of us?		c Have you come to get rid of us?
d I know you, who you are:		d I know you, who you are:
e God's holy man!"		e God's holy man."
25a But Jesus yelled at it,		35a But Jesus yelled at it,
b "Shut up and get out of him!"		b "Shut up and get out of him!"
26a Then the unclean spirit threw the man into convulsions,		c Then the demon threw the man down in full view of everyone
b and letting out a loud shriek		d and came out of him
c it came out of him.		e without doing him any harm.
27a And they were all so amazed		36a And so amazement came over them all
b that they asked themselves,		b and they would say to one another,
c "What's this?		c "What kind of message is this?
d A new kind of teaching backed by authority!		d With authority and power
e He gives orders even to unclean spirits		e he gives orders to unclean spirits,
f and they obey him!"		f and they leave."
28 So his fame spread rapidly everywhere throughout Galilee and even beyond.		37 So rumors about him began to spread to every corner of the surrounding region.

1:21a Mark frequently switches tense from past to present and present to past as he narrates. The translators have preserved these shifts to reflect the colloquial nature of Mark's speech.

1:25a *Jesus* is probably a clarifying or harmonizing (Luke) addition.

K8: Jesus Gives Orders to an Unclean Spirit

✩ **Mark 11:18** Mark ◊ 1:22

[18]And the ranking priests and the scholars heard this and kept looking for a way to get rid of him. (The truth is that they stood in fear of him, and that the whole crowd was astonished at his teaching.)

✩ **Matt 13:54** ◊ Mark 1:21–22

[54]And he came to his hometown and resumed teaching them in their synagogue, and they were astounded and said so: "What's the source of this wisdom and these miracles?"

✩ **Matt 22:33** ◊ Mark 1:22

[33]And when the crowd heard, they were stunned by his teaching.

✩ **John 7:15** ◊ Mark 1:22

[15]The Judeans were taken aback, saying, "This man is uneducated; how come he's so articulate?"

✩ **John 7:46** ◊ Mark 1:22

[46]The deputies answered, "No one ever talked like this!"

✩ **John 6:69** ◊ Mark 1:24

[69]"We have become believers and are certain that you are God's holy one."

✩ **InThom 19:2–5** ◊ Mark 1:22

[2]After Passover they began the journey home. But while on their way, the child Jesus went back up to Jerusalem. His parents, of course, assumed that he was in the traveling party. [3]After they had traveled one day, they began to look for him among their relatives. When they did not find him, they were worried and returned again to the city to search for him.

[4]After three days they found him in the temple area, sitting among the teachers, listening to the law and asking them questions. [5]All eyes were on him, and everyone was astounded that he, a mere child, could interrogate the elders and teachers of the people and explain the main points of the law and the parables of the prophets.

K9: Jesus Heals Simon's Mother-in-law

Mark 1:29–31	Matt 8:14–15	Luke 4:38–39
1 29 a They left the synagogue right away and b entered the house of Simon and Andrew along with James and John. 30 a Simon's mother-in-law was in bed with a fever, b and they told him about her right away. 31 a He went up to her, b took hold of her hand, c raised her up, d and the fever disappeared. e Then she started looking after them.	**8** 14 a And when Jesus came to Peter's house, b he noticed his mother-in-law lying sick with a fever. 15 a He touched her hand **c** Then she got up b and the fever disappeared. d and started looking after him.	**4** 38 a He got up from the synagogue b and entered the house of Simon. c Simon's mother-in-law was suffering from a high fever, d and they made an appeal to him on her behalf. 39 a He stood over her, b rebuked the fever, **d** She immediately got up c and it disappeared. e and started looking after them.

K10: Sick and Demon-Possessed Come to Jesus

Mark 1:32–34	Matt 8:16–17	Luke 4:40–41
1 32 a In the evening, b at sundown, c they would bring all the sick and demon-possessed to him. 33 And the whole town would crowd around the door. 34 a On such occasions he cured many people afflicted with various diseases b and drove out many demons. c He would never let the demons speak, d because they realized who he was.	**8** 16 a In the evening, b they brought many who were demon-possessed to him. c He drove out the spirits with a command, d and all those who were ill he cured. 17 a In this way Isaiah's prophecy b came true: c "He took away our illnesses d and carried off our diseases."	**4** 40 a As the sun was setting, b all those who had people sick with various diseases brought them to him. c He would lay his hands on each one of them d and cure them. 41 a Demons would also come out of many of them b screaming, c and saying, d "You son of God, you!" e But he would rebuke them f and not allow them to speak, g because they knew that he was the Anointed.

K9: Jesus Heals Simon's Mother-in-law

✿ **Mark 13:3** ◊ Mark 1:29

³And as he was sitting on the Mount of Olives across from the temple, Peter would ask him privately, as would James and John and Andrew. . . .

K10: Sick and Demon-Possessed Come to Jesus

✿ **Mark 3:7–12**

⁷Then Jesus withdrew with his disciples to the sea, and a huge crowd from Galilee followed. When they heard what he was doing, a huge crowd from Judea, ⁸and from Jerusalem and Idumea and across the Jordan, and from around Tyre and Sidon, collected around him. ⁹And he told his disciples to have a small boat ready for him on account of the crowd, so they would not mob him. (¹⁰After all, he had healed so many, that all who had diseases were pushing forward to touch him.) ¹¹The unclean spirits also, whenever they faced him, would fall down before him and shout out, "You son of God, you!" ¹²But he always warned them not to tell who he was.

✿ **Mark 6:55** ◊ Mark 1:32

⁵⁵and they ran around over the whole area and started bringing those who were ill on mats to wherever he was rumored to be.

✿ **Matt 12:16** ◊ Mark 1:34

¹⁶And he warned them not to disclose his identity.

K11: Jesus Steals Away

Mark 1:35–39	**Matt 4:23–25**	**Luke 4:42–44**

1 35a And rising early,
   b while it was still very dark,
   c he went outside
   d and stole away to an isolated place,
   e where he started praying.
36   Then Simon and those with him hunted him down.
37a When they had found him
   b they say to him,
   c "They're all looking for you."
 	
38a But he replies:
   b "Let's go somewhere else,
   c to the neighboring villages,
   d so I can speak there too,
 	
   e since that's what I came for."
39a So he went all around Galilee
   b speaking in their synagogues
 	
   c and driving out demons.
		4 42a The next morning
		
		   b he went outside
		   c and withdrew to an isolated place.
		
		   d Then the crowds came looking for him,
		   e and when they got to him
		
		   f they tried to keep him from leaving them.
		43a He said to them,
		
		   b "I must declare God's imperial rule to the other towns as well;
		   c after all, this is why I was sent."
		44**b** of Judea.
		   a And he continued to speak in the synagogues

	4 23a And he toured all over Galilee,
	   b teaching in their synagogues,
	
	   c proclaiming the news of ⟨Heaven's⟩ imperial rule,
	   d and healing every disease and every ailment the people had.
	24a And his reputation spread through the whole of Syria.
	   b They brought him everyone who was ill,
	   c who suffered from any kind of disease or was in intense pain,
	   d who was possessed,
	   e who was epileptic,
	   f or a paralytic,
	   g and he cured them.
	25 And huge crowds followed him from Galilee and Decapolis and Jerusalem and Judea and from across the Jordan.	

1:35c–d Some mss omit *went outside and* (W *pc* it).

GREEK AND ROMAN MONETARY SYSTEMS

Greek Coins

1 talent = 60 minas
1 mina = 50 staters (gold)
1 stater = 2 drachmas (silver)
1 drachma = 6 obols (bronze)

Roman Coins

1 aureus (gold) = 25 denarii (silver)
1 denarius = 4 sestercia
1 sestertius = 2 dupondii
1 dupondius = 2 asses
1 as = 4 quadrants

1 drachma = 1 denarius

The *sestertius* depicts the laureated bust of Gaius Caligula (37–41 C.E.). The obverse inscription reads C.CAESAR DIVI AVG. P.M. TR.P. IIII P.P. The reverse portrays the emperor speaking to his troops from a low platform before a camp chair. The inscription reads ADLOCVT COH.

Photograph and description courtesy of Numismatics Fine Arts, Inc., Los Angeles, and the Institute for Antiquity and Christianity, Claremont, CA.

K12: Jesus Cures a Leper

Mark 1:40–45	**Matt 8:1–4**	**Luke 5:12–16**

Matt 8:1–4

8 1a When he came down from the mountain,
  b huge crowds followed him.

Luke 5:12–16

5 12a And it so happened
   b while he was in one of the towns,
   c there was this man covered with leprosy.
   d Seeing Jesus,
   f and begged him,
   e he knelt with his face to the ground
      cf. Luke 5:12f
   g "Sir,
   h if you want to,
   i you can make me clean."

Mark 1:40–45

1 40a Then a leper comes up to him,

  b pleads with him,
  c falls down on his knees,
  d and says to him,

  e "If you want to,
  f you can make me clean."
41a Although Jesus was indignant,
  b he stretched out his hand,
  c touched him,
  d and says to him,
  e "Okay—
  f you're clean!"
42a And right away the leprosy disappeared,
  b and he was made clean.

43a And Jesus snapped at him,
  b and dismissed him curtly
44a with this warning:
  b "See that you don't tell anyone anything,
  c but go,
  d have a priest examine ⟨your skin⟩.
  e Then offer for your cleansing
  f what Moses commanded,

  g as evidence ⟨of your cure⟩."
45a But after he went out,
  b he started telling everyone

  c and spreading the story,
  d so that ⟨Jesus⟩ could no longer enter a town openly,
  e but had to stay out in the countryside.
  f Yet they continued to come to him from everywhere.

Matt 8:1–4 (cont.)

2a Just then a leper appeared,

  b bowed down to him,
  c and said,
  d "Sir,
  e if you want to,
  f you can make me clean."
3a And he stretched out his hand,
  b touched him,
  c and says,
  d "Okay—
  e you're clean!"

  f At once his leprosy was cleansed away.

4a Then Jesus warns him:
  b "See that you don't tell anyone,

  c but go,
  d have a priest examine ⟨your skin⟩.
  e Then offer the gift
  f that Moses commanded,

  g as evidence ⟨of your cure⟩.

Luke 5:12–16 (cont.)

13a Jesus stretched out his hand,

  c and says,
  d "Okay—
  e you're clean!"
  f And at once the leprosy disappeared.

      cf. Luke 5:14a
14a He ordered him to tell no one.

  b "But go,
  c have a priest examine ⟨your skin⟩.
  d Then make an offering,
  e as Moses commanded,
  f for your cleansing,
  g as evidence ⟨of your cure⟩."

15a Yet the story about him spread around all the more.
      cf. Luke 5:15a
      cf. Luke 5:16a

      cf. Luke 5:16a

  b Great crowds would gather to hear him
  c and to be healed of their sicknesses.
16a But he would withdraw to isolated places
  b and pray.

1:41a The reading adopted, *indignant* (ὀργισθείς), is supported by the Old Latin tradition (a d ff² r¹) and D. It comports in tone with

1:43. The alternative, *he was moved* (σπλαγνισθείς), softens the offensive term and is therefore probably a scribal emendation.

1:45d Greek: *he.*

K12: Jesus Cures a Leper

GEger 2:1–4

1 a Just then a leper comes up to him
◊ 1:40a

 b and says, ◊ 1:40d
"Teacher, Jesus, in wandering around
with lepers and eating with them in the
inn, I became a leper myself.

2 a If you want to, ◊ 1:40e

 b I'll be made clean." ◊ 1:40f

3 a The master said to him, ◊ 1:41d

 b "Okay— ◊ 1:41e

 c you're clean!" ◊ 1:41f

 d And at once his leprosy vanished
from him. ◊ 1:42a

⁴Jesus says to him,

4 b "Go ◊ 1:44c

 c and have the priests examine ⟨your
skin⟩. ◊ 1:44d

 d Then offer for your cleansing what
Moses commanded— ◊ 1:44e
and no more sinning."

cf. Lev 13–14, esp. 14:2–20 ◊ Mark 1:44

SYNAGOGUE AT CAPERNAUM

The synagogue at Capernaum is usually dated II/III c.e. The main building, rectangular in shape, was bordered on the east by a courtyard. The main building had a second story which functioned as a gallery for the hall below. On the main floor, stone benches ran along the walls to provide seats for the congregation. Photo courtesy of Ambrose Edens.

K13: Jesus Cures a Paralytic

Mark 2:1–12	**Matt 9:1–8**	**Luke 5:17–26**

Matt 9:1–8

9 1a After he got on board the boat,
   b he crossed over

   c and came to his own town.

Mark 2:1–12

2 1a Some days later
   b he went back to Capernaum
   c and was rumored to be at home.
   2a And many people crowded around
   b so there was no longer any room,
     even outside the door.
   c Then he started speaking to them.

Luke 5:17–26

5 17a And it so happened one day,

   b as he was teaching,
   c that the Lord's healing power was
     with him.
   d Now Pharisees and teachers of the
     Law,
   e who had come from every village of
     Galilee
   f and Judea and from Jerusalem,
   g were sitting around.

3a Some people then show up
 b with a paralytic being carried by four
   of them.

2a The next thing you know,
 b some people were bringing a
   paralytic lying on a bed.

18a The next thing you know,
  b some men appeared, carrying a
    paralyzed person on a bed.
  c They attempted to bring him in
  d and lay him before ⟨Jesus⟩.

4a And when they were not able to get
   near him
 b on account of the crowd,
 c they removed the roof above him.
 d After digging it out,
 e they lowered the mat on which the
   paralytic was lying.

19a But finding no way to get him in

  b on account of the crowd,
  c they went up onto the roof

  d and lowered him on his pallet
    through the tiles
  e into the middle of the crowd
  f in front of Jesus.

5a When Jesus noticed their trust,
 b he says to the paralytic,

 c "Child, your sins are forgiven."

c When Jesus noticed their trust,
d he said to the paralytic,
e "Take courage, child,
f your sins are forgiven."

20a When Jesus noticed their trust,
  b he said,

  c "Mister, your sins have been
    forgiven you."

6a Some of the scholars were sitting
   there
 b and silently wondering:
7a "Why does that fellow say such
   things?
 b He's blaspheming!

 c Who can forgive sins except the one
   God?"

3a At that
 b some of the scholars

 c said to themselves,

 d "This fellow blasphemes!"

21a And the scholars and the Pharisees

  b began to raise questions:

  c "Who is this that utters
    blasphemies?
  d Who can forgive sins except God
    alone?"

Mark	**Matt**	**Luke**
2 8a And right away,		
b because Jesus sensed in his spirit	**9** 4a Because he understood	**5** 22a Because Jesus was aware
c that they were raising questions like this among themselves,	b the way they thought,	b of their questions,
d he says to them:	c Jesus said,	c he responded to them,
e "Why do you entertain questions about these things?	d "Why do you harbor evil thoughts?	d "Why do you entertain such questions?
9a Which is easier,	5a Which is easier:	23a Which is easier:
b to say to the paralytic,	b to say,	b to say,
c 'Your sins are forgiven,'	c 'Your sins are forgiven,'	c 'Your sins have been forgiven you,'
d or to say,	d or to say,	d or to say,
e 'Get up,	e 'Get up	e 'Get up
f pick up your mat		
g and walk'?"	f and walk'?"	f and walk'?"
10a But so that you may realize	6a But so that you may realize	24a But so that you may realize
b that on earth the son of Adam has authority to forgive sins,	b that on earth the son of Adam has authority to forgive sins,	b that on earth the son of Adam has authority to forgive sins,
c he says to the paralytic,	c he then says to the paralytic,	c he said to the paralyzed man,
11a "You there,		d "You there,
b get up,	d "Get up,	e get up,
c pick up your mat	e pick up your bed	f pick up your pallet
d and go home!"	f and go home."	g and go home."
12a And he got up,	7a And he got up	25a And immediately he stood up in front of them,
b picked his mat right up,		b picked up what he had been lying on,
c and walked out	b and went to his home.	c and went home
d as everyone looked on.		
		d praising God.
e So they all became ecstatic,	8a When the crowds saw this,	26a They all became ecstatic,
		c but they were also filled with fear
	b they became fearful,	b and they began to extol God,
f extolled God,	c and extolled God,	
g and exclaimed,		d and exclaimed,
h "We've never seen the likes of this!"		e "We saw some incredible things today!"
	d for giving such authority to humans.	

2:10b *On earth* appears to be a harmonizing reading borrowed from Matt and Luke; omit W *pc* b q.

2:10b *son of Adam* (Greek: υἱὸς τοῦ ἀνθρώπου) replaces traditional *son of man*.

The phrase may mean *any person, any human*, or it may refer to the heavenly redeemer figure of Daniel, Mark 13, and the book of Revelation. *Adam* recalls the first human being at creation, the primal human being, who stands for any person, male or female. Just as the phrase *son of a prophet* means any descendant of a prophet, so *son of Adam* refers to any descendant of Adam. To be entirely correct, the phrase should be translated *son or daughter of Adam* to indicate that it refers to a generic human being.

Under the influence of Dan 7:13–14, 8:15–17, and 10:15–17, the phrase took on messianic overtones. The one in human form is contrasted with the other forms in Daniel's vision, which are non-human in form. The one in human form then becomes the redeemer who comes on clouds at the end of the age (Mark 13:26).

☆ **John 5:8–9a** ◊ Mark 2:11–12

⁸"Get up, pick up your mat and walk around," Jesus tells him.

⁹And at once the man recovered; he picked up his mat and started walking.

Table 2

Parables and Sayings

Parables	Mark	Sayings (*continued*)	Mark
Sower, Soils, Seeds	4:3–8	No Sign for This Generation	8:12c–e
Mustard Seed	4:30b–32	Unseeing Eyes, Unhearing Ears	8:15d,
Seed & Harvest	4:26b–29		8:17c–19b,
Leased Vineyard	12:1b–8		8:20a–b,
Returning Landlord	13:34–37		8:21b
		Son of Adam Will Die	8:31
Sayings	**Mark**	Saving One's Life	8:34c–38
God's Imperial Rule	1:15	Some Standing Here	9:1b–d
No Doctor Needed	2:17	Elijah Must Come	9:12–13
Groom's Friends Don't Fast	2:19b–20	Son of Adam Will Die	9:31
Patches & Wineskins	2:21–22	Number One	9:35
Sabbath Day For Adam	2:27–28	Accepting a Child	9:37
Satan Divided	3:23c–26	For and Against	9:39c–41
Powerful Man's House	3:27	Hand, Foot & Eye	9:42–50
Blasphemies	3:28–29	Divorce	10:2–9,
Two Good Ears	4:9		10:11–12
Secret of God's Imperial Rule	4:11b–12	Let the Children	10:14d–15
Understanding the Sower	4:13b–20	Needle's Eye	10:23c,
Lamp Under the Bushel	4:21b–e		10:24c–25,
Hidden Brought to Light	4:22		10:27c–e,
Two Good Ears	4:23		10:29–30
The Same Standard	4:24b–25	First, Last	10:31
No Respect	6:4	Son of Adam Will Die	10:33–34
On the Road	6:8–9	Mountains Into the Sea	11:22–25
On the Town	6:10b–11d	Son of David	12:35–37
Human Tradition	7:6b–8	Scholars in Long Robes	12:38–40
	7:9b–13	Signs of the Times	13:1–33
What Comes Out Defiles	7:14b–15	Too Bad	14:21
	7:18b–19	Sleep On	14:41
	7:20b–23	Destroy This Temple	14:58
Bread to the Dogs	7:27b–d		

K14.1: Jesus Teaches by the Sea

Mark 2:13   **Matt**   **Luke**

2 13a Again he went out by the sea.
    b And, with a huge crowd gathered
      around him,
    c he started teaching.

K14.2: Levi Becomes a Follower

Mark 2:14   **Matt 9:9**   **Luke 5:27–28**

2 14a As he was walking along,   9 9a As Jesus was walking along there,   5 27a After these events he went out
    b he caught sight of Levi, the son of   b he caught sight of a man   b and observed a toll collector named
      Alphaeus,   Levi
    c sitting at the toll booth,   c sitting at the toll booth,   c sitting at the toll booth.
                                             d one named Matthew,
    d and he says to him,   e and he says to him,   d He said to him,
    e "Follow me!"   f "Follow me!"   e "Follow me!"
                                                                                  28a Leaving everything behind,
    f And Levi got up   g And he got up   b he got up,
    g and followed him.   h and followed him.   c and followed him.

K14.3: Jesus Dines with Toll Collectors

Mark 2:15–17   **Matt 9:10–13**   **Luke 5:29–32**

15a Then Jesus happens to recline at   10a And it so happened while he was   29a And Levi gave him a great banquet
    table in ⟨Levi's⟩ house,   dining in ⟨Matthew's⟩ house,   in his house,
                                           b that many toll collectors and sinners
                                             surprisingly showed up just then
    b along with many toll collectors and   c and dined with Jesus and his   b and a large group of toll collectors
      sinners and Jesus' disciples.   disciples.   and others were dining with them.
    c (Remember, there were many of
      these people
    d and they were all following him.)
2 16a And whenever the Pharisees'   9 11a And whenever the Pharisees saw
    scholars saw   this,
    b him eating with sinners and toll
      collectors,
    c they would question his disciples: b they would question his disciples: 5 30a The Pharisees and their scholars
                                                                                     would complain to his disciples:
    d "What's he doing eating with toll   c "Why does your teacher eat with toll   b "Why do you people eat and drink
      collectors and sinners?"   collectors and sinners?"   with toll collectors and sinners?"
   17a When Jesus overhears,   12a When Jesus overheard,
    b he says to them: b he said,   31a In response Jesus said to them:
    c "Since when do the able-bodied need   c "Since when do the able-bodied need   b "Since when do the healthy need a
      a doctor?   a doctor?   doctor?
    d It's the sick who do.   d It's the sick who do.   c It's the sick who do.

2:14b Some witnesses read *James:* (cf. Mark   **2:16a** Some witnesses read *the scholars and the*
3:18) D Θ *f*¹³ 565 it (in part) *al.*   *Pharisees:* A C (D) K Θ Π *f*¹ *f*¹³ *al.*
  2:15a Diners customarily reclined at meals;   **2:16d** Some witnesses add *and drinking:* (cf.
they did not normally sit on chairs.   Luke 5:30) A K Π *f*¹ 28 33 *al.*

K14.1: Jesus Teaches by the Sea

K14.2: Levi Becomes a Follower

GEbi 2 ◊ Mark 2:14

At any rate, in the gospel that they call "According to Matthew," which is not complete but adulterated and mutilated—they call it the "Hebrew" gospel—is found the following:

[1]There was this man named Jesus, who was about thirty years old, who chose us. [2]And when he came to Capernaum, he entered the house of Simon, who was nicknamed Peter. He then began to speak as follows:

[3]"As I was walking along by the lake of Tiberias, I chose John and James, sons of Zebedee, and Simon and Andrew and Thaddeus and Simon the Zealot and Judas the Iscariot. [4]Then I summoned you, Matthew, while you were sitting at the toll booth, and you followed me. [5]Therefore, I want you to be twelve apostles, to symbolize Israel."

Epiphanius, *Haer.* 30.13.2

K14.3: Jesus Dines with Toll Collectors

✩ **Luke 15:1–2** ◊ Mark 2:16

[1]Now the toll-collectors and sinners kept crowding around Jesus so they could hear him. [2]But the Pharisees and the scholars would complain to each other: "This fellow welcomes sinners and eats with them."

POxy1224 5:1–2 ◊ Mark 2:16–17

[1]When the scholars an[d Pharise]es and priests observ[ed hi]m, they were indignant [because he reclined ⟨at table⟩ in the com]pany of sin[ners]. [2]But Jesus overheard [them and said,] Those who are we[ll don't need a doctor.]

Mark	Matt	Luke

	13a Go
	  b and learn what this means,
	  c 'It's mercy I desire instead of sacrifice.'
	  d After all, I did not come to enlist religious folks but sinners!"	

2 17e I did not come to enlist religious folks but sinners!"		5 32 I have not come to enlist religious folks to change their hearts, but sinners!"

K15: Why Don't Your Disciples Fast?

Mark 2:18–22	Matt 9:14–17	Luke 5:33–39
2 18a John's disciples and the Pharisees were in the habit of fasting, b and they come		
	9 14a Then the disciples of John come up to him,	
c and ask him,	b and ask:	5 33a They said to him,
d "Why do the disciples of John fast,	c "Why do we fast, and the Pharisees fast,	b "The disciples of John are always fasting c and offering prayers,
e and the disciples of the Pharisees,	*cf. Matt 9:14c*	d and so are those of the Pharisees,
f but your disciples don't?"	d but your disciples don't?"	e but yours just eat and drink."
19a And Jesus said to them:	15a And Jesus said to them,	34a And Jesus said to them,
b "The groom's friends can't fast	b "The groom's friends can't mourn	b "You can't make the groom's friends fast
c while the groom is around, can they?	c as long as the groom is around, can they?	c as long as the groom is around, can you?
d So long as the groom is around, e you can't expect them to fast.		
20a But the days will come	d But the days will come	35a But the days will come

b when the groom is taken away from them,
  c and then they will fast,
  d on that day.
	e when the groom is taken away from them,
	  f and then they will fast.
		b when the groom is taken away from them,
		  c and then they will fast,
		  d in those days."

		36a He then gave them a proverb:

21a Nobody sews a piece of unshrunk cloth on an old garment,
  cf. Mark 2:21a
	16a Nobody puts a piece of unshrunk cloth on an old garment,
	  cf. Matt 9:16a
		b "Nobody tears a piece from a new garment
		  c and puts it on an old one,

b otherwise the new, unshrunk patch pulls away from the old
  c and creates a worse tear.
	b since the patch pulls away from the garment
	  c and creates a worse tear.
		d since the new one will tear
		  e and the piece from the new will not match the old.

2:19a *Jesus* is probably a harmonizing addition
(cf. Matt); omit D W *pc* it (in part).

Justin, *Apology* **1.15.8** ◊ Mark 2:17

[8]He spoke as follows: "I did not come to call the pious but sinners to repentance." The heavenly Father, you see, prefers the repentance of the sinner rather than their punishment.

K15: Why Don't Your Disciples Fast?

Thom 47:1–5

[1]Jesus said, "A person cannot mount two horses or bend two bows. [2]And a slave cannot serve two masters, otherwise that slave will honor the one and offend the other.

Matt 11:18–19 ◊ Mark 2:18

[18]And the ranking priests and the scholars heard this and kept looking for a way to get rid of him. (The truth is that they stood in fear of him, and that the whole crowd was astonished at his teaching.) [19]And when it grew dark, they made their way out of the city.

☆ **Luke 7:33–34** ◊ Mark 2:18

[33]"Just remember, John the Baptist appeared on the scene, eating no bread and drinking no wine, and you say, 'He is demented.' [34]The son of Adam appeared on the scene both eating and drinking, and you say, 'There's a glutton and a drunk, a crony of toll collectors and sinners!'"

☆ **Luke 18:12** ◊ Mark 2:18

[12]'I fast twice a week, I give tithes of everything that I acquire.'

☆ **Thom 27:1–2** ◊ Mark 2:19–20

[1]"If you do not fast from the world, you will not find the ⟨Father's⟩ domain. [2]If you do not observe the sabbath day as a sabbath day, you will not see the Father."

☆ **Thom 104:1–3** ◊ Mark 2:19–20

[1]They said to Jesus, "Come, let us pray today, and let us fast."
[2]Jesus said, "What sin have I committed, or how have I been undone? [3]Rather, when the groom leaves the bridal suite, then let people fast and pray."

☆ **John 3:29–30** ◊ Mark 2:19–20

[29]The bride belongs to the groom, and the best man stands with him and is happy enough just to be close at hand. So I am content. [30]He can only grow in importance; my role can only diminish.

☆ **Did 8:1** ◊ Mark 2:20

[1]Don't hold your fasts with the hypocrites. They fast each week on Mondays and Thursdays. You should fast on Wednesdays and Fridays.

5 a An old patch is not sewn onto a new garment,

b since it would create a tear."

	Mark	**Matt**	**Luke**

2 22a And nobody pours young wine into old wineskins,
   b otherwise the wine will burst the skins,

   c and destroy both the wine and the skins.
   d Instead, young wine is for new wineskins."

9 17a Nor do they pour young wine into old wineskins,
   b otherwise the wineskins burst,

   c the wine gushes out,
   d and the wineskins are destroyed.

   e Instead, they put young wine in new wineskins
   f and both are preserved."

5 37a And nobody pours young wine into old wineskins,
   b otherwise the young wine will burst the wineskins,

   c it will gush out,
   d and the wineskins will be destroyed.

   38 Instead, young wine must be put into new wineskins.

   39a Besides, nobody wants young wine

   b after drinking aged wine:
   c As they say,
   d 'Aged wine is just fine!'"

K16: What Is Permitted on the Sabbath?

	Mark 2:23–28	**Matt 12:1–8**	**Luke 6:1–5**

2 23a It so happened
   b that he was walking along through the grainfields on the sabbath day,

   c and his disciples began to strip heads of grain as they walked along.

24a And the Pharisees started to argue with him:
   b "See here,
   c why are they doing
   d what's not permitted on the sabbath day?"
25a And he says to them:
   b "Haven't you ever read what David did
   c when he found it necessary,
   d when both he and his companions were hungry?
26a He went into the house of God,
   b when Abiathar was high priest,
   c and ate the consecrated bread,

   d and even gave some to his men to eat.

12 1a On that occasion
   b Jesus walked through the grainfields on the sabbath day.
   c His disciples were hungry
   d and began to strip heads of grain

   e and chew them.
2a When the Pharisees saw this,
   b they said to him,

   c "See here,
   d your disciples are doing
   e what's not permitted on the sabbath day."
3a He said to them,
   b "Haven't you read what David did

   c when he and his companions were hungry?
4a He went into the house of God,

   b and ate the consecrated bread,

6 1a It so happened
   b that he was walking through grainfields on a sabbath day,

   c and his disciples would strip some heads of grain,
   d husk them in their hands,
   e and chew them.

2a Some of the Pharisees said,

   b "Why are you doing
   c what's not permitted on the sabbath day?"
3a And Jesus answered them,
   b "Haven't you read what David did

   c when he and his companions were hungry?
4a He went into the house of God,

   b took and ate the consecrated bread himself,
   c and gave some to his men to eat?

2:22d Some mss omit: *Instead, young wine is for new wineskins* (D it [in part]).

Thom

47 4a Young wine is not poured into old
        wineskins,
     b or they might break,

     c and aged wine is not poured into a
        new wineskin,
     d or it might spoil.

3b and immediately wants to drink new
      wine.
     a Nobody drinks aged wine

K16: What is Permitted on the Sabbath?

☆ InThom 2:1–7

[1]When this boy, Jesus, was five years old, he was playing at the ford of a rushing stream. [2]He was collecting the flowing water into ponds and made the water instantly pure. He did this with a single command. [3]He then made soft clay and shaped it into twelve sparrows. He did this on the sabbath day, and many other boys were playing with him.

[4]But when a Jew saw what Jesus was doing while playing on the sabbath day, he immediately went off and told Joseph, Jesus' father: "See here, your boy is at the ford, and has taken mud and fashioned twelve birds with it, and so has violated the sabbath."

[5]So Joseph went there, and as soon as he spotted him he shouted, "Why are you doing what's not permitted on the sabbath?"

[6]But Jesus simply clapped his hands and shouted to the sparrows: "Be off, fly away, and remember me, you who are now alive!" And the sparrows took off and flew away noisily.

[7]The Jews watched with amazement, then left the scene to report to their leaders what they had seen Jesus doing.

Deut 23:25 (Lxx) ◊ Mark 2:23

[25]If you go into your neighbor's grain-field, you can gather heads of grain by hand, but you can not use a sickle on your neighbor's grain.

Exod 20:10 (Lxx) ◊ Mark 2:24

[10]The seventh day is a sabbath day to the Lord your God. You are not to do any work on that day, nor is your son and daughter. Your servants, male and female, are to refrain from work, as are your ox, your beast of burden and all your other animals, along with the proselytes who live among you.

Deut 5:14 (Lxx) ◊ Mark 2:24

[14]The seventh day is a sabbath day to the Lord your God. You are not to do any work on that day, nor are your sons or your daughters. Your servants, male and female, are to refrain from work, as are your ox, your beast of burden, and all your other animals, along with the proselytes who live among you, so your servants, male and female, and rest as well as you.

1 Sam 21:2–7 (Lxx) ◊ Mark 2:25–26

[2]David comes to the priest Ahimelech at Nob. Ahimelech was alarmed at meeting him and said to him, "Why are you alone? Why is no one with you?" [3]David replied to the priest, "The king has given me an order this day and has said to me, 'No one is to know about the mission on which I am sending you and concerning which I have given you orders.' I have made an appointment with my young companions at a place called 'God's trust' (Phellani Alemoni). [4]Now, then, I hope you have five loaves ⟨of bread⟩ on hand. Give me whatever you can find." [5]The priest replied to David, "I don't have any unconsecrated bread on hand. All I have is consecrated loaves. If your companions have had no contact with women, they may eat." [6]In response David said to the priest, "We have indeed abstained from women yesterday and the day before. When I go out on a mission, my companions are ritually pure, even when it is an ordinary mission. Consequently, my vessels will certainly be sanctified today." [7]And Ahimelech the priest gave the consecrated bread to David but there was no bread other than the consecrated bread. The consecrated bread was removed from the presence of the Lord and replaced with freshly baked bread as soon as the former was taken away.

Mark	Matt	Luke
2 26e No one is permitted to eat this bread,	**12** 4c which no one is permitted to eat— not even David or his companions—	**6** 4d No one is permitted to eat this bread
f except the priests!	d except the priests alone!	e except the priests alone!"
	5a Or haven't you read in the Law	
	b that during the sabbath day the priests violate the sabbath in the temple	
	c and are held blameless?	
	6a Yet I say to you,	
	b someone greater than the temple is here.	
	7a And if you had known what this means,	
	b 'It's mercy I desire instead of sacrifice,'	
	c you would not have condemned those who are blameless.	
27a And he continued:		5a And he used to say to them,
b "The sabbath day was created for Adam and Eve,		
c not Adam and Eve for the sabbath day.		
28 So, the son of Adam lords it even over the sabbath day."	8 Remember, the son of Adam lords it over the sabbath day."	b "The son of Adam lords it over the sabbath day."

K17: Jesus Heals on the Sabbath Day

Mark 3:1–6	Matt 12:9–14	Luke 6:6–11
		6 6a On another sabbath day,
		b it so happened
3 1a Then he went back to the synagogue,	**12** 9a And when he had moved on,	c that he entered the synagogue
	b he went into their synagogue.	d and taught.
b and a fellow with a crippled hand was there.	10a Just then a fellow with a crippled hand appeared,	e A fellow was there whose right hand was crippled.
2a So they kept an eye on him,		7a And the scholars and the Pharisees watched him carefully,
b to see whether he would heal the fellow on the sabbath day,		b to see if he would heal on the sabbath day,
c so they could denounce him.	d so they could discredit him.	c so they could find some excuse to denounce him.
		8a However, he knew their motives,
	b and they asked him,	b and he said to the fellow with the crippled hand,
3a And he says to the fellow with the crippled hand,		c "Get up and stand here in front of everybody."
b "Get up here in front of everybody."		d And he got to his feet and stood there.

2:28 Greek (κύριος): or *is lord (master) of*
  The Greek term can be translated *sir* (a polite form of address for superiors), *lord* (equivalent to the British title = person of substance,

achievement, translated in SV as *patron*), *Lord* (as a title suitable for a divinized oriental monarch), or even *Lord = God* (so used frequently in the LXX, the Greek version of the

Hebrew scriptures). The term probably functioned at more than one level for the evangelists. It clearly functioned variously in the earlier levels of the tradition.

☆ **Thom 27:1–2** ◊ Mark 2:27–28

[1] "If you do not fast from the world, you will not find the ⟨Father's⟩ domain. [2]If you do not observe the sabbath day as a sabbath day, you will not see the Father."

Lev 24:5–9 (LXX) ◊ Mark 2:26

[5]You are to take the finest wheat flour and make twelve loaves out of it. A loaf is to contain two-tenths ⟨of a measure⟩. [6]You are to place them in two piles, six loaves to the pile, on a clean table before the Lord. [7]And on the piles you are to place pure frankincense and salt. And they will serve as memorial loaves placed before the Lord. [8]They are always to be set out before the Lord each sabbath, as a perpetual covenant on behalf of the people of Israel. [9]These ⟨loaves⟩ are for Aaron and his sons. They will eat them in the sanctuary, since for him this is the most sacred of all the sacrifices to the Lord, a perpetual rite.

K17: Jesus Heals on the Sabbath Day

☆ **Luke 14:1–6**

[1]And so one sabbath day, when Jesus happened to have dinner at the house of a prominent Pharisee, they were keeping an eye on him. [2]This man who had dropsy suddenly showed up.

[3]Jesus addressed the legal experts and Pharisees: "Is it permitted to heal on the sabbath day, or not?"

[4]But they were silent.

So he took the man, healed him, and sent him on his way.

[5]Then he said to them, "Suppose your son or your ox falls down a well, would any of you hesitate for a second to pull him out on the sabbath day?"

[6]And they had no response to this.

☆ **InThom 2:1–7**

[1]When this boy, Jesus, was five years old, he was playing at the ford of a rushing stream. [2]He was collecting the flowing water into ponds and made the water instantly pure. He did this with a single command. [3]He then made soft clay and shaped it into twelve sparrows. He did this on the sabbath day, and many other boys were playing with him.

[4]But when a Jew saw what Jesus was doing while playing on the sabbath day, he immediately went off and told Joseph, Jesus' father: "See here, your boy is at the ford, and has taken mud and fashioned twelve birds with it, and so has violated the sabbath."

[5]So Joseph went there, and as soon as he spotted him he shouted, "Why are you doing what's not permitted on the sabbath?"

[6]But Jesus simply clapped his hands and shouted to the sparrows: "Be off, fly away, and remember me, you who are now alive!" And the sparrows took off and flew away noisily.

[7]The Jews watched with amazement, then left the scene to report to their leaders what they had seen Jesus doing.

GNaz 4 ◊ Mark 3:1

In the gospel that the Nazoreans and Ebonites use ⟨in the story of the healing of the man with the crippled hand⟩, this man who had a crippled hand is described as a stonemason who called for help with words like this: "I was a stonemason making a living with my hands. I plead with you, Jesus, give me back my health so that I won't have to beg for my food in shame."

Jerome, *Comm. in Mattheum* 2 on 12:13

Mark	**Matt**	**Luke**
3 4a Then he asks them,	*cf. Matt 12:11a*	**6** 9a Then Jesus queried them: b "I ask you,
b "On the sabbath day is it permitted to do good or to do evil, c to save life or to destroy it?" d But they maintained their silence.	**12** 10c "Is it permitted to heal on the sabbath day?"	c on the sabbath day is it permitted to do good or to do evil, d to save life or to destroy it?"
	11a He asked them, b "If you had only a single sheep, c and it fell into a ditch on the sabbath day, d wouldn't you grab it and pull it out?	**14** 5a Then he said to them, b "Suppose your son or your ox c falls down a well, d would any of you hesitate for a second to pull him out on the sabbath day?"
	12a A person is worth considerably more than a sheep. b So, it is permitted to do good on the sabbath day!"	
5a And looking right at them b with anger, c exasperated at their obstinacy, d he says to the fellow, e "Hold out your hand!" f He held it out g and his hand was restored.	13a Then he says to the fellow, b "Hold out your hand!" c He held it out d and it was restored e to health like the other.	10a And he looked right at all of them, b and said to him, c "Hold out your hand!" d He did e and his hand was restored.
6a Then the Pharisees went right out with the Herodians b and hatched a plot against him, c to get rid of him.	14a The Pharisees went out b and hatched a plot against him c to get rid of him.	11a But they were filled with rage b and discussed among themselves c what to do with Jesus.

☆ **John 11:53** ◊ Mark 3:6

⁵³So from that day on they began plotting how to kill him.

Table 3

Pronouncement Stories

		Mark
1.	Jesus Steals Away	1:35–39
2.	Jesus Cures a Paralytic	2:1–12
3.	Jesus Dines with Toll Collectors	2:16–17
4.	Why Don't Your Disciples Fast?	2:18–22
5.	What Is Permitted on the Sabbath?	2:23–28
6.	Jesus Heals on the Sabbath Day	3:1–6
7.	Scholars Accuse Jesus	3:22-30
8.	True Relatives	3:31–35
9.	Secret of God's Imperial Rule	4:10–20
10.	No Respect at Home	6:1–6
11.	Unwashed Hands	7:1–13
12.	Greek Woman's Daughter	7:24–30
13.	The Pharisees Demand a Sign	8:11–12
14.	The Son of Adam Must Suffer	8:31–33
15.	Elijah Must Come First	9:9–13
16.	Number One Is Last	9:33–37
17.	For and Against	9:38–40
18.	Is Divorce Permitted?	10:2–9
19.	Let the Children Come	10:13–16
20.	The Man with Money	10:17–22
21.	The Needle's Eye	10:23–27
22.	Jesus' Cup and Baptism	10:35–45
23.	The Temple as Hideout	11:15–17
24.	The Fig Tree Without Figs	11:20–25
25.	Who Gave You the Authority?	11:27–33
26.	Is It Permissible to Pay the Tax?	12:13–17
27.	Whose Wife Will She Be?	12:18–27
28.	Which Commandment?	12:28–34
29.	Whose Son Is the Anointed?	12:35–37
30.	The Widow's Pittance	12:41–44
31.	What Wonderful Buildings!	13:1–2

THIRD GALILEAN

K18: Jesus Withdraws to the Sea

Mark 3:7–12	**Matt 12:15–21**	**Luke 6:17–19**
	12 15 a Aware of this,	
3 7a Then Jesus withdrew with his disciples to the sea,	b Jesus withdrew from there,	
		6 17a On the way down with them,
		b Jesus stopped at a level place.
b and a huge crowd from Galilee followed.	c and huge crowds followed him,	c There was a huge crowd of his disciples
c When they heard what he was doing,		*cf. Luke 6:18a*
d a huge crowd from Judea,		d and a great throng of people from all Judea
8a and from Jerusalem and Idumea		e and Jerusalem
b and across the Jordan,		
c and from around Tyre and Sidon, collected around him.		f and the coast of Tyre and Sidon.
		18a They came to hear him
9a And he told his disciples		b and to be healed of their diseases.
b to have a small boat ready for him on account of the crowd,		
c so they would not mob him.		
10a (After all, he had healed so many,	d and he healed all of them.	
b that all who had diseases were pushing forward to touch him.)		
		19a And everyone in the crowd tried to touch him,
		b since power would flow out from him
		c and heal them all.
11a The unclean spirits also,		18c Those who were tormented by unclean spirits were cured.
b whenever they faced him,		
c would fall down before him		
d and shout out,		
e "You son of God, you!"		
12a But he always warned them	16a And he warned them	
b not to tell who he was.	b not to disclose his identity,	
	17 so what was spoken through Isaiah the prophet would come true:	
	18a Here is my servant whom I have selected,	
	b my favored of whom I fully approve.	
	c I will put my spirit upon him,	
	d and he will announce judgment for foreigners.	
	19a He will not be contentious,	
	b nor loud-mouthed,	
	c nor will anyone hear his voice on main street.	

K18: Jesus Withdraws to the Sea

☆ **Matt 4:25** ◊ Mark 3:7–8

²⁵And huge crowds followed him from Galilee and Decapolis and Jerusalem and Judea and from across the Jordan.

☆ **Mark 6:56** ◊ Mark 3:10

⁵⁶And wherever he would go, into villages, or towns, or onto farms, they would lay out the sick in the marketplaces and beg him to let them touch the fringe of his cloak. And all those who managed to touch it were cured!

☆ **Matt 14:36** ◊ Mark 3:10

³⁶And they begged him just to let them touch the fringe of his cloak, And all those who managed to touch ⟨it⟩ were cured!

☆ **Luke 4:41** ◊ Mark 3:11–12

⁴¹Demons would also come out of many of them screaming, and saying, "You son of God, you!" But he would rebuke them and would not allow them to speak, because they knew that he was the Anointed.

Mark	Matt	Luke

	1220a He is not about to break a crushed reed,	
	b and he's not one to snuff out a smoldering wick,	
	c until he brings forth a decisive victory,	
	21 and foreigners will center their hope on him.	

K19: Jesus Forms the Twelve

Mark 3:13–19	**Matt 10:1–4**	**Luke 6:12–16**

		6 12a During that time, it so happened that
		b he went out to the mountain to pray,
		c and spent the night in prayer to God.
3 13a Then he goes up on the mountain		13a The next day,
b and summons those he wanted,	**10** 1a And summoning his twelve disciples	b he called his disciples
c and they came to him.		
14a He formed a group of twelve		c and selected twelve of them,
b to be his companions,		
	cf. Matt 10:2a	d whom he named apostles:
c and to be sent out to speak,		
15 and to have authority to drive out demons.	b he gave them authority to drive out unclean spirits	
	c and to heal every disease and every ailment.	
	2a The names of the twelve apostles were these:	*cf. Luke 6:13d*
16 And to Simon he gave the nickname Rock,	b first, Simon, also known as Rock,	14a Simon, whom he nicknamed Rock,
cf. Mark 3:18a		
17a and to James, the son of Zebedee,	c and Andrew his brother,	b and Andrew his brother,
b and to John, his brother,	d and James the son of Zebedee	c and James
c he also gave a nickname, Boanerges,	e and John his brother,	d and John,
d which means "Thunder Brothers";		
18a and Andrew	*cf. Matt 10:2c*	*cf. Luke 6:14b*
b and Philip	3a Philip	e and Philip,
c and Bartholomew	b and Bartholomew,	f and Bartholomew,
d and Matthew	**d** and Matthew the toll collector,	15a and Matthew,
e and Thomas	c Thomas,	b and Thomas,
f and James, the son of Alphaeus;	e James the son of Alphaeus,	c and James the son of Alphaeus,
g and Thaddeus	f and Thaddaeus,	
h and Simon the Zealot;	4a Simon the Zealot,	d and Simon who was called the Zealot,
19a and Judas Iscariot,	b and Judas of Iscariot,	16a and Judas the son of James,
b who, in the end, turned him in.	c the one who, in the end, turned him in.	b and Judas Iscariot,
		c who turned traitor.

3:14a Some mss add: *whom he named apostles* (ℵ B C* ⊖ *f*¹³ 28 1195 *al*); cf. Luke 6:13d.

3:16 Some mss insert before *And to Simon: So he appointed the twelve* (ℵ B C* Δ 565 *pc*).

△ **Acts 1:12–14** ◊ Mark 3:16–19

[12]Then they returned to Jerusalem from the Mount of Olives, as it is called. It is near Jerusalem, only a sabbath day's travel away. [13]And when they arrived, they went to the upper room where they had been staying: Peter and John and James and Andrew, Philip and Thomas, Bartholomew and Matthew, James the son of Alphaeus, and Simon the Zealot, and Judas son of James. [14]This whole group was busily engaged in prayer, along with the women, and Mary, the mother of Jesus, and his brothers.

△ **GEbi 2**

At any rate, in the gospel that they call "According to Matthew," which is not complete but adulterated and mutilated—they call it the "Hebrew" gospel—is found the following:

[1]There was this man named Jesus, who was about thirty years old, who chose us. [2]And when he came to Capernaum, he entered the house of Simon, who was nicknamed Peter. He then began to speak as follows:

[3]"As I was walking along by the lake of Tiberias, I chose John and James, sons of Zebedee, and Simon and Andrew and Thaddeus and Simon the Zealot and Judas the Iscariot. [4]Then I summoned you, Matthew, while you were sitting at the toll booth, and you followed me. [5]Therefore, I want you to be twelve apostles, to symbolize Israel."

Epiphanius, *Haer*. 30.13.2

K19: Jesus Forms the Twelve

Mark 6:7 ◊ Mark 3:13–15

[7]Then he summoned the twelve and started sending them out in pairs and giving them authority over unclean spirits.

Luke 9:1–2 ◊ Mark 3:13–15

[1]He called the twelve together and gave them power and authority over all demons and to heal diseases. [2]He sent them out to announce God's imperial rule and to heal the sick.

John 1:42 ◊ Mark 3:16

[42]And he took him to Jesus.

When Jesus laid eyes on him, he said "You're Simon, John's son; you're going to be called Kephas" (which means Peter ⟨or Rock⟩).

☆ **John 6:70–71** ◊ Mark 3:19

[70]Jesus responded to them, "Isn't why I chose you twelve? Even so, one of you is a devil." ([71]He was of course referring to Judas, son of Simon Iscariot, one of the twelve, who was going to turn him in.)

K20.1: Jesus' Relatives Come to Get Him

Mark 3:20–21	**Matt 12:22–23**	**Luke 11:14**
3 20a Then he goes home,		
b and once again a crowd gathers,		
c so they could not even grab a bite to eat.		
21a When his relatives heard about it,		
b they came to get him.		
c (You see, they thought he was out of his mind.)		
	12 22a Then they brought to him a blind and mute person	**11** 14a Jesus was driving out a demon that was mute,
	b who was demon-possessed,	
	c and he cured him	b and when the demon had departed
	d so the mute was able both to speak and to see.	c the mute man spoke.
	23a And the entire crowd was beside itself	d And the crowds were amazed.
	b and would say,	
	c "This fellow can't be the son of David, can he?"	

K20.2: Scholars Accuse Jesus

Mark 3:22–30	**Matt 12:24–32**	**Luke 11:15–23, 12:10**
3 22a And the scholars	**12** 24a But when the Pharisees heard of it,	
b who had come down from Jerusalem		
c would say,	b they said,	**11** 15a But some of them said,
d "He is under the control of Beelzebul"		
e and "He drives out demons in the name of the head demon!"	c "This fellow drives out demons only in the name of Beelzebul, the head demon."	b "He drives out demons in the name of Beelzebul, the head demon."
		16 Others were testing him by demanding a sign from heaven.
23a And after calling them over,	25a But he knew how they thought,	17a But he knew what they were thinking,
b he would speak to them in riddles:	b and said to them:	b and said to them:
c "How can Satan drive out Satan?		
24a After all, if a government is divided against itself,	c "Every government divided against itself is devastated,	c "Every government divided against itself is devastated,
b that government cannot endure.		
25a And if a household is divided against itself,	d and every town or household divided against itself won't survive.	d and a house divided against a house falls.
b that household won't be able to survive.		

3:21c Mark occasionally provides explanatory asides for the reader, as in this case. In Greek these are often introduced by *for* (γάρ): 3:10, 6:14b, 31d, 52a, 7:3a, 9:6, 11:13h. The translators have put these asides in parentheses.

3:23b Greek παραβολή: The Greek term covers a wider range of speech forms than the English cognate *parable* suggests. The translators have therefore translated *riddle, analogy, parable*, depending on the context: 4:2, 10, 11, 13, 30, 33, 34, 7:17, 12:1, 12, 13:28.

K20.1: Jesus' Relatives Come to Get Him

☆ John 7:20 ◊ Mark 3:21

²⁰The crowd answered, "You're out of your mind! Who's trying to kill you?"

☆ John 8:48 ◊ Mark 3:21

⁴⁸The Judeans replied, "Aren't we right to say, 'You're a Samaritan and out of your mind'?"

☆ John 8:52 ◊ Mark 3:21

⁵²To this the Judeans retorted, "Now we're certain you're out of your mind! ⟨Even⟩ Abraham died, and so did the prophets, and here you are claiming, 'All who obey my teaching will certainly never taste death.'"

☆ John 10:20 ◊ Mark 3:21

²⁰Many of them were saying, "He's out of his mind and crazy. Why pay any attention to him?"

K20.2: Scholars Accuse Jesus

Matt 9:32–34

³²Just as they were leaving, they brought to him a mute who was demon-possessed. ³³And after the demon had been driven out, the mute started to speak. And the crowd was amazed and said, "Nothing like this has ever been seen in Israel."

34a But the Pharisees were saying,
   ◊ 3:22c
   b "He drives out demons in the name of the head demon." ◊ 3:22e

Mark	Matt	Luke
3 26 a So if Satan rebels against himself b and is divided, c he cannot endure d but is done for.	**12** 26 a So if Satan drives out Satan, b he is divided against himself. c In that case, how will his domain endure?	**11** 18 a If Satan is divided against himself b —since you claim I drive out demons in Beelzebul's name— c how will his domain endure?
	27 a Even if I drive out demons in Beelzebul's name, b in whose name do your own people drive ⟨them⟩ out? c In that case, they will be your judges. 28 a But if by God's spirit b I drive out demons, c then for you God's imperial rule has arrived.	19 a If I drive out demons in Beelzebul's name, b in whose name do your own people drive ⟨them⟩ out? c In that case, they will be your judges. 20 a But if by God's finger b I drive out demons, c then for you God's imperial rule has arrived.
27 a No one can enter a powerful man's house b to steal his belongings c unless he first ties him up. d Only then does he loot his house.	29 a Or how can someone enter a powerful man's house b and steal his belongings, c unless he first ties him up? d Only then does he loot his house.	
		21 a When a strong man is fully armed b and guards his courtyard, c his possessions are safe. 22 a But when a stronger man attacks b and overpowers him, c he takes the weapons on which he was relying d and divides up his loot.
	30 a The one who isn't with me is against me, b and the one who doesn't gather with me scatters.	23 a The one who isn't with me is against me, b and the one who doesn't gather with me scatters."
28 a I swear to you, b all offenses c and whatever blasphemies humankind might blaspheme d will be forgiven them.	31 a That's why I tell you: b every offense c and blasphemy d will be forgiven humankind, e but the blasphemy of the spirit won't be forgiven. 32 a And the one who speaks a word against the son of Adam b will be forgiven;	**12** 10 a And everyone who utters a word against the son of Adam b will be forgiven;
29 a But whoever blasphemes against the holy spirit b is never ever forgiven, c but is guilty of an eternal sin."	c but the one who speaks a word against the holy spirit d won't be forgiven, either in this age or in the one to come."	c but whoever blasphemes against the holy spirit d won't be forgiven.

3:28a *I swear to you* translates Greek ἀμὴν λέγω ὑμῖν: *amen* introduces solemn declarations in the gospels, always on the lips of Jesus. At the conclusion of prayers, *amen* may be translated *so be it* (Greek: γένοιτο). The translators considered translating the phrase *so help me (God)*, but concluded that *I swear to you* catches the solemn, serious tone of the pronouncements introduced by it.

Thom 35:1–2 ◊ Mark 3:27

[1]Jesus said, "One can't enter a strong man's house and take it by force without tying his hands. [2]Then one can loot his house."

△ **Thom 21:1–10** ◊ Mark 3:27

[1]Mary said to Jesus, "What are your disciples like?"

[2]He said, "They are like little children living in a field that is not theirs. [3]When the owners of the field come, they will say, 'Give us back our field.' [4]They take off their clothes in front of them in order to give it back to them, and they return their field to them. [5]For this reason I say, if the owners of a house know that a thief is coming, they will be on guard before the thief arrives, and will not let the thief break into their house (their domain) and steal their possessions. [6]As for you, then, be on guard against the world. [7]Prepare yourselves with great strength, so the robbers can't find a way to get to you, for the trouble you expect will come. [8]Let there be among you a person who understands. [9]When the crop ripened, he came quickly carrying a sickle and harvested it. [10]Anyone here with two good ears had better listen!"

Thom 44:1–3 ◊ Mark 3:28–29

[1]Jesus said, "Whoever blasphemes against the Father will be forgiven, [2]and whoever blasphemes against the son will be forgiven, [3]but whoever blasphemes against the holy spirit will not be forgiven, either on earth or in heaven."

✢ **Did 11:7** ◊ Mark 3:28–29

You are not to test or examine any prophet who is speaking under the influence of the spirit. Understand, every other sin will be forgiven, but this sin will not be forgiven.

Mark	**Matt**	**Luke**

3 30a (Remember, it was they who had started the accusation,
   b "He is controlled by an unclean spirit.")

K20.3: True Relatives

Mark 3:31–35	**Matt 12:46–50**	**Luke 8:19–21**

3 31a Then his mother and his brothers arrive.
   b While still outside,

   c they send in and ask for him.

  32a A crowd was sitting around him,
   b and they say to him,
   c "Look, your mother and your brothers
   d and sisters
   e are outside
   f looking for you."
  33a In response he says to them:

   b "My mother and brothers—whoever are they?"
  34a And looking right at those seated around him in a circle,
   b he says,
   c "Here are my mother and my brothers.
  35a Whoever does God's will,

   b that's my brother and sister and mother!"

12 46a While he was still speaking to the crowds,
   b his mother and brothers showed up outside;
   c they had come to speak to him.

  47a Someone said to him,
   b "Look, your mother and your brothers

   c are outside
   d wanting to speak to you."
  48a In response he said to the one speaking to him,
   b "My mother and my brothers—whoever are they?"
  49a And he pointed to his disciples

   b and said,
   c "Here are my mother and my brothers.
  50a For whoever does the will of my Father in heaven,
   b that's my brother and sister and mother."

8 19a Then his mother and his brothers came to him,
   b but they could not reach him because of the crowd.

  20a When he was told,
   b "Your mother and your brothers

   c are outside
   d and want to see you,"
  21a he replied to them,

   b "My mother and my brothers are those who
   c listen to God's message and do it."

3:32d The phrase: *and sisters* is found in a few mss (A D Γ *al*); most mss omit it.

K20.3: True Relatives

GEbi 5 ◊ Mark 3:31–35

They deny that he was human, I suppose because of what the Savior said when it was reported to him:
[1]"Look, your mother and your brothers are outside."
[2]"My mother and brothers—whoever are they?" [3]And he pointed to his disciples and said, "These are my brothers and mother and sisters, [4]those who do the will of my Father."
Epiphanius, *Haer.* 30.14.5

Thom 99:1–3 ◊ Mark 3:31–35

1 a The disciples said to him, ◊ 3:32b
   b "Your brothers and your mother
      ◊ 3:32c
   c are standing outside." ◊ 3:32e
2 a He said to them, ◊ 3:34b
   b "Those here who do what my Father
      wants ◊ 3:35a
   c are my brothers and my mother.
      ◊ 3:35b
[3]They are the ones who will enter my Father's domain."

✫ **John 15:14** ◊ Mark 3:35

[14]"You are my friends if you follow my orders."

2 Clem 9:11 ◊ Mark 3:35

For the Lord said, "My brothers are those who do the will of my Father."

TEACHING IN PARABLES

K21.1: Jesus Teaches from a Boat

Mark 4:1	Matt 13:1–2	Luke 8:4a–b
	13 1 a That same day, b Jesus left the house	
4 1 a Once again he started to teach b beside the sea. c An enormous crowd gathers around him,	c and sat beside the sea. 2 a Huge crowds gathered around him,	**8** 4 a Since a huge crowd was now gathering, b and people were making their way to him from town after town,
d so he climbs into a boat e and sits there on the water f facing the huge crowd on the shore.	b so he climbed into a boat c and sat down, d while the entire crowd stood on the sea shore.	

K21.2: Parable of the Sower, Seeds, Soils

Mark 4:2–9	Matt 13:3–9	Luke 8:4c–8
4 2 a He would then teach them many things in parables. b In the course of his teaching he would tell them: 3 a "Listen to this! b This sower went out to sow.	**13** 3 a He told them many things in parables: b "This sower went out to sow.	**8** 4 c he told them some such parable as this: 5 a "A sower went out to sow his seed;
4 a While he was sowing, b some seed fell along the path,	4 a While he was sowing, b some seed fell along the path,	b and while he was sowing, c some seed fell along the path, d and was trampled under foot,
c and the birds came d and ate it up. 5 a Other seed fell on rocky ground b where there wasn't much soil, c and it came up right away because the soil had no depth.	c and the birds came d and ate it up. 5 a Other seed fell on rocky ground b where there wasn't much soil, c and it came up right away because the soil had no depth.	e and the birds of the sky f ate it up. 6 a Other seed fell on the rock;
		b when it grew, c it withered because it lacked moisture.
6 a But when the sun came up b it was scorched, c and because it had no root d it withered.	6 a When the sun came up b it was scorched, c and because it had no roots d it withered.	

4:2 *would teach* and *would tell* (Greek imperfect tense): the imperfect tense is often used by Mark to indicate things Jesus characteristically, or typically, or habitually did. Matthew and Luke usually historicize this tense as a simple past (Greek: aorist). Cf. Mark 4:10–11, 21a, 24a, 26a, 30a, 33b, 34a, b, and often elsewhere.

K21.1: Jesus Teaches from a Boat

☆ **Luke 5:1–3** ⫤ Mark 4:1

[1]On one occasion, when the crowd pressed him to hear the word of God, he was standing by the lake of Gennesaret. [2]He noticed two boats moored there at the shore; the fishermen had left them and were washing their nets. [3]He got into one of the boats, the one belonging to Simon, and asked him to put out a little from the shore. Then he sat down and began to teach the crowds from the boat.

K21.2: Parable of the Sower, Seeds, Soils

Thom 9:1–5

9 1 a Jesus said,

b "Look, the sower went out,

c took a handful (of seeds),
d and scattered (them).
2 a Some fell on the road,
b and the birds came
c and gathered them.
3 a Others fell on rock,

☆ **InThom 12:1–4** ⫤ Mark 4:2–9

[1]Again, during the sowing season, the child went out with his father to sow their field with grain. While his father was sowing, the child Jesus sowed one measure of grain. [2]When he had harvested and threshed it, it yielded one hundred measures. [3]Then he summoned all the poor in the village to the threshing floor and gave them grain. Joseph carried back what was left of the grain. [4]Jesus was eight years old when he did this miracle.

☆ **SecJas 8:1–4** ⫤ Mark 4:2–9

[1]When we heard these things, we became distressed. [2]But when he saw that we were distressed, he said, "This is why I say this to you, that you may know yourselves. [3]For heaven's domain is like a head of grain which sprouted in a field. And when it ripened, it scattered its fruit and, in turn, filled the field with heads of grain for another year. [4]You also: be eager to reap for yourselves a head of the grain of life, so that you may be filled with the domain."

b and they didn't take root in the soil
c and didn't produce heads of grain.

Mark	**Matt**	**Luke**
4 7a Still other seed fell among thorns,	**13** 7a Still other seed fell among thorns,	**8** 7a Still other seed fell among thorns;
b and the thorns came up	b and the thorns came up	b the thorns grew with it
c and choked it,	c and choked them.	c and choked it.
d so that it produced no fruit.		
8a Finally, some seed fell on good earth	8a Other seed fell on good earth	8a Other seed fell on fertile earth;
b and started producing fruit.	b and started producing fruit:	c it produced fruit
c The seed sprouted		
d and grew:		b and when it matured,
e one part had a yield of thirty,	e and a third a yield of thirty.	
f another part sixty,	d another a yield of sixty,	
g and a third part one hundred."	c One part had a yield of one hundred,	d a hundredfold."
9a And as usual		e During his discourse,
b he said:		f he would call out,
c "Anyone here with two good ears	9a Anyone here with two ears	g "Anyone here with two good ears
d had better listen!	b had better listen!	h had better listen!"

K21.3: Secret of God's Imperial Rule

Mark 4:10–12	**Matt 13:10–17**	**Luke 8:9–10**
4 10a Whenever he went off by himself,	**13** 10a And his disciples came up	
	b and said to him,	
b those close to him, together with the twelve, would ask him about the parables.	c "Why do you instruct them only in parables?"	**8** 9 His disciples asked him what this parable was all about.
11a And he would say to them:	11a In response he said to them,	10a He replied,
b "You have been given the secret of God's imperial rule;	b "You have been given the privilege of knowing the secrets of Heaven's imperial rule,	b "You have been given the privilege of knowing the secrets of God's imperial rule;
c but to those outside everything is presented in parables,	c but that privilege has not been granted to anyone else.	c but the rest get only parables,
	12a In fact, to those who have,	
	b more will be given,	
	c and then some;	
	d and from those who don't have,	
	e even what they do have will be taken away!	
12a so that 'They may look with eyes wide open but never quite see,	13a That is why I tell them parables,	d so that 'They may look but not see,
	b because 'When they look they don't really see	
b and may listen with ears attuned but never quite understand,	c and when they listen they don't really hear or understand.'	e listen but not understand.'
	14a Moreover, in them the prophecy of Isaiah comes true, the one which says,	
	b 'You listen closely,	
	c yet you won't ever understand,	
	d and you look intently	
	e but won't ever see.	

Thom

4 a Others fell on thorns,

 b and they choked the seeds

 c and worms ate them.
5 a And others fell on good soil,
 b and it produced a good crop:

 c it yielded sixty per measure
 d and one hundred twenty per
 measure."

K21.3: Secret of God's Imperial Rule

SecJas 6:5–6 ◊ Mark 4:10–12

[5]I first spoke with you parabolically, and you did not understand. Now I am speaking with you openly, and you do not perceive. [6]Nevertheless, for me you were a parable among parables, and the disclosure of openness.

☆ **Thom 62:1** ◊ Mark 4:11

[1]Jesus said, "I disclose my mysteries to those [who are worthy] of [my] mysteries."

John 9:39 ◊ Mark 4:12

[39]Jesus said, "I came into this world to hand down this verdict: the blind are to see and those with sight are to be blind."

Isa 6:9–10 (LXX) ◊ Mark 4:12

[9]And he said, "Go and tell this people, 'You listen closely, yet you won't ever understand,
and you look intently but won't ever see.'
[10]For the mind of this people has grown dull,
 and their ears are hard of hearing,
 and they have shut their eyes,
otherwise they might actually see with their eyes,
 and hear with their ears,
and understand with their minds,
 and turn around and I would heal them."

Jer 5:21 (LXX) ◊ Mark 4:12

[21]Pay attention to these things, you foolish and senseless people, who have eyes but do not see, who have ears, but do not hear.

Ezek 12:2 (LXX) ◊ Mark 4:12

[2]O son of Adam, you live in the midst of wrongdoers, those who have eyes to see but don't see; who have ears to hear but don't hear.

Mark	Matt	Luke
	13 15a "For the mind of this people has grown dull,	
	b and their ears are hard of hearing,	
	c and they have shut their eyes,	
	d otherwise they might actually see with their eyes,	
	e and hear with their ears,	
	f and understand with their minds,	
4 12c otherwise they might turn around	g and turn around	
d and find forgiveness'!"	h and I would heal them.	
	16a How privileged are your eyes	
	b because they see,	
	c and your ears	
	d because they hear.	
	17a I swear to you,	
	b many prophets and righteous ones have longed to see what you see	
	c and didn't see it,	
	d and to hear what you hear	
	e and didn't hear it."	

K21.4: Understanding the Sower

Mark 4:13–20	Matt 13:18–23	Luke 8:11–15
4 13a Then he says to them:		
b "You don't get this parable,		
c so how are you going to understand other parables?		
	13 18 "You there, pay attention to the interpretation of the sower.	**8** 11a "Now this is the interpretation of the parable.
14 The 'sower' is 'sowing' the message.		b The 'seed' is God's message.
15a The first group are the ones 'along the path':	19e this is the one who is sown 'along the path.'	12a Those 'along the path' are those who have listened to it,
b here the message 'is sown,'	a When anyone listens to the message of ⟨Heaven's⟩ imperial rule	
c but when they hear,	b and does not understand it,	
d Satan comes right along	c the evil one comes	b but then the devil comes
e and steals the message that has been 'sown' into them.	d and steals away what was sown in the heart:	c and steals the message from their hearts,
		d so they won't trust
		e and be saved.
16a The second group are the ones sown 'on rocky ground.'	20a The one who is sown 'on rocky ground'	13a Those 'on the rock' are those who,
b Whenever they listen to the message,	b is the one who listens to the message	b when they listen to the message,
c right away they receive it happily.	c and right away receives it happily.	c receive it happily.
17a Yet they do not have their own 'root'	21a However, this one lacks its own 'root'	d But they 'have no root':
b and so are short-lived.	b and so is short-lived.	e they trust for the moment
c When distress or persecution comes because of the message,	c When distress or persecution comes because of the message,	
d such a person becomes easily shaken right away.	d such a person becomes easily shaken right away.	f but fall away when they are tested.

K21.4: Understanding the Sower

✩ **SecJas 6:16–18** ◊ Mark 4:13–20

[16]"Become eager for instruction. For the first prerequisite for instruction is faith, the second is love, the third is works; now from these comes life. [17]For instruction is like a grain of wheat. When they sowed it they had faith in it; and when it sprouted they loved it, because they envisioned many grains in place of one; and when they worked they were sustained, because they prepared it for food, then kept the rest in reserve to be sown. [18]So it is possible for you, too, to receive for yourselves heaven's domain: unless you receive it through knowledge, you will not be able to discover it."

Mark	**Matt**	**Luke**

Mark   **Matt**   **Luke**

Mark

4 18a And the third group are those sown 'among the thorns.'
   b These are the ones who have listened to the message,

19a but the worries of the age
   b and the seductiveness of wealth
   c and the yearning for everything else come
   d and 'choke' the message
   e and they become 'fruitless.'
20a And the final group are the ones sown 'on good earth.'
   b They are the ones who listen to the message
   c and take it in

   d and 'produce fruit,

   e here thirty,
   f there sixty,
   g and there one hundred.'"

Matt

1322a And the one sown 'into the thorns'

   b is the one who listens to the message,

   c but the worries of the age
   d and the seductiveness of wealth

   e 'choke' the message
   f and it becomes 'fruitless.'
23a The one who is sown 'on the good earth'
   b is the one who listens to the message

   c and understands,

   d who really 'produces fruit

   e and yields
   h and there thirty.'"
   g there sixty,
   f here a hundred,

Luke

8 14a What 'fell into the thorns'

   b represents those who listen,

   c but as they continue on,
   d they are 'choked' by the worries
   e and wealth
   f and pleasures of life,

   g and they do not come to maturity.
15a But the seed 'in good earth'

   b stands for those who listen to the message
   c and hold on to it with a good and fertile heart,
   d and 'produce fruit' through perseverance.

K21.5: Placing the Lamp

Mark 4:21–23   **Matt 5:15, 10:26**   **Luke 8:16–17**

Mark 4:21–23

4 21a And he would say to them:
   b "Since when is the lamp brought in

   c to be put under the bushel basket

   d or under the bed?
   e It's put on the lampstand, isn't it?

22a After all, there is nothing hidden
   b except to be brought to light,

   c nor anything kept secret
   d that won't be exposed.

23a If anyone here has two good ears,
   b use them!"

Matt 5:15, 10:26

5 15a "Nor do people light a lamp

   b and put it under a bushel basket

   c but rather on a lamp stand,
   d where it sheds light for everyone in the house."
1026a "So don't be afraid of them.
   b After all, there is nothing veiled
   c that won't be unveiled

   d or hidden
   e that won't be made known."

Luke 8:16–17

8 16a "No one lights a lamp
   b and covers it with a pot

   c or puts it under a bed;
   d rather, one puts it on a lampstand,
   e so that those who come in can see the light.

17a After all, there is nothing hidden
   b that won't be brought to light,

   c nor kept secret
   d that won't be made known
   e and exposed."

K21.5: Placing the Lamp

Luke 11:33, 12:2	**Thom 33:2–3, 5:2, 6:5–6**	**POxy654 5:2–3, 6:5**

11 33 a "No one lights a lamp
  b and then puts it in a cellar
  c or under a bushel basket,
 	
  d but rather on a lampstand
  e so that those who come in can see the light."
	33 2 a "After all, no one lights a lamp
	   cf. Thom 33:2c
	  b and puts it under a basket,
	  c nor does one put it in a hidden place.
	
	 3 a Rather, one puts it on a lampstand
	  b so that all who come and go will see its light."	

12 2 a "There is nothing veiled
  b that won't be unveiled,
 	
  c or hidden
  d that won't be made known."
	5 2 a "For there is nothing hidden
	  b that won't be revealed."
	 6 5 a "After all, there is nothing hidden
	  b that won't be revealed,
	 6 a and there is nothing covered up
	  b that will remain undisclosed."
		5 2 a ["... For there is nothing] hidden
		  b that [wo]n't [become] exposed, ...
		 6 5 a [After all, there is nothing] hidden
		  b [that won't be exposed].
		
		 5 3 a and ⟨nothing⟩ buried
		  b that [won't be raised]."

K21.6: The Same Standard

Mark 4:24–25	**Matt 7:2, 13:12**	**Luke 8:18**
4 24a And he went on to say to them: b "Pay attention to what you hear!		8 18a "So pay attention to how you're listening!
	7 2a "Don't forget, the judgment you hand out b will be the judgment you get back.	
c The standard you apply d will be the standard applied to you, e and then some.	c And the standard you apply, d will be the standard applied to you." *cf. Matt 13:12c*	
25a In fact, to those who have, b more will be given, *cf. Mark 4:24e* c and from those who don't have, d even what they do have will be taken away!"	13 12a "In fact, to those who have, b more will be given, c and then some; d and from those who don't have, e even what they do have will be taken away!"	b in fact, to those who have c more will be given, d and from those who don't have, e even what they seem to have will be taken away."

K21.7: Seed and Harvest

Mark 4:26–29	**Matt**	**Luke**
4 26a And he would say: b "God's imperial rule is like this: c Suppose someone sows seed on the ground, 27a and sleeps and rises night and day, b and the seed sprouts c and matures, d although the sower is unaware of it. 28a The earth produces fruit on its own, b first a shoot, c then a head, d then mature grain on the head. 29a But when the grain ripens, b all of a sudden ⟨that farmer⟩ sends for the sickle, c because it's harvest time."		

K21.6: The Same Standard

Matt 25:29   **Luke 19:26**   **Thom 41:1–2**

25 29 a "To everyone who has
b more will be given
c and then some,
d and from those who don't have,
e even what they have will be taken away."

19 26 a He replied,
b "I tell you,
c to everyone who has,
d more will be given;

e but from those who don't have,
f even what they do have will be taken away."

41 1 a Jesus said,

b "Those who have something in hand
c will be given more,

2 a and those who have nothing
b will be deprived of even the little they have."

Luke 6:37–38

37"Don't pass judgment, and you won't be judged; Don't condemn, and you won't be condemned; forgive, and you'll be forgiven. 38Give, and it will be given to you: they'll put in your lap a full measure, packed down, sifted and overflowing.
38 e For the standard you apply ◊ 4:24c
f will be the standard applied to you."
◊ 4:24d

1 Clem 13:2 ◊ Mark 4:24

2The standard you apply will be the standard applied to you.

PolPhil 2:3 ◊ Mark 4:24

3The standard you apply will be the standard applied to you.

K21.7: Seed and Harvest

☆ **Matt 13:24–30**   △ **Thom 21:1–10** ◊ Mark 4:29   ☆ **SecJas 8:1–4**

24He spun out another parable for them: "Heaven's imperial rule is like someone who sowed good seed in his field. 25And while everyone was asleep, his enemy came and scattered weed seed ground in his wheat and stole away. 26 And when the crop sprouted and produced heads, then the weeds also appeared. 27The owner's slaves came and asked him, 'Master, didn't you sow good seed in your field? Then why are there weeds everywhere?' 28He replied to them, 'Some enemy has done this.' The slaves said to him, 'Do you want us then to go and pull the weeds?' 29He replied, 'No, otherwise you'll root out the wheat at the same time as you pull the weeds. 30 Let them grow up together until the harvest, and at harvest time I'll say to the harvesters, "Gather the weeds first and bind them in bundles to burn, but gather the wheat into my granary." ' "

1Mary said to Jesus, "What are your disciples like?"
2He said, "They are like little children living in a field that is not theirs. 3When the owners of the field come, they will say, 'Give us back our field.' 4They take off their clothes in front of them in order to give it back to them, and they return their field to them. 5For this reason I say, if the owners of a house know that a thief is coming, they will be on guard before the thief arrives, and will not let the thief break into their house (their domain) and steal their possessions. 6As for you, then, be on guard against the world. 7Prepare yourselves with great strength, so the robbers can't find a way to get to you, for the trouble you expect will come. 8Let there be among you a person who understands. 9When the crop ripened, he came quickly carrying a sickle and harvested it. 10Anyone here with two good ears had better listen!"

1When we heard these things, we became distressed. 2But when he saw that we were distressed, he said, "This is why I say this to you, that you may know yourselves. 3For heaven's domain is like a head of grain which sprouted in a field. And when it ripened, it scattered its fruit and, in turn, filled the field with heads of grain for another year. 4You also: be eager to reap for yourselves a head of the grain of life, so that you may be filled with the domain."

Joel 4:13 (LXX) ◊ Mark 4:29

13Dispatch pruning shears because the fruit is ripe. Get in there and stomp around, because the wine press is full. The catch-basin is running over because their wickedness has multiplied.

K21.8: Parable of the Mustard Seed

Mark 4:30–32	**Matt 13:31–33**	**Luke 13:18–21**

4 30a And he would say:
  b "To what should we compare God's imperial rule,
  c or what parable should we use for it?

31a Consider the mustard seed:

  b When it is sown on the ground,
  c though it is the smallest of all the seeds on the earth,
32a —yet when it is sown,
  b it comes up,
  c and becomes the biggest of all garden plants,

  d and produces branches,
  e so that the birds of the sky
  f can nest in its shade."

13 31a He put another parable before them with these words:
  b "Heaven's imperial rule is like a mustard seed
  c that a man took
  d and sowed in his field.
32a Though it is the smallest of all seeds,

  b yet, when it has grown up,
  c it is the largest of garden plants,

  d and becomes a tree,

  e so that the birds of the sky come
  f and roost in its branches."
33a He told them another parable:

  b "Heaven's imperial rule is like leaven
  c that a woman took
  d and concealed in fifty pounds of flour
  e until it was all leavened."

13 18a Then he would say:
  b "What is God's imperial rule like?

  c What does it remind me of?

19a It is like a mustard seed

  b that a man took
  c and tossed into his garden.

  d It grew

  e and became a tree,

  f and the birds of the sky
  g roosted in its branches."
20a He continued:
  b "What does God's imperial rule remind me of?
21a It is like leaven

  b that a woman took
  c and concealed in fifty pounds of flour
  d until it was all leavened."

K21.9: Only in Parables

Mark 4:33–34	**Matt 13:34–35**	**Luke**

4 33a And with the help of many such parables
  b he would speak his message to them
  c according to their ability to comprehend.
34a Yet he would not say anything to them,
    except by way of parable,
  b but would spell everything out in private to his own disciples.

13 34a Jesus spoke all these things to the crowds in parables.

  b And he would not say anything to them,
    except by way of parable,
35a so that what was spoken through the prophet would come true:
  b "I will open my mouth in parables,
  c I will utter matters kept secret since the foundation of the world."

K21.8: Parable of the Mustard Seed

Thom 20:1–4	Dan 4:20–22 (LXX) ◊ Mark 4:32	Dan 4:12 (LXX) ◊ Mark 4:32
20 1 a The disciples said to Jesus, b "Tell us what heaven's imperial rule is like." 2 a He said to them, b "It's like a mustard seed. 3 ⟨It's⟩ the smallest of all seeds, 4 a but when it falls on prepared soil, b it produces a large branch c and becomes a shelter for birds of the sky."	[20]The tree which you saw, the great and powerful tree, whose crown reaches the sky, and whose branches cover the whole earth; [21]whose leaves are splendid, and whose fruit is abundant and provides nourishment for all; under it dwell the wild beasts and in its branches nest the birds of the sky— [22]You are ⟨that tree⟩ O King, since you have become glorious and strong, your magnificence has increased and your dominion extends to the ends of the earth.	[12]Its branches were nearly four miles long, and all the beasts of the earth found shade under it, and in it the birds of the skies built nests. Its fruit was abundant and beautiful, and supplied all living creatures.

K21.9: Only in Parables

ACROSS THE SEA

K22: Jesus Rebukes the Wind and the Sea

Mark 4:35–41	Matt 8:18, 23–27	Luke 8:22–25
	8 18a When Jesus saw the crowds around him,	
		8 22a One day Jesus and his disciples happened to get into a boat,
4 35a Later in the day,		
b when evening had come,		
c he says to them,	b he gave orders	b and he said to them,
d "Let's go across to the other side."	c to cross over to the other side.	c "Let's cross to the other side of the lake."
36a After sending the crowd away,		
b they took him along		
c since he was in the boat,	23a When he got into a boat,	
	b his disciples followed him.	
d and other boats accompanied him.		d So they shoved off.
37a Then a great squall comes up	24a And just then a great storm broke on the sea,	23c A squall descended on the lake;
b and the waves begin to pound against the boat,	b so that the boat was swamped by the waves;	
c so that the boat suddenly began to fill up.		d they were being swamped,
		e and found themselves in real danger.
38a He was in the stern		a And as they sailed
b sleeping on a cushion.	c but he was asleep.	b he fell asleep.
c And they wake him up	25a And they came	24a And they came
d and say to him,	b and woke him up,	b and woke him up,
e "Teacher, don't you care that we are going to drown?"	c and said,	c and said,
	d "Master, save us! We are going to drown!"	d "Master, master, we are going to drown!"
39a Then he got up	26d Then he got up	e He got up
b and rebuked the wind	e and rebuked the winds	f and rebuked the wind
c and said to the sea,	f and the sea,	g and the rough water;
d "Be quiet, shut up!"		
e The wind then died down		h and they settled down,
f and there was a great calm.	g and there was a great calm.	i and there was a calm.
40a He said to them,	a He says to them,	25a Then he said to them,
b "Why are you so cowardly?	b "Why are you so cowardly?	
c You still don't trust, do you?"	c Don't you trust me at all?"	b "Where is your trust?"
41a And they were completely terrified	27a And everyone marveled,	c Although they were terrified, they marveled,
b and would say to one another,	b saying,	d saying to one another,
c "Who can this fellow be,	c "What kind of person is this,	e "Who can this fellow be,
d that even the wind and the sea obey him?"	d that even the winds and the sea obey him?"	f that he commands even winds and water
		g and they obey him?"

92

K22: Jesus Rebukes the Wind and the Sea

Jonah 1:4, 5b (LXX) ◊ Mark 4:37–38

[4]And the Lord aroused a wind on the sea, and a tidal wave appeared in the water, and the ship started to break up. [5]But Jonah went down into the bowels of the ship, fell asleep and began to snore.

K23: The Gerasene Demon

Mark 5:1–20	**Matt 8:28–34**	**Luke 8:26–39**

5 1 a And they came to the other side of the sea,
　b to the region of the Gerasenes.

2 a And when he got out of the boat,
　b suddenly a person controlled by an unclean spirit
　c came from the tombs to accost him.

3 a This man made his home in the tombs,
　b and nobody was able to bind him, not even with a chain,
4 a because, though he had often been bound with fetters and with chains,
　b he would break the fetters
　c and pull the chains apart,
　d and nobody could subdue him.
5 a And day and night he would howl among the tombs and across the hills
　b and keep bruising himself on the stones.
6 a And when he saw Jesus from a distance,
　b he ran up

　c and knelt before him
7 a and, shouting at the top of his voice,
　b he says,
　c "What do you want with me, Jesus, you son of the most high God?
　d For God's sake,
　e don't torment me!"

8 a —because he had been saying to it:

　b "Come out of that fellow, you filthy spirit!"

8 28 a And when he came to the other side,
　b to the region of the Gadarenes,

　c he was met by two demoniacs

　d who came out from the tombs.
　e They were so hard to deal with
　f that no one could pass along that road.

29 a And just then they shouted,

　b "What do you want with us, you son of God?

　c Did you come here ahead of time to torment us?"

8 26 a They sailed
　b to the region of the Gerasenes,
　c which lies directly across from Galilee.
27 a As he stepped out on land,
　b this man from the town who was possessed by demons met him.

　c For quite some time he had been going without clothes
　d and hadn't lived in a house but stayed in the tombs instead.

28 a When he saw Jesus,

　b he screamed
　c and fell down before him,
　d and said at the top of his voice,

　e "What do you want with me, Jesus, you son of the most high God?
　f I beg you,
　g don't torment me."

29 a (You see, he was about to command the unclean spirit to get out of the man.

　b It seems, the demon had taken control of him many times;
　c the man had been kept under guard,
　d bound with chains and fetters,
　e but he would break the bonds
　f and be driven by the demon into the wilderness.)

5:1b *Gerasenes* (cf. Matt 8:28, Luke 8:26) ℵ* B D it vg cop^sa; *Gadarenes* A C K *f*¹³ syr (in part); *Gergesenes* ℵ^c L Δ Θ *f*¹ syr (in part) cop^bo.

K23: The Gerasene Demon

☆ **Mark 1:24** ◊ Mark 5:7

²⁴"Jesus! What do you want with us, you Nazarene? Have you come to get rid of us? I know you, who you are: God's holy man!"

☆ **Mark 1:34** ◊ Mark 5:7

³⁴On such occasions he cured many people afflicted with various diseases and drove out many demons. He would never let the demons speak, because they realized who he was.

☆ **Mark 3:11** ◊ Mark 5:7

¹¹The unclean spirits also, whenever they faced him, would fall down before him and shout out, "You son of God, you!"

☆ **John 2:4** ◊ Mark 5:7

⁴Jesus replies to her, "Woman, what is it with you and me? It's not my time yet."

Mark	Matt	Luke
5 9a And ⟨Jesus⟩ started questioning him: b "What's your name?" c "My name is Legion," d he says, e "because there are many of us."		**8** 30a Jesus questioned him, b "What is your name?" c "Legion," d he said, e because many demons had entered him.
10 And it kept begging him over and over not to expel them from their territory.		31 They kept begging him not to order them to depart into the abyss.
11 Now over there by the mountain a large herd of pigs was feeding.	**8** 30 And a large herd of pigs was feeding off in the distance.	32a Now over there a large herd of pigs was feeding on the mountain;
12a And so they bargained with him:	31a And the demons kept bargaining with him: b "If you drive us out, c send us into the herd of pigs."	b and they bargained with him
b "Send us over to the pigs so we may enter them!"		c to let them enter those pigs.
13a And he agreed.		d And he agreed.
	32a And he said to them, b "Get out ⟨of him⟩!"	
b And then the unclean spirits came out	c And they came out	33a Then the demons came out of the fellow
c and entered the pigs,	d and went into the pigs,	b and entered the pigs,
d and the herd rushed down the bluff into the sea,	e and suddenly all the herd rushed down the bluff into the sea	c and the herd rushed down the bluff into the lake
e about two thousand of them,		
f and drowned in the sea.	f and drowned in the water.	d and was drowned.
14a And the herdsmen ran off	33a The herdsmen ran off,	34a When the herdsmen saw what had happened, b they ran off
b and reported it in town and out in the country.	b and went into town	c and reported it in town and out in the country.
	c and reported everything, d especially about the demoniacs.	
c And they went out to see what had happened.	34a And what do you know, the whole town came out to meet Jesus.	35a And people came out to see what had happened.
15a And they come to Jesus b and notice the demoniac	b And when they saw him,	b They came to Jesus c and found d the fellow from whom the demons had gone,
c sitting d with his clothes on e and with his wits about him, f the one who had harbored Legion, g and they got scared.		e sitting at the feet of Jesus, f with his clothes on g and his wits about him;
16a And those who had seen b told them what had happened to the demoniac, c and all about the pigs.		h and they got scared. 36a Those who had seen it b explained how the demoniac had been cured.

5:9a Greek: *he.*

5:9c *Legion* is a unit of the Roman army, in the Imperial period numbering about 5,300 soldiers.

➡

Mark	Matt	Luke
5 17 And they started begging him to go away from their region.	8 34c they begged him to move on from their district.	8 37a Then the entire populace of the Gerasene region asked him to leave them;
		b for they were gripped by a great fear.
18a And as ⟨Jesus⟩ was getting into the boat,		c So he got into a boat
		d and went back.
b the ex-demoniac kept pleading with him to let him go along.		38a The man from whom the demons had departed begged to go with him;
19a And he would not let him,		b but he dismissed him,
b but says to him,		c saying,
c "Go home to your people		39a "Return home,
d and tell them what your patron has done for you—		b and tell the story of what God has done for you."
e how he has shown mercy to you."		
20a And he went away		c And he went his way,
b and started spreading the news in the Decapolis		d spreading the news throughout the whole town
c about what Jesus had done for him,		e about what Jesus had done for him.
d and everybody would marvel.		

K24.1: Jairus Begs for Jesus' Help

Mark 5:21–24a	Matt 9:18–19c	Luke 8:40–42b
		8 40a Now when Jesus returned,
5 21a When Jesus had again crossed over to the other side,		b the crowd welcomed him,
b a large crowd gathered around him,		c for they were all waiting for him.
c and he was beside the sea.		
	9 18a Just as he was saying these things to them,	41a Just then
22a And one of the synagogue officials comes,	b one of the officials came,	b a man named Jairus, a synagogue official, came up to Jesus.
b Jairus by name,		
c and as soon as he sees him,		
d he falls at his feet	c kept bowing down to him,	d He fell at Jesus' feet
23a and pleads with him		e and begged him to come to his house,
b and begs,	d and said,	
c "My little daughter is on the verge of death,	e "My daughter has just died.	42a because his only child, a twelve-year-old daughter, was dying.
d so come	f But come	
e and put your hands on her	g and put your hand on her	
f so she may be cured and live!"	h and she will live."	
	19a And Jesus got up	
24a And ⟨Jesus⟩ set out with him.	b and followed him,	b As ⟨Jesus⟩ was walking along,
	c along with his disciples.	

5:19d Greek (κύριος): *lord.*   **5:21a** Some mss add *in the boat.*   **5:24a** Greek: *he.*

K24.2: Jesus Cures a Woman with a Vaginal Flow

Mark 5:24b–34	**Matt 9:20–22**	**Luke 8:42c–48**
5 24b And a large crowd started following c and shoving against him.		**8** 42c the crowd milled around him.
25 And there was a woman who had had a vaginal flow for twelve years,	**9** 20a And just then a woman who had suffered from ⟨vaginal⟩ bleeding for twelve years	43a A woman who had had a vaginal flow for twelve years

26a who had suffered much under many doctors,
  b and who had spent everything she had,
  c but hadn't been helped at all,
 	
  d but instead had gotten worse.
		
		  b and had found no one able to heal her,

27a When ⟨this woman⟩ heard about Jesus,
  b she came up from behind in the crowd
  c and touched his cloak.
	
	  b came up from behind
	
	  c and touched the hem of his cloak.
		
		44a came up behind him,
		
		  b and touched the hem of his cloak.

28a (No doubt she had been figuring,
  b "If I could just touch his clothes,
  c I'll be cured!")
	21a She had been saying to herself,
	  b "If I only touch his cloak,
	  c I'll be cured."	

29a And the vaginal flow stopped instantly
  b and she sensed in her body that she was cured of her illness.
		
		  c Immediately her flow of blood stopped.

30a And suddenly,
  b because Jesus realized that power had drained out of him,
  c he turned around
  d and started asking the crowd,
  e "Who touched my clothes?"		

31a And his disciples said to him,
  b "You see the crowd
  c jostling you around
  d and you're asking,
  e 'Who touched me?'"
		45a Then Jesus said,
		  b "Who touched me?"
		  c When everyone denied it,
		  d Peter said,
		  e "Master, the crowds are pressing in
		  f and jostling you!"
		46a But Jesus insisted:
		  b "Someone touched me;
		  c I can tell that power has drained out of me."

32 And he started looking around to see who had done this.	22a When Jesus turned around	

33a Although the woman got scared
 	
  b and started trembling—
  c she realized what she had done—
  d she came
  e and fell down before him
  f and told him the whole truth.
		47a And when the woman saw
		  b that she had not escaped notice,
		
		  c she came forward trembling,
		  d and fell down before him.
		  e In front of all the people she explained why she had touched him,
		  f and how she had been immediately healed.

	b and saw her,	

5:27a Greek: *she.*

K24.2: Jesus Cures a Woman with a Vaginal Flow

☆ **Mark 6:56** ◊ Mark 5:27–33

☆ **Matt 14:36** ◊ Mark 5:27–33

☆ **Luke 6:19** ◊ Mark 5:27–33

[56]And wherever he would go, into villages, or towns, or onto farms, they would lay out the sick in the marketplaces and beg him to let them touch the fringe of his cloak. And all those who managed to touch it were cured!

[36]And they begged him just to let them touch the fringe of his cloak. And all those who managed to touch ⟨it⟩ were cured!

[19]And everyone in the crowd tried to touch him, since power would flow out from him and heal them all.

Table 4

Miracle Stories

Healing Stories	Mark
1. Jesus Gives Orders to an Unclean Spirit	1:21–28
2. Jesus Heals Simon's Mother-in-law	1:29–31
3. Sick and Demon-Possessed Come to Jesus	1:32–34
4. Jesus Cures a Leper	1:40–45
5. Jesus Cures a Paralytic	2:1–12
6. Jesus Heals on the Sabbath Day	3:1–6
7. The Gerasene Demon	5:1–20
8. Jesus Cures Jairus' Daughter	5:21–24a, 35–43
9. Jesus Cures the Woman with a Vaginal Flow	5:24b–34
10. Greek Woman's Daughter	7:24–30
11. Jesus Cures a Deaf-Mute	7:31–37
12. Jesus Cures a Blind Man	8:22–26
13. The Man with the Mute Spirit	9:14–29
14. Jesus Cures Blind Bartimaeus	10:46–52

Nature Wonders	Mark
15. Jesus Rebukes the Wind and the Sea	4:35–41
16. Loaves and Fish for Five Thousand	6:35–44
17. Jesus Walks on the Sea	6:45–52
18. Loaves and Fish for Four Thousand	8:1–9

Epiphanies	Mark
19. John Baptizes Jesus	1:9–11
20. Jesus, Elijah, Moses on the Mountain	9:2–8

Mark	Matt	Luke
5 34a He said to her,	**9** 22c he said,	**8** 48a Jesus said to her,
b "Daughter, your trust has cured you.	d "Take courage, daughter,	
c Go in peace,	e your trust has cured you."	b "Daughter, your trust has cured you;
d and farewell to your illness."		c go in peace."
	f And the woman was cured right then and there.	

K24.3: Jesus Cures Jairus' Daughter

Mark 5:35–43	Matt 9:23–26	Luke 8:49–55
5 35a While he was still speaking,		**8** 49a While he is still speaking,
b the synagogue official's people approach		b someone from the synagogue official's house comes
c and say,		c and says,
d "Your daughter has died;		d "Your daughter is dead;
e why keep bothering the teacher?"		e don't bother the teacher further."
36a When Jesus overheard this conversation,		50a When Jesus heard this,
b he says to the synagogue official,		b he answered him,
c "Don't be afraid,		c "Don't be afraid;
d just have trust!"		d just have trust,
		e and she'll be cured."
37a And he wouldn't let anyone follow along with him		51a When he arrived at the house,
b except Peter and James and John, James' brother.		b he wouldn't allow anyone to go in with him
cf. Mark 5:40c		c except Peter and John and James,
38a When they come to the house of the synagogue official,	**9** 23a And when Jesus came into the home of the official	d and the child's father and mother.
b he notices a lot of clamor	b and saw the mourners with their flutes,	
c and people crying and wailing,	c and the crowd making a disturbance,	52a Everyone was crying
		b and grieving over her,
39a and he goes in		
b and says to them,	24a he said,	c but he said,
	b "Go away;	
c "Why are you carrying on like this?		d "Don't cry;
d The child hasn't died;	c you see, the girl hasn't died	e she hasn't died
e she's sleeping."	d she's sleeping."	f she's sleeping."
40a And they started laughing at him.	e And they started laughing at him.	53a But they started laughing at him,
b But he runs everyone out	25a When the crowd had been thrown out,	
c and takes the child's father and her mother		b certain that she had died.
d and his companions		*cf. Luke 8:51d*
e and goes in where the child is.	b he came in	

☆ **Mark 10:52** ◊ Mark 5:34

[52]And Jesus said to him, "Be on your way, your trust has cured you." And right away he regained his sight, and he started following him on the road.

☆ **Luke 7:50** ◊ Mark 5:34

[50]And he said to the woman, "Your trust has saved you; go in peace."

☆ **Luke 17:19** ◊ Mark 5:34

[19]And he said to him, "Get up and be on your way; your trust has cured you."

☆ **Luke 18:42** ◊ Mark 5:34

[42]Jesus said to him, "Then use your eyes; your trust has cured you."

K24.3: Jesus Cures Jairus' Daughter

	Mark	**Matt**	**Luke**

5 41 a And he takes the child by the hand
  b and says to her,
  c *"talitha koum"*
  d (which means, "Little girl,"
  e I say to you,
  f "Get up!").

42 a And the little girl got right up
  b and started walking around.
  c (Incidentally, she was twelve years
    old.)
  d And they were downright ecstatic.
43 a And he gave them strict orders

  b that no one should learn about this,
  c and he told them to give her
    something to eat.

9 25 c and took her by the hand

  d and raised the little girl up.

26 And his reputation spread all around
    that region.

8 54 a He took her by hand
  b and called out,

  c "Child,

  d get up!"

55 a Her breathing returned
  b and she immediately got up.

56 **a** Her parents were quite ecstatic;
  b but he commanded them not to tell
    anyone what had happened.

55 c He ordered them to give her
    something to eat.

5:41c Aramaic: טְלִיתָא קוּם.

SILVER DENARIUS

The silver *denarius* depicts the bearded, laureated bust of the youthful Emperor Nero. The obverse inscription reads NERO CAESAR, continuing on the reverse with the words AVGVSTVS GERMANICVS. The reverse depicts a togate and radiate standing figure of Nero. He faces forward, holding a branch in his right hand and a figure of Victory on a globe in his left. This figure very possibly represents the colossal statue of Nero as the sungod Sol which the emperor set up before his Golden House (*Domus Aurea*) in Rome. The statue, executed in gilt bronze by Zenodorus, stood 30 meters tall. When it was moved during the reign of Hadrian, the task required 24 elephants. While the statue no longer exists, memory of it may be preserved in the name of the Colosseum which was built on the site of the Golden House.

Photo and description courtesy of Numismatic Fine Arts, Inc., Los Angeles, and the Institute for Antiquity and Christianity, Claremont, CA.

K25: No Respect at Home

Mark 6:1–6   **Matt 13:53–58**   **Luke**

13 53 a And so
    b when Jesus had finished these parables,
    c he moved on from there.
54 a And he came to his hometown

6 1 a Then he left that place,
    b and he comes to his hometown,
    c and his disciples follow him.
2 a When the sabbath day arrived,
    b he started teaching in the synagogue;
      b and resumed teaching them in their synagogue,
    c and many who heard him were astounded
      c so they were astounded
    d and said so:
      d and said so:
        cf. Matt 13:56b
    e "Where's he getting this?"
    f and "What's the source of all this wisdom?"
      e "What's the source of this wisdom
    g and "Who gave him the right to perform such miracles?
      f and these miracles?
3 a This is the carpenter, isn't it?
      55 a This is the carpenter's son, isn't it?
    b Isn't he Mary's son?
      b Isn't his mother called Mary?
    c And who are his brothers, if not James and Judas and Simon?
      c And aren't his brothers James and Joseph and Simon and Judas?
    d And who are his sisters, if not our neighbors?"
      56 a And aren't all his sisters neighbors of ours?
      b So where did he get all this?"
    e And they were resentful of him.
      57 a And they were resentful of him.
4 a Jesus used to tell them:
      b Jesus said to them,
    b "No prophet goes without respect
      c "No prophet goes without respect,
    c except on his home turf and among his relatives and at home!"
      d except on his home turf and at home!"
5 a He was unable to perform a single miracle there,
      58 a And he did not perform many miracles there
    b except that he did cure a few by laying hands on them,
6 a though he was always shocked at their lack of trust.
      b because of their lack of trust.
    b And he used to go around the villages teaching in a circuit.

‡ Luke 4:16–30

[16]When he came to Nazareth, where he had been brought up, he went to the synagogue on the sabbath day, as was his custom. He stood up to do the reading [17]and was handed the scroll of the prophet Isaiah. He unrolled the scroll and found the place where it was written: [18]"The spirit of the Lord is upon me, because he has anointed me to bring good news to the poor. He has sent me to announce pardon for prisoners and recovery of sight to the blind; to set free the oppressed, [19]to proclaim the year of the Lord's amnesty." [20]After rolling up the scroll, he gave it back to the attendant, and sat down; and the attention of everyone in the synagogue was riveted on him.

[21]He began by saying to them, "Today this scripture has come true as you listen."

[22]And they all began voicing approval of him, and marveling at the pleasing speech that he delivered; and would remark, "Isn't this Joseph's son?"

[23]And he said to them, "No doubt you will quote me that proverb, 'Doctor, cure yourself,' and you'll tell me, 'Do here in your hometown what we've heard you've done in Capernaum.'" [24]Then he said, "The truth is, no prophet is welcome on his home turf. [25]I can assure you, there were many widows in Israel in Elijah's time, when the sky was dammed up for three and a half years, and a severe famine swept through the land. [26]Yet Elijah was not sent to any of them, but instead to a widow in Zarephath near Sidon. [27]In addition, there were many lepers in Israel in the prophet Elisha's time; yet none of them was made clean, except Naaman the Syrian."

[28]Everyone in the synagogue was filled with rage when they heard this. [29]They rose up, ran him out of town, and led him to the brow of the hill on which their town was built, intending to hurl him over it. [30]But he slipped away through the throng and went on his way.

K25: No Respect at Home

✩ John 7:15 ◊ Mark 6:2

[15]The Judeans were taken aback, saying, "This man is uneducated; how come he's so articulate?"

John 4:44 ◊ Mark 6:4

([44]Remember, ⟨Jesus⟩ himself had observed, "A prophet gets no respect on his own turf.")

POxy1 31:1–2 ◊ Mark 6:4

[1]Jesus says, "No prophet is welcome on his home turf; [2]doctors don't cure those who know them."

Thom 31:1–2 ◊ Mark 6:4

[1]Jesus said, "No prophet is welcome on his home turf; [2]doctors don't cure those who know them."

✩ Matt 9:35 ◊ Mark 6:6

[35]And Jesus went about all the towns and villages, teaching in their synagogues and proclaiming the gospel of ⟨Heaven's⟩ imperial rule and healing every disease and ailment.

K26: Jesus Sends the Twelve Out in Pairs

Mark 6:7–13	Matt 10:1, 5–15	Luke 9:1–6
6 7a Then he summoned the twelve b and started sending them out in pairs c and giving them authority over unclean spirits.	**10** 1a And summoning his twelve disciples 5**a** Jesus sent out these twelve 1b he gave them authority c to drive out unclean spirits. d and to heal every disease and every ailment. 5b after he had given them these instructions: c "Don't travel foreign roads d and don't enter a Samaritan town, 6 but go rather to the lost sheep of the house of Israel. 7a Go b and announce: c 'Heaven's imperial rule is closing in.' 8a Heal the sick, b raise the dead, c cleanse the lepers, d drive out demons. e You have received freely, f so freely give.	**9** 1a He called the twelve together 2**a** He sent them out 1b and gave them power and authority over all demons c and to heal diseases. 2b to announce c God's imperial rule d and to heal the sick.
8a And he instructed them b not to take anything on the road, c except a staff: d no bread, e no knapsack, f no spending money, 9a but to wear sandals, b and to wear no more than one shirt.	10**d** or a staff; **a** don't take a knapsack for the road, 9 Don't get gold or silver or copper coins for spending money, 10**c** or sandals **b** or two shirts, **e** for 'the worker deserves to be fed.'	3a He said to them, b "Don't take anything for the road: c neither staff **e** neither bread d nor knapsack, f nor money; g no one is to take two shirts.
10a And he went on to say to them: b "Wherever you enter someone's house, c stay there until you leave town.	11a Whichever town or village you enter, b find out who is deserving; c stay there until you leave. 12a When you enter a house, b greet it. 13a And if the house is deserving, b give it your peace blessing, c but if it is unworthy, d withdraw your peace blessing.	4a And whichever house you enter, b stay there and leave from there.
11a And whatever place does not welcome you b or listen to you, c get out of there d and shake the dust off your feet in witness against them." 12a So they went out b and announced that people should turn their lives around,	14a And if anyone does not welcome you, b or listen to your words, c as you are going out of that house or town d shake the dust off your feet.	5a And wherever they do not welcome you, b leave the town c and shake the dust from your feet in witness against them." 6a And they set out b and went from village to village, c bringing good news

K26: Jesus Sends the Twelve Out in Pairs

✫ Mark 3:14–15 ◊ Mark 6:7

[14]He formed a group of twelve to be his companions, and to be sent out to speak, [15]and to have authority to drive out demons.

✫ Thom 14:4 ◊ Mark 6:10

[4]When you go into any region and walk about in the countryside, when people take you in, eat what they serve you and heal the sick among them.

✫ Luke 22:35 ◊ Mark 6:8

[35]And he said to them, "When I sent you out with no purse or knapsack or sandals, you weren't short of anything, were you?"

△ Luke 10:1–16

[1]After this the Lord appointed seventy-two others and sent them on ahead of him in pairs to every town and place that he himself intended to visit. [2]He would say to them, "Although the crop is good, still there are few to harvest it. So beg the harvest boss to dispatch workers to the fields. [3]Get going; look, I'm sending you out like lambs into a pack of wolves. [4]Carry no purse, no knapsack, no sandals. Don't greet anyone on the road. [5]Whenever you enter a house, first say, 'Peace to this house.' [6]If peaceful people live there, your peace will rest on them. But if not, it will return to you. [7]Stay at that house, eating and drinking whatever they provide, for workers deserve their wages. Do not move from house to house. [8]Whenever you enter a town and they welcome you, eat whatever is set before you. [9]Cure the sick there and tell them, 'God's imperial rule is closing in.' [10]But whenever you enter a town and they do not receive you, go out into its streets and say, [11]'Even the dust of your town that sticks to our feet, we wipe off against you. But know this: God's imperial rule is closing in.' [12]I tell you, on that day Sodom will be better off than that town.

[13]"Damn you, Chorazin! Damn you, Bethsaida! If the miracles done in you had been done in Tyre and Sidon, they would have sat in sackcloth and ashes and changed their ways long ago. [14]But Tyre and Sidon will be better off at the judgment than you. [15]And you, Capernaum, you don't think you'll be exalted to heaven, do you? No, you'll go to Hell.

[16]"Whoever hears you hears me, and whoever rejects you rejects me, and whoever rejects me rejects the one who sent me."

✫ Did 11:4–6

[4]Every emissary who comes to you is to be welcomed as you would the Lord. [5]Emissaries are to stay only one day. If necessary, they may stay a second day. If they stay three days, they are frauds. [6]When emissaries depart, they are to take bread enough to last only until they reach their next night's hospitality. If they ask for money, they are frauds.

| **Mark** | **Matt** | |

Mark

6 13a and they often drove out demons,
   b and they anointed many sick people
      with oil
   c and healed ⟨them⟩.

Matt

10 15a I swear to you,
    b the land of Sodom
    c and Gomorrah will be better off on
       judgment day than that town."

9 6d and healing everywhere.

K27: King Herod Beheads John

| **Mark 6:14–29** | **Matt 14:1–12** | **Luke 9:7–9** |

Mark 6:14–29

6 14a King Herod heard about it—

   b by now, ⟨Jesus'⟩ reputation had
      become well known—

   c and people kept saying that John the
      Baptizer had been raised from the
      dead
   d and that, as a consequence,
      miraculous powers were at work in
      him.
15a Some spread the rumor that he was
      Elijah,
   b while others reported that he was a
      prophet
   c like one of the prophets.
16a When Herod got wind of it, he
      started declaring,
   b "John, the one I beheaded,
   c has been raised!"

17a Earlier Herod himself had sent
      someone to arrest John
   b and put him in chains
   c in a dungeon,
   d on account of Herodias, his brother
      Philip's wife,
   e because he had married her.
18a You see, John had said to Herod,
   b "It is not right for you to have your
      brother's wife!"

Matt 14:1–12

14 1 On that occasion Herod the tetrarch
       heard the rumor about Jesus

2a and said to his servants,

   b "This is John the Baptizer.
   c He's been raised from the dead;
   d that's why miraculous powers are at
      work in him."

3a Herod, remember, had arrested
      John,
   b put him in chains,
   c and thrown him in prison,
   d on account of Herodias, his brother
      Philip's wife.

4a John, for his part, had said to him,
   b "It is not right for you to have her."

Luke 9:7–9

9 7a Now Herod the tetrarch heard about
       everything that was happening.

   b He was perplexed
   c because some were saying that John
      had been raised from the dead,

8a some that Elijah had appeared,

   b and others that one of the ancient
      prophets had come back to life.

9a Herod said,

   b "John I beheaded;

   c but this one about whom I hear such
      things—who is he?"
   d And he was curious to see him.

6:13c The object *them* is supplied from the
context.
                        6:14b Greek: *his*.

☆ **Mark 8:28** ◊ Mark 6:14–15

²⁸In response they said to him, "⟨Some say, 'You are⟩ John the Baptist,' and others, 'Elijah,' but others, 'One of the prophets.'"

☆ **John 1:19–21** ◊ Mark 6:14–15

¹⁹This is what John had to say when the Judeans sent priests and Levites from Jerusalem to ask him, "Who are you?"

²⁰He made it clear—he wouldn't deny it—"I'm not the Anointed." ²¹And they asked him, "Then what are you? Are you Elijah?" And he replies, "I am not." "Are you the Prophet?" He answered, "No."

K27: King Herod Beheads John

☆ **Matt 16:14** ◊ Mark 6:14–15

¹⁴They said, "Some ⟨say, 'He is⟩ John the Baptist,' but others, 'Elijah,' and others, 'Jeremiah or one of the prophets.'"

☆ **Luke 9:19** ◊ Mark 6:14–15

¹⁹They said in response, "⟨Some say, 'You are⟩ John the Baptist,' while others, 'Elijah,' and still others, 'One of the ancient prophets has come back to life.'"

Luke 3:19–20 ◊ Mark 6:17–18

¹⁹But Herod the tetrarch, who had been denounced by John over the matter of Herodias, his brother's wife, ²⁰topped off all his other crimes by shutting John up in prison.

Mark	Matt	Luke
19a So Herodias nursed a grudge against him		
b and wanted to eliminate him,	5a And while ⟨Herod⟩ wanted to kill him,	
c but she couldn't manage it,		
20a because Herod was afraid of John.	b he was afraid of the crowd	
b He knew that he was an upright and holy man,	c because they regarded ⟨John⟩ as a prophet.	
c and so protected him,		
d and, although he listened to him frequently,		
e he was very confused,		
f yet he listened to him eagerly.		
21a Now a festival day came,	6a On Herod's birthday,	
b when Herod gave a banquet on his birthday		
c for his courtiers,		
d and his commanders,		
e and the leading citizens of Galilee.		
22a And the daughter of Herodias came in		
b and captivated Herod and his dinner guests	c and captivated Herod,	
c by dancing.	b the daughter of Herodias danced for them	
d The king said to the girl,		
e "Ask me for whatever you wish		
f and I'll grant it to you!"		
23a Then he swore an oath to her,	7a so he swore an oath	
b "I'll grant you whatever you ask for,	b and promised to give her whatever she asked.	
c up to half my domain!"		
24a She went out		
b and said to her mother,		
c "What should I ask for?"		
d And she replied,	8a Prompted by her mother,	
e "The head of John the Baptist!"		
25a She promptly hastened back		
b and made her request:	b she said,	
c "I want you to give me the head of John the Baptist on a platter, right now!"	c "Give me the head of John the Baptist right here on a platter."	
26a The king grew regretful,	9a The king was sad,	
c but, on account of his oath	b but, on account of his oath	
d and his dinner guests,	c and his dinner guests,	
b he didn't want to refuse her.	d he ordered that it be done.	
27a So right away the king sent for the executioner	10a And he sent	
b and commanded him to bring his head.		

Esth 5:3 (LXX) ◊ Mark 6:23

³The king said, "What do you want, Esther? Anything up to half of my domain is yours for the asking."

Esth 7:2 (LXX) ◊ Mark 6:23

²On the second day as they were having a drink, the king said to Esther: "What, Queen Esther, is your request? What is your petition? Anything up to half of my domain is yours."

Table 5

Chains of Miracle Stories

1a. Jesus Rebukes the Wind and the Sea Mark 4:35–42	1b. Jesus Walks on the Sea Mark 6:45–52
2a. The Gerasene Demon Mark 5:1–20	2b. Jesus Cures a Blind Man Mark 8:22–26
3a. Jesus Cures Jairus' Daughter Mark 5:21–24a, 35–43	3b. Greek Woman's Daughter Mark 7:24b–30
4a. Jesus Cures the Woman with a Vaginal Flow Mark 5:24b–34	4b. Jesus Cures a Deaf-Mute Mark 7:31–37
5a. Loaves and Fish for Five Thousand Mark 6:35–44	5a. Loaves and Fish for Four Thousand Mark 8:1–9

1a. Jesus Cures a Paralytic Mark 2:1–12	1b. The Lame Man at the Pool John 5:1–18
2a. Loaves and Fish for Five Thousand Mark 6:35–44	2b. Loaves and Fish for Five Thousand John 6:1–15
3a. Jesus Walks on the Sea Mark 6:45–52	3b. Jesus Walks on the Sea John 6:16–21
4a. Jesus Cures a Blind Man Mark 8:22–26	4b. Jesus Cures the Man Born Blind John 9:1–7
5a. Jesus Raises a Young Man SecMk 1:1–10	5b. Jesus Raises Lazarus John 11:1–44

Mark	Matt	Luke

6 27c And he went away
d and beheaded ⟨John⟩ in prison.
28a He brought his head on a platter

b and presented it to the girl,
c and the girl gave it to her mother.
29a When his disciples heard about it,
b they came
c and got his body
d and put it in a tomb.

b and had John beheaded in prison.
11a ⟨John's⟩ head was brought on a platter
b and presented to the girl,
c and she gave it to her mother.

12a Then his disciples came
b and got his body
c and buried him.
d Then they went
e and told Jesus.

K28: The Twelve Report

Mark 6:30–34	Matt 14:13–14	Luke 9:10–11

6 30a Then the apostles regroup around Jesus
b and they reported to him
c everything that they had done and taught.
31a And he says to them:
b "You come privately to an isolated place
c and rest a little."
d (Remember, many were coming and going
e and they didn't even have a chance to eat.)

9 10a On their return

b the apostles reported to him
c what they had done.

14 13a When Jesus got word of ⟨John's death⟩,

d Taking them along,
e Jesus withdrew privately to a town called Bethsaida.

32 So they went away in the boat privately to an isolated place.

b he sailed away quietly to an isolated place.

33a But many noticed them leaving
b and figured it out

c The crowds got wind ⟨of his departure⟩

11a But the crowds found this out

c and raced there on foot from all the towns
d and got there ahead of them.

d and followed him on foot from the towns.

b and followed him.

34a When he came ashore,
b he saw a huge crowd

14a When he stepped ashore,
b he saw this huge crowd,

c and was moved by them,
d because they 'resembled sheep without a shepherd,'
e and he started teaching them at length.

c took pity on them,

c He welcomed them,

d spoke to them about God's imperial rule,
e and cured those in need of treatment.

d and healed their sick.

6:27d Greek: *him.*

K28: The Twelve Report

Luke 10:17 ◊ Mark 6:30

[17]The seventy-two returned with joy, saying, "Lord, even the demons submit to us when we invoke your name!"

Matt 9:36 ◊ Mark 6:34

[36]When he saw the crowd, he was moved by them because they were in trouble and helpless, like sheep without a shepherd.

Num 27:15–17 (Lxx) ◊ Mark 6:34

[15]Moses said to the Lord, [16]"The Lord God of the spirits and the whole human race should appoint someone over the community [17]who will precede them when they return; who will lead them out and lead them in. And then the community will not resemble a flock of sheep without a shepherd."

1 Kgs 22:17 (Lxx) ◊ Mark 6:34

[17]Then Micaiah said, "It is not so. I have seen the whole of Israel scattered about on the mountains, like sheep without a shepherd." And the Lord said, "They have no leader. Let everyone return to his or her house in peace."

K29: Loaves and Fish for Five Thousand

Mark 6:35–44	**Matt 14:15–21**	**Luke 9:12–17**
6 35a And when the hour had already grown late,	**14**15a When it was evening	**9** 12a As the day began to draw to a close,
b his disciples would approach him	b the disciples approached him,	b the twelve approached him
c and say,	c and said,	c and said,
d "This place is desolate	d "This place is desolate	
e and it's late.	e and it's already late.	
36a Send them away	f Send the crowd away	d "Send the crowd away,
b so that they can go to the farms and villages around here	g so that they can go to the villages	e so that they can go to the villages and farms around here
c to buy something to eat."	h and buy food for themselves."	f and find food and lodging;
		g for we are in a desolate place here."
37a But in response he said to them,	16a Jesus said to them,	13a But he said to them,
	b "They don't need to leave;	
b "Give them something to eat yourselves!"	c give them something to eat yourselves!"	b "Give them something to eat yourselves."
c And they say to him,	17a But they say to him,	c They said,
d "Are we to go out	b "We have nothing here except five loaves of bread	d "All we have are five loaves
	c and two fish."	e and two fish—
		f unless we go ourselves
e and buy half a year's wages worth of bread		g and buy food for all these people."
f and donate it for their meal?!"		
		14a (There were about five thousand men.)
38a So he says to them,	18a He said,	b He said to his disciples,
b "How many loaves do you have?		
c Go look."		
d And when they find out,		
e they say,		
f "Five,	*cf. Matt 14:17b*	*cf. Luke 9:13d*
g and two fish."	*cf. Matt 14:17c*	*cf. Luke 9:13e*
	b "Bring them here to me."	
39a Next he instructed them all to sit down	19a And he told the crowd to sit down on the grass,	c "Have them sit down in groups of about fifty."
b and eat,		
c some over here,		
d some over there,		
e on the green grass.		
40a So they sat down group by group,		15a They did so,
b in hundreds and in fifties.		b and got them all seated.
41a And he took the five loaves	b and he took the five loaves	16a Then he took the five loaves
b and the two fish,	c and two fish,	b and two fish,
c looked up to the sky,	d and looking up to the sky	c looked up to the sky,
d gave a blessing,	e he gave a blessing,	d gave a blessing,
e and broke the bread apart,	f and breaking it apart	e and broke them,
f and started giving it to his disciples	g he gave the bread to the disciples,	f and started handing them out to the disciples
g to pass around to them,	h and the disciples ⟨gave it⟩ to the crowd.	g to pass around to the crowd.
h and even the two fish they shared with everybody.		

6:37e Greek: *two hundred denarii*; a denarius would feed a family of four for about three days.

K29: Loaves and Fish for Five Thousand

• Mark 8:1–9

[1]And once again during that same period, when there was a huge crowd without anything to eat, he calls the disciples aside and says to them, [2]"I feel sorry for the crowd, because they have already spent three days with me and now they've run out of food. [3]If I send these people home hungry, they will collapse on the road—in fact, some of them have come from quite a distance."

[4]And his disciples answered him, "How can anyone feed these people bread out here in this desolate place?"

[5]And he started asking them, "How many loaves do you have?"

> 5c They replied, ◊ 6:38e
> d "Seven." ◊ 6:38f
> 6a Then he orders the crowd to sit down on the ground. ◊ 6:39a
> b And he took the seven loaves, ◊ 6:41a
> c gave thanks, ◊ 6:41d
> d and broke them into pieces, ◊ 6:41e
> e and started giving ⟨them⟩ to his disciples to hand out; ◊ 6:41f
> f and they passed them around to the crowd.
> 7a They also had a few small fish. ◊ 6:41g

When he had blessed them, he told them to hand those out as well.

> 8a They had more than enough to eat ◊ 6:42
> b then they picked up seven big baskets of leftover scraps. ◊ 6:43
> 9a There were about four thousand people there. ◊ 6:44

Then he started sending them away.

☆ Mark 14:22 ◊ Mark 6:41

[22]And as they were eating, he took a loaf, gave a blessing, broke it into pieces and offered it to them. And he said, "Take some, this is my body!"

☆ Matt 26:26 ◊ Mark 6:41

[26]As they were eating, Jesus took a loaf, gave a blessing, and broke it into pieces. And he offered it to the disciples, and said, "Take some and eat; this is my body."

• Matt 15:32–39

[32]Then Jesus called his disciples aside and said: "I feel sorry for the crowd because they have already spent three days with me and now they've run out of food. And I don't want to send these people away hungry for fear they'll collapse on the road."

[33]And the disciples say to him, "How can we get enough bread here in this desolate place to feed so many people?"

[34]Jesus says to them, "How many loaves do you have?"

> 34c They replied, ◊ 6:38e
> d "Seven, ◊ 6:38f
> e plus a few fish." ◊ 6:38g
> 35 And he ordered the crowd to sit down on the ground. ◊ 6:39a
> 36a And he took the seven loaves ◊ 6:41a
> b and the fish ◊ 6:41b
> c and gave thanks ◊ 6:41d
> d and broke them into pieces, ◊ 6:41e
> e and started giving ⟨them⟩ to the disciples, ◊ 6:41f
> f and the disciples ⟨started giving them⟩ to the crowds.
> 37a And everyone had more than enough to eat. ◊ 6:42
> b Then they picked up seven baskets of leftover scraps. ◊ 6:43
> 38a Those who had eaten numbered four thousand, ◊ 6:44
> b not counting women and children.

[39]And after he sent the crowds away, he got into the boat and went to the Magadan region.

☆ Luke 22:19 ◊ Mark 6:41

[19]And he took a loaf, gave thanks, broke it into pieces, offered it to them, and said, "This is my body which is offered for you. Do this as my memorial."

☆ Luke 24:30 ◊ Mark 6:41

[30]And so, as soon as he took his place at table with them, he took a loaf, and gave a blessing, broke it, and started passing it out to them.

☆ Acts 27:35 ◊ Mark 6:41

[35]After he had said these things, he took a piece of bread, gave thanks to God in front of everybody, broke it up, and began to eat.

John 6:1–15

[1]After these events, Jesus crossed to the far side of the sea of Galilee, ⟨also know as the sea of⟩ Tiberias. [2]A huge crowd was following him, because they wanted to see the miracles he was performing on the sick. [3]Jesus climbed up the mountain, and he sat down there with his disciples. [4]It was about time for the Jewish celebration of Passover.

[5]Jesus looks up and sees a big crowd approaching him, and he says to Philip, "Where are we going to get enough bread to feed this mob?" ([6]He was saying this to test him; you see, Jesus already knew what he was going to do.)

> 7a "Half a year's wages wouldn't buy enough bread for everyone to have a bite," ◊ 6:37e
> b Philip said.

[8]One of his disciples, Andrew, Simon Peter's brother, says to him, [9]"There is a lad here

> 9b with five loaves of barley bread ◊ 6:38f
> c and two fish; ◊ 6:38g

but what does that amount to for so many?" [10]Jesus said,

> 10b "Have the people sit down." ◊ 6:39a
> c (They were in a grassy place.) ◊ 6:39e
> d So they sat down; ◊ 6:40a
> e the men alone numbered about five thousand. ◊ 6:44
> 11a Jesus took the loaves, ◊ 6:41a
> b gave thanks, ◊ 6:41d
> c and passed them around to the people sitting there, ◊ 6:41g
> d along with the fish and all of them had as much as they wanted. ◊ 6:41h
> 12a And when they had eaten their fill,

he says to his disciples, "Gather up the leftovers so that nothing goes to waste."

> 13 So they gathered them up
> 13b and filled twelve baskets with scraps ◊ 6:43

from the five barley loaves—from what was left over. [14]When these folks saw the miracle he had peformed they would say, "Yes indeed! This is undoubtedly the Prophet who is to come into the world." [15]Jesus perceived that they were about to come and make him king by force, so he retreated once again to the mountain by himself.

Mark	Matt	Luke
42 Everybody had more than enough to eat.	20a And everyone had more than enough to eat.	17a And everybody had more than enough to eat.
43 Then they picked up twelve baskets full of leftovers, including some fish.	b Then they picked up twelve baskets full of leftovers.	b Then the leftovers were collected, twelve baskets full.
44 And the number of men who had some bread came to five thousand.	21a The number of men who had eaten came to about five thousand,	14a (There were about five thousand men.)
	b not counting women and children.	

K30: Jesus and His Disciples Depart

Mark 6:45–46	Matt 14:22–23	Luke
6 45a And right away	14 22a And right away	
b he made his disciples embark in the boat	b he made the disciples get in a boat	
c and go ahead to the opposite shore	c and go ahead of him to the other side,	
d toward Bethsaida,		
e while he himself dispersed the crowd.	d while he dispersed the crowds.	
46a And once he got away from them,	23a After he had dispersed the crowds,	
b he went off to the mountain to pray.	b he went up to the mountain privately to pray.	
	c He remained there alone	
	d well into the evening.	

K31: Jesus Walks on the Sea

Mark 6:47–52	Matt 14:24–33	Luke
6 47a When evening came,		
b the boat was in the middle of the sea,	14 24a By this time the boat was already some distance from the land	
c and he was alone on the land.	b and was being pounded by waves	
48a When he saw they were having a rough time making headway,		
b because the wind was against them,	c because the wind was against them.	
c at about three o'clock in the morning	25a About three o'clock in the morning	
d he comes toward them walking on the sea	b he came toward them walking on the sea.	
e and intending to go past them.		

6:47b Some mss read πάλαι, *already* ($\mathfrak{P}^{45}$ D *f*¹
28 *pc* it vg); the corresponding text in Matt
(14:24) has ἤδη, which also means *already*.

2 Kgs 4:42–44 (LXX)

42And a man came from Baithsarisa, and brought to the man of God, by way of first fruits, twenty barley loaves and fruit cakes, and told him, "Give it to the people and let them eat." 43And his servant said, "How in the world can I set this before a hundred men?" He replied, "Give it to the people and let them eat. For the Lord says, 'They shall eat and have some left over.'" 44And they ate and had some left over, just as the Lord had said.

K30: Jesus and His Disciples Depart

Mark 8:10 ◊ Mark 6:45

10And he got right into the boat with his disciples and went to the Dalmanoutha district.

Matt 15:39 ◊ Mark 6:45

39And after he sent the crowds away, he got into the boat and went to the Magadan region.

John 6:15 ◊ Mark 6:46

15Jesus perceived that they were about to come and make him king by force, so he retreated once again to the mountain by himself.

K31: Jesus Walks on the Sea

John 6:16–21

16a As evening approached, ◊ 6:47a his disciples went down to the sea. 17They boarded a boat and were trying to cross the lake to Capernaum. It had already gotten dark, and Jesus still had not joined them.

18a A strong wind began to blow ◊ 6:48b and the sea was getting rough. 19When they had rowed about three or four miles,

19b they catch sight of Jesus walking on the lake ◊ 6:49a

and coming towards the boat.

19d They were frightened, ◊ 6:50b

20a but he says to them, ◊ 6:50d

b "Don't be afraid! It's me." ◊ 6:50e

21Then they would have taken him on board, but the boat instantly arrived at the shore they had been making for.

Mark	Matt	Luke
49a But when they saw him walking on the sea,	26a But when the disciples saw him walking on the sea,	
b they thought he was a ghost	b they were terrified.	
c and they cried out.	c "It's a ghost," they said,	
50a By now they all saw him	d and cried out in fear.	
b and were terrified.	*cf. Matt 14:24b*	
c But right away he spoke with them		
d and says to them,	27a Right away Jesus spoke to them,	
e "Take heart, it's me!	b saying,	
f Don't be afraid."	c "Take heart, it's me!	
	d Don't be afraid."	
	28a In response Peter said,	
	b "Master, if it's really you,	
	c order me to come across the water to you."	
	29a He said,	
	b "Come on."	
	c And Peter got out of the boat	
	d and walked on the water	
	e and came toward Jesus.	
	30a But with the strong wind in his face,	
	b he started to panic.	
	c And when he began to sink,	
	d he cried out,	
	e "Master, save me."	
	31a Right away Jesus extended his hand	
	b and took hold of him	
	c and says to him,	
	d "You don't have enough trust!	
	e Why did you hesitate?"	
51a And he climbed into the boat with them,	32a And by the time they had climbed into the boat,	
b and the wind died down.	b the wind had died down.	
c By this time they were completely dumbfounded.		
52a (You see, they hadn't understood about the loaves;		
b they were being obstinate.)		
	33a Then those in the boat paid homage to him,	
	b saying,	
	c "You really are God's son."	

☆ **Luke 24:37** ◊ Mark 6:49

[37]But they were terrified and frightened, and figured that they were seeing a ghost.

☆ **Mark 8:17** ◊ Mark 6:52

[17]And because he was aware of this, he says to them: "Why are you puzzling about your lack of bread? You still aren't using your heads, are you? You still haven't got the point, have you? Are you just dense?"

K32: Many Sick Are Brought to Jesus

Mark 6:53–56	**Matt 14:34–36**	**Luke**
6 53a Once they had crossed over to land, b they landed at Gennesaret c and dropped anchor. 54a As soon as they had gotten out of the boat, b people recognized him right away, 55a and they ran around over the whole area b and started bringing those who were ill on mats to wherever he was rumored to be. 56a And wherever he would go, b into villages, c or towns, d or onto farms, e they would lay out the sick in the marketplaces f and beg him g to let them touch the fringe of his cloak. h And all those who managed to touch it were cured!	**14** 34a Once they had crossed over b they landed at Gennesaret. 35a And the local people recognized him b and sent word into the whole surrounding area c and brought him all who were ill. 36a And they begged him b just to let them touch the fringe of his cloak. c And all those who managed to touch ⟨it⟩ were cured!	

K32: Many Sick Are Brought to Jesus

△ **John 6:22–24**

[22]The next day, the crowd, which was still on the other side of the lake, remembered that there had been only one boat there, and that Jesus had not gotten into that boat with the disciples, but that his disciples had set off alone. [23]Other boats came out from Tiberias, near the place where they had eaten bread. [24]So when the crowd saw that neither Jesus nor his disciples were there, they, too, got into boats and set out for Capernaum looking for Jesus.

☆ **Mark 5:27–33** ◊ Mark 6:56

[27]When ⟨this woman⟩ heard about Jesus, she came up from behind in the crowd and touched his cloak. ([28]No doubt she had been figuring, "If I could just touch his clothes, I'll be cured!") [29]And the vaginal flow stopped instantly, and she sensed in her body that she was cured of her illness.

[30]And suddenly, because Jesus realized that power had drained out of him, he turned around and started asking the crowd, "Who touched my clothes?"

[31]And his disciples said to him, "You see the crowd jostling you around and you're asking, 'Who touched me?'"

[32]And he started looking around to see who had done this. [33]Although the woman got scared and started trembling—she realized what she had done—she came and fell down before him and told him the whole truth.

☆ **Matt 9:20–21** ◊ Mark 6:56

[20]And just then a woman who had suffered from vaginal bleeding for twelve years came up from behind and touched the hem of his cloak. [21]She had been saying to herself, "If I only touch his cloak, I'll be cured."

☆ **Luke 8:43–47** ◊ Mark 6:56

[43]A woman who had had a vaginal flow for twelve years, and had found no one able to heal her, [44]came up behind him, and touched the hem of his cloak. Immediately her flow of blood stopped.

[45]Then Jesus said, "Who touched me?"

When everyone denied it, Peter said, "Master, the crowds are pressing in and jostling you!"

[46]But Jesus insisted: "Someone touched me; I can tell that power has drained out of me."

[47]And when the woman saw that she had not escaped notice, she came forward trembling, and fell down before him. In front of all the people she explained why she had touched him, and how she had been immediately healed.

DISCOURSE ON DEFILEMENT

K33: Unwashed Hands

Mark 7:1–13	Matt 15:1–9	Luke
7 1a The Pharisees gather around him, b along with some of the scholars, c who had come from Jerusalem.	15 1a Then the Pharisees b and scholars c from Jerusalem d come to Jesus,	Luke
2a When they notice some of his disciples b eating their meal with defiled hands, c that is to say, without washing their hands		
3a (you see, the Pharisees and the Judeans generally wouldn't think of eating b without first washing their hands in a particular way, c always observing the tradition of the elders,		
4a and they won't eat when they get back from the marketplace without washing again, b and there are many other traditions they cherish, c such as the washing of cups and jugs and kettles),		
5a the Pharisees and the scholars start questioning him: b "Why don't your disciples live up to the tradition of the elders, c instead of eating bread d with defiled hands?"	e and say, 2a "Why do your disciples deviate from the traditions of the elders? c before they eat bread." b For instance, they don't wash their hands	
6a And he answered them, b "How accurately Isaiah depicted you phonies c when he wrote: d 'This people honors me with their lips, e but their heart stays far away from me. 7a Their worship of me is empty, b because they insist on teachings that are human commandments.' 8a You have set aside God's commandment b and hold fast to human tradition!"	7a "You phonies, b how accurately Isaiah depicted you, c when he said, 8a 'This people honors me with their lips, b but their heart strays far away from me. 9a Their worship of me is empty, b because they insist on teachings that are human regulations.'"	

7:3b Greek: *with the fist*: some mss substitute *frequently* (πυκνά).

7:4c Some mss add: *and beds* (A D K W X Θ Π f¹ f¹³ 28c 33 *pm*).

K33: Unwashed Hands

△ POxy840 2:1–9

[1]And taking ⟨the disciples⟩ along, he led them into the inner sanctuary itself, and began walking about in the temple precinct.

[2]This Pharisee, a leading priest, Levi by name, also entered, ran into them, and said to the Savior, "Who gave you permission to wander around in this inner sanctuary and lay eyes on these sacred vessels, when you have not performed your ritual bath, and your disciples have not even washed their feet? [3]Yet in a defiled state you have invaded this sacred place, which is ritually clean. No one walks about in here, or dares lay eyes on these sacred vessels, unless they have bathed themselves and changed clothes."

[4]And the Savior stood up immediately, with his disciples, and replied, "Since you are here in the temple, I take it you are clean."

[5]He replies to ⟨the Savior⟩, "I am clean. I bathed in the pool of David, you know, by descending into it by one set of steps and coming up out of it by another. [6]I also changed to white and ritually clean clothes. Only then did I come here and lay eyes on these sacred vessels."

[7]In response the Savior said to him: "Damn the blind who won't see. You bathe in these stagnant waters where dogs and pigs wallow day and night. [8]And you wash and scrub the outer layer of skin, just like prostitutes and dance-hall girls, who wash and scrub and perfume and paint themselves to entice men, while inwardly they are crawling with scorpions and filled with all sorts of corruption. [9]But my disciples and I—you say we are unbathed —have bathed in lively life-giving water that comes down from . . . But damn those . . ."

GEger 3:1–6 ◊ Mark 7:6–7

[1]They come to him and interrogate him as a way of putting him to the test. [2]They ask, "Teacher, Jesus, we know that you are [from God], since the things you do put you above all the prophets. [3]Tell us, then, is it permissible to pay to rulers what is due them? Should we pay them or not?" [4]Jesus knew what they were up to, and became indignant. [5]Then he said to them, "Why do you pay me lip service as a teacher, but not [do] what I say? [6]How accurately Isaiah prophesied about you when he said, 'This people honors me with their lips, but their heart stays far away from me; their worship of me is empty, [because they insist on teachings that are human] commandments . . .'"

Isa 29:13 (LXX) ◊ Mark 7:6–7

[13]And the Lord said, "This people draws near ⟨and⟩ honors me with their lips, but their heart stays far away from me. Their worship of me is empty, because they insist on teachings that are human commandments."

123

Mark	Matt	Luke

7 9a Or he would say to them,
  b "How expert you've become at putting aside God's commandment
  c to establish your own tradition.
10a For instance, Moses said,
  b 'Honor your father and your mother'
  c and 'Those who curse their father or mother will surely die.'
11a But you say,
  b 'If people say to their father or mother,
  c "Whatever I might have spent to support you is *korban*"'
  d (which means "consecrated to God"),
12 you no longer let those persons do anything for their father or mother.
 	
13a So you end up invalidating God's word with your own tradition,
  b which you then perpetuate.
  c And you do all kinds of other things like that!"
	15 3a In response he asked them,
	  b "Why do you also break God's commandment
	  c because of your tradition?
	  4a You remember God said,
	  b 'Honor your father and mother'
	  c and 'Those who curse their father or mother will surely die.'
	  5a But you say,
	  b 'If people say to their father or mother,
	  c "Whatever I might have spent to support you
	  d has been consecrated to God,"
	
	  6a they certainly should not honor their father or mother.'
	  b So you end up invalidating God's word because of your tradition."	

K34: What Comes Out Defiles

Mark 7:14–23	Matt 15:10–20	Luke

7 14a Once again he summoned the crowd
  b and would say to them:
  c "Listen to me, all of you,
  d and try to understand!
15a What goes into you can't defile you;
 	
  b what comes out of you can.
 	
16 If anyone has two good ears, use them!"
	15 10a And he summoned the crowd
	  b and said to them,
	  c "Listen
	  d and try to understand.
	11a What goes into your mouth doesn't defile you;
	  b what comes out of your mouth does."
	
	12a The disciples came
	  b and said to him,
	  c "Don't you realize that the Pharisees
	  d who heard this remark
	  e were offended by it?"
	13a He responded:
	  b "Every plant
	  c which my heavenly Father does not plant
	  d will be rooted out.	

7:11c Aramaic: קָרְבָּן.   7:16 Omit ℵ B L *pc.*

Exod 20:12 (LXX) ◊ Mark 7:10

[12]"Honor your father and mother so things will go well for you and so you will have a long life on the good land that the Lord your God gives you."

Lev 20:9 (LXX) ◊ Mark 7:10

[9]"Whoever speaks evil of father or mother has to be put to death. That person has spoken evil of father or mother and so is subject to the ⟨appropriate⟩ penalty."

Exod 21:16 (LXX; MT 21:17) ◊ Mark 7:10

[16]Those who curse their father or mother will surely die.

Deut 5:16 ◊ Mark 7:10

[16]"Honor your father and mother as the Lord your God commanded you, so things may go well with you and so you may have a long life on the land the Lord your God gives you."

K34: What Comes Out Defiles

Thom 14:1–5 ◊ Mark 7:15

[1]Jesus said to them, "If you fast, you will bring sin upon yourselves, [2]and if you pray, you will be condemned, [3]and if you give to charity, you will harm your spirits. [4]When you go into any region and walk about in the countryside, when people take you in, eat what they serve you and heal the sick among them. [5]After all, what goes into your mouth won't defile you; what comes out of your mouth will."

Mark	Matt	Luke
	1514a Never mind them.	
	b They are blind guides of blind people!	
	c If one blind person guides another,	
	d both will end up in some ditch."	
	15a Then Peter replied,	
7 17a When he entered a house away from the crowd,		
b his disciples started questioning him about the riddle.	b "Explain the riddle to us."	
18a And he says to them:	16a He said,	
b "Are you as dim-witted as the rest?	b "Are you still as dim-witted as the rest?	
c Don't you realize	17a Don't you realize	
d that nothing from outside can defile by going into a person,		
19a because it doesn't get to the heart		
	b that everything that goes into the mouth	
b but passes into the stomach,	c passes into the stomach	
c and comes out in the outhouse?"	d and comes out in the outhouse?	
d (This is how everything we eat is purified.)		
20a And he went on to say,		
b "It's what comes out of a person	18a But the things that come out of the mouth	
	b come from the heart,	
c that defiles.	c and those things defile a person.	
21a For from out of the human heart issue wicked intentions:	19a For out of the heart emerge evil intentions:	
b sexual immorality,	d sexual immorality,	
c thefts,	e thefts,	
	f false witnesses,	
d murders,	b murders,	
22a adulteries,	c adulteries,	
b envies,		
c wickedness,		
d deceit,		
e promisuity,		
f an evil eye,		
g blasphemy,	g blasphemies.	
h arrogance,		
i lack of good sense.		
23a All these evil things come from the inside out		
b and defile the person."		
	20a These are the things that defile a person.	
	b However, eating with unwashed hands	
	c doesn't defile anybody."	

K35: Greek Woman's Daughter

Mark 7:24–30	**Matt 15:21–28**	Luke
7 24a From there he got up	15 21a So Jesus left there,	
b and went away to the regions of Tyre.	b and withdrew to the district of Tyre and Sidon.	
c Whenever he visited a house		
d he wanted no one to know,		
e but he could not escape notice.		
25a Instead, suddenly a woman	22a And this Canaanite woman from those parts appeared	
	b and cried out,	
	c "Have mercy on me, sir, you son of David.	
b whose daughter had an unclean spirit	d My daughter is severely possessed."	
	23a But he did not respond at all.	
	b And his disciples came	
	c and began to complain:	
	d "Get rid of her,	
	e because she is badgering us."	
	24a But in response he said,	
	b "I was sent only to the lost sheep of the house of Israel."	
c heard about him,	25a She came	
d and came	b and bowed down to him,	
e and fell down at his feet.		
26a The woman was a Greek,		
b by race a Phoenician from Syria.		
c And she started asking him to drive the demon out of her daughter.	c saying,	
	d "Sir, please help me."	
27a He responded to her like this:	26a In response he said,	
b "Let the children be fed first,		
c since it isn't good to take bread out of children's mouths	b "It's not right to take bread out of children's mouths	
d and throw it to the dogs!"	c and throw it to the dogs."	
28a But as a rejoinder she says to him,	27a But she said,	
b "Sir, even the dogs under the table get to eat scraps	b "Of course, sir, but even the dogs eat the scraps	
c ⟨dropped by⟩ children!"	c that fall from their master's table."	

7:24b Some mss add: *and Sidon*: D L W Δ Θ
28 *al*, which is probably a harmonizing reading
derived from Matt 15:21.

7:28b Greek (κύριος): *Sir* or *Master* or *Lord*.

Mark	**Matt**	**Luke**
7 29a Then he said to her,	1528a Then in response Jesus said to her,	
b "For that retort,		
c be on your way,	b "My good woman, your trust is enormous!	
	c Your wish is as good as fulfilled."	
d the demon has come out of your daughter."	d And her daughter was cured at that moment.	
30a She returned home		
b and found the child lying on the bed		
c and the demon gone.		

K36: Jesus Cures a Deaf-Mute

Mark 7:31–37	**Matt 15:29–31**	**Luke**
7 31a Then he left the regions of Tyre	1529a Then Jesus left there	
b and traveled through Sidon to the Sea of Galilee,	b and went to the Sea of Galilee.	
c through the middle of the region known as the Decapolis.		
32a And they bring him a deaf-mute		
b and plead with him to lay his hand on him.		
33a Taking him aside from the crowd in private,		
b he stuck his fingers into the man's ears		
c and spat		
d and touched his tongue.		
34a And looking up to the sky,		
b he groaned		
c and says to him,		
d "*ephphatha*"		
e (which means,		
f "Be opened!").		
35a And his ears opened up,		
b and right away his speech impediment was removed,		
c and he started speaking properly.		
36a Then he ordered them to tell no one.		
b But no matter how much he enjoined them,		
c they spread it around all the more.		

7:34d Aramaic: אֶתְפְּתַח.

Mark	Matt	Luke

Mark

7 37a And they were completely
       dumbfounded.
   b "He's done everything
   c and has done it quite well,"
   d they said;
   e "he even makes the deaf hear and the
       mute speak!"

Matt

15 29c And he climbed the mountain
    d and sat there.
30 a And huge crowds came to him
   b and brought with them the lame,
   c the blind,
   d the maimed,
   e the mute,
   f and many others,
   g and they crowded around his feet
   h and he healed them.
31 a As a result, the crowd was astonished
   b when they saw the mute now
       speaking,
   c the maimed made strong,
   d and the lame walking
   e and the blind seeing.
   f And they gave all the credit to the
       God of Israel.

K37: Loaves and Fish for Four Thousand

Mark 8:1–10	**Matt 15:32–39**	• **Mark 6:35–45**

Mark 8:1–10

8 1a And once again during that same period,
 b when there was a huge crowd without anything to eat,
 c he calls the disciples aside
 d and says to them,
 2a "I feel sorry for the crowd,
 b because they have already spent three days with me
 c and now they've run out of food.
 3a If I send these people home hungry,
 b they will collapse on the road
 c —in fact, some of them have come from quite a distance."
 4a And his disciples answered him,
 b "How can anyone feed these people bread out here in this desolate place?"
 5a And he started asking them,
 b "How many loaves do you have?"
 c They replied,
 d "Seven."
 6a Then he orders the crowd to sit down on the ground.
 b And he took the seven loaves,
 c gave thanks,
 d and broke them into pieces,
 e and started giving ⟨them⟩ to his disciples to hand out;
 f and they passed them around to the crowd.
 7a They also had a few small fish.
 b When he had blessed them,
 c he told them to hand those out as well.
 8a They had more than enough to eat.
 b Then they picked up seven big baskets of leftover scraps.
 9a There were about four thousand people there.
 b Then he started sending them away.

Matt 15:32–39

15 32a Then Jesus called his disciples aside
 b and said:
 c "I feel sorry for the crowd
 d because they have already spent three days with me
 e and now they've run out of food.
 f And I don't want to send these people away hungry,
 g for fear they'll collapse on the road."
 33a And the disciples say to him,
 b "How can we get enough bread here in this desolate place to feed so many people?"
 34a Jesus says to them,
 b "How many loaves do you have?"
 c They replied,
 d "Seven,
 e plus a few fish."
 35 And he ordered the crowd to sit down on the ground.
 36a And he took the seven loaves
 b and the fish
 c and gave thanks,
 d and broke them into pieces,
 e and started giving ⟨them⟩ to the disciples,
 f and the disciples ⟨started giving them⟩ to the crowds.
 37a And everyone had more than enough to eat.
 b Then they picked up seven baskets of leftover scraps.
 38a Those who had eaten numbered 4,000,
 b not counting women and children.
 39a And after he sent the crowds away,

• **Mark 6:35–45**

35And when the hour had already grown late, his disciples would approach him and say, "This place is desolate and it's late. 36Send them away so that they can go to the farms and villages around here to buy something to eat."
37But in response he said to them, "Give them something to eat yourselves!"
And they say to him, "Are we to go out and buy half a year's wages worth of bread and donate it for their meal?!"
 38a So he says to them, ◊ 8:5a
 b "How many loaves do you have? ◊ 8:5b
Go look."
 And when they find out,
 e they say, ◊ 8:5c
 f "Five, ◊ 8:5d
 g and two fish."
 39a Next he instructed them all to sit down ◊ 8:6a
and eat, some over here, some over there, on the green grass. So they sat down group by group, in hundreds and in fifties.
 41a And he took the five loaves ◊ 8:6a
 b and the two fish,
looked up to the sky,
 d gave a blessing, ◊ 8:6c
 e and broke the bread apart, ◊ 8:6d
 f and started giving it to his disciples to pass around to them, ◊ 8:6e
 g and even the two fish they shared with everybody. ◊ 8:7a
 42 Everybody had more than enough to eat. ◊ 8:8
 43 Then they picked up twelve baskets full of leftovers, including some fish. ◊ 8:8c
 44 And the number of men who had some bread came to five thousand. ◊ 8:9a
45And right away
 b he made his disciples embark in the boat ◊ 8:10a
and go ahead to the opposite shore toward Bethsaida,
 e while he himself dispersed the crowd. ◊ 8:9b

• Matt 14:15–22

¹⁵When it was evening the disciples approached him, and said, "This place is desolate and it's already late. Send the crowd away so that they can go to the villages and buy food for themselves."

¹⁶Jesus said to them, "They don't need to leave; give them something to eat yourselves!"

¹⁷But they say to him,

17b "We have nothing here except five loaves of bread ◊ 8:5d

c and two fish."

18a He said, ◊ 8:5a

"Bring them here to me."

19a And he told the crowd to sit down on the grass, ◊ 8:6a

b and he took the five loaves ◊ 8:6b

c and two fish,

and looking up to the sky

19e he gave a blessing, ◊ 8:6c

f and breaking it apart ◊ 8:6d

g he gave the bread to the disciples, ◊ 8:6e

h and the disciples ⟨gave it⟩ to the crowd. ◊ 8:6f

20a And everybody had more than enough to eat. ◊ 8:8

b Then they picked up twelve baskets full of leftovers. ◊ 8:8c

21a The number of people who had eaten came to about five thousand, ◊ 8:9a

b not counting women and children.

²²And right away

22b he made the disciples get in a boat ◊ 8:10a

and go ahead of him to the other side,

22d while he dispersed the crowds. ◊ 8:9b

Matt 9:36 ◊ Mark 8:1–3

³⁶When he saw the crowd, he was moved by them because they were in trouble and helpless, like sheep without a shepherd.

Mark 14:22 ◊ Mark 8:6

²²And as they were eating, he took a loaf, gave a blessing, broke it into pieces and offered it to them. And he said, "Take some; this is my body!"

△ **Luke 9:12–17**

¹²As the day began to draw to a close, the twelve approached him and said, "Send the crowd away, so that they can go to the villages and farms around here and find food and lodging; for we are in a desolate place here."

¹³But he said to them, "Give them something to eat yourselves."

They said, "All we have are five loaves

13d and two fish— ◊ 8:5d

e unless we go ourselves

and buy food for all these people."

⟨14a There were about five thousand men.⟩ ◊ 8:9a

b He said to his disciples, ◊ 8:5a

c "Have them sit down in groups of about fifty." ◊ 8:6a

¹⁵They did so, and got them all seated.

16a Then he took the five loaves ◊ 8:6b

b and two fish,

looked up to the sky,

16d gave a blessing, ◊ 8:6c

e and broke them, ◊ 8:6d

f and started handing them out to the disciples to pass around to the crowd. ◊ 8:6e

17a And everybody had more than enough to eat. ◊ 8:8

b Then the leftovers were collected, twelve baskets full. ◊ 8:8b

☆ **Matt 26:26 ◊ Mark 8:6**

²⁶As they were eating, Jesus took a loaf, gave a blessing, and broke it into pieces. And he offered it to the disciples, and said, "Take some and eat; this is my body."

☆ **Luke 22:19 ◊ Mark 8:6**

¹⁹And he took a loaf, gave thanks, broke it into pieces, offered it to them, and said, "This is my body which is offered for you. Do this as my memorial."

☆ **Luke 24:30 ◊ Mark 8:6**

³⁰And so, as soon as he took his place at table with them, he took a loaf, and gave a blessing, broke it, and started passing it out to them.

☆ **Acts 27:35 ◊ Mark 8:6**

³⁵After he had said these things, he took a piece of bread, gave thanks to God in front of everybody, broke it up, and began to eat.

△ **John 6:1–15**

¹After these events, Jesus crossed to the far side of the sea of Galilee, ⟨also known as the Sea of⟩ Tiberias. ²A huge crowd was following him, because they wanted to see the miracles he was performing on the sick. ³Jesus climbed up the mountain, and he sat down there with his disciples. ⁴It was about time for the Jewish celebration of Passover.

⁵Jesus looks up and sees a huge crowd approaching him, and he says to Philip, "Where are we going to get enough bread to feed this mob?" ⟨⁶He was saying this to test him; you see, Jesus already knew what he was going to do.⟩

⁷"Half a year's wages wouldn't buy enough bread for everyone to have a bite," Philip said.

⁸One of his disciples, Andrew, Simon Peter's brother, says to him, ⁹"There's a lad here

9b with five loaves of barley bread ◊ 8:5d

c and two fish;

but what does that amount to for so many?"

¹⁰Jesus said,

10b "Have the people sit down." ◊ 8:6a

⟨They were in a grassy place.⟩

10d So they sat down; ◊ 8:9a

e the men alone numbered about five thousand.

11a Jesus took the loaves, ◊ 8:6b

b gave thanks, ◊ 8:6c

c and passed them around to ◊ 8:6f

d the people sitting there, ◊ 8:7a

e along with the fish, and all of them had as much as they wanted.

12a And when they had eaten their fill, ◊ 8:8b

he says to his disciples, "Gather up the leftovers so nothing goes to waste."

¹³So they gathered them up

13b and filled twelve baskets with scraps ◊ 8:8c

from the five barley loaves—from what was left over. ¹⁴When these folks saw the miracle he had performed they would say, "Yes indeed! This is undoubtedly the Prophet who is to come into the world." ¹⁵Jesus perceived that they were about to come and make him king by force, so he retreated once again to the mountain by himself.

	Mark	**Matt**	**Luke**
	8 10a And he got right into the boat with his disciples	**15** 39b he got into the boat	
	b and went to the Dalmanoutha district.	c and went to the Magadan region.	

K38: The Pharisees Demand a Sign

Mark 8:10–13	**Matt 15:39b, 16:1–4**	**Luke**
8 10a And he got right into the boat with his disciples	**15** 39b he got into the boat	
b and went to the Dalmanoutha district.	c and went to the Magadan region.	
11a The Pharisees came out	**16** 1a And the Pharisees and Sadducees came,	
b and started to argue with him.		
c To test him,	b and to put him to the test	
d they demanded a sign in the sky.	c they asked him to show them a sign in the sky.	
12a He groaned under his breath		
b and says,	2a In response he said to them,	
	b "When it's evening,	
	c you say,	
	d 'It'll be fair weather	
	e because the sky looks red.'	
	3a Early in the morning,	
	b ⟨you say,⟩	
	c 'The day will bring winter weather	
	d because the sky looks red and dark.'	
	e You know how to read the face of the sky,	
	f but you can't discern the signs of the times.	
c "Why does this generation insist on a sign?	4a An evil and immoral generation seeks a sign,	
d I swear to God,		
e this generation won't get any sign!"	b yet no sign will be given it	
	c except the sign of Jonah."	
13a And turning his back on them,	d And he turned his back on them	
b he got back in the boat		
c and crossed over to the other side.	e and walked away.	

8:10b Some mss read *Magadan* (cf. Matt 15:39).

2 Kgs 4:42–44 (LXX)

⁴²And a man came from Baithsarisa, and brought to the man of God, by way of first fruits, twenty barley loaves and fruit cakes, and told him, "Give it to the people and let them eat." ⁴³And his servant said "How in the world can I set this before a hundred men?" He replied, "Give it to the people and let them eat. For the Lord says, 'They shall eat and have some left over.'" ⁴⁴And they ate and had some left over, just as the Lord had said.

K38: The Pharisees Demand a Sign

△ **Matt 12:38–42**

³⁸Then some of the scholars and Pharisees responded to him, "Teacher, we would like to see a sign from you." ³⁹In response he said to them, "An evil and immoral generation insists on a sign, and no sign will be given it, except the sign of Jonah the prophet. ⁴⁰You see, just as 'Jonah was in the belly of a sea monster for three days and three nights,' so the son of Adam will be in the bowels of the earth for three days and three nights. ⁴¹At judgment time, the citizens of Nineveh will come back to life along with this generation and condemn it, beacause they had a change of heart in response to Jonah's message. Yet take note: what is right here is greater than Jonah.

⁴²At judgment time, the queen of the south will be brought back to life along with this generation, and she will condemn it, because she came from the ends of the earth to listen to Solomon's wisdom. Yet take note: what is right here is greater than Solomon."

△ **Luke 11:29–32**

²⁹As more and more people were crowding around him, he began to say, "This generation is an evil generation. It insists on a sign, but it will be given no sign except the sign of Jonah. ³⁰You see, just as Jonah became a sign for the Ninevites, so the son of Adam will be a sign for this generation. ³¹At judgment time, the queen of the south will be brought back to life along with members of this generation, and she will condemn them, because she came from the ends of the earth to listen to Solomon's wisdom. Yet take note: what is right here is greater than Solomon. ³²At judgment time, the citizens of Nineveh will come back to life, along with this generation, and condemn it, because they had a change of heart in response to Jonah's message. Yet take note: what is right here is greater than Jonah."

☆ **Luke 12:54–56**

⁵⁴He would also say to the crowds, "When you see a cloud rising in the west, right away you say that it's going to rain; and so it does. ⁵⁵And when the wind blows from the south, you say we're in for scorching heat; and we are. ⁵⁶You phonies! You know the lay of the land and can read the face of the sky, so why don't you know how to interpret the present time?"

☆ **Luke 11:16** ◊ Mark 8:11

¹⁶Others were testing him by demanding a sign from heaven.

☆ **John 6:30** ◊ Mark 8:11

³⁰They asked him, "What miracle are you going to perform so we can see it and come to believe in you? What 'labor' are you going to perform?"

K39: Bread and Leaven

Mark 8:14–21	**Matt 16:5–12**	Luke

16 5a And the disciples came to the
opposite shore,
  b but they forgot to bring any bread.

8 14a They forgot to bring any bread
  b and had nothing with them in the
boat except one loaf.

15a Then he started giving them
directives:
  b "Look,"
  c he says,
  d "watch out for the leaven of the
Pharisees and the leaven of Herod!"

6a Jesus said to them,

  b "Look, take care
  c and guard against the leaven of the
Pharisees and Sadducees."

16a They began looking quizzically at
one another

7a Now they looked quizzically at each
other,
  b saying,
  c "We didn't bring any bread."

  b because they didn't have any bread.
17a And because he was aware of this,
  b he says to them:
  c "Why are you puzzling

8a Because Jesus was aware of this,
  b he said,
  c "Why are you puzzling,
  d you with so little trust,

  d about your lack of bread?
  e You still aren't using your heads, are
you?
  f You still haven't got the point, have
you?
  g Are you just dense?

  e because you don't have any bread?
9a You still aren't using your heads, are
you?

18a Though you have eyes,
  b you still don't see,
  c and though you have ears,
  d you still don't hear!
  e Don't you even remember

  b You don't remember the five loaves
for the five thousand
  c and how many baskets you carried
away, do you?

19a how many baskets full of scraps you
picked up
  b when I broke up the five loaves for
the five thousand?"
  c "Twelve,"
  d they reply to him.
20a "When I broke up the seven loaves
for the four thousand,

10a Nor the seven loaves for four
thousand
  b and how many big baskets you filled?

  b how many big baskets full of scraps
did you pick up?"
  c And they say,
  d "Seven."
21a And he repeats,
  b "You still don't understand, do
you?"

11a How can you possibly think
  b I was talking to you about bread?
  c Just be on guard against the leaven of
the Pharisees and Sadducees."

8:15d Some mss read: *the Herodians* ($\mathfrak{P}^{45}$ W Θ
$f^1 f^{13}$ 28 *pc*) (cf. Mark 3:6).

K39: Bread and Leaven

Luke 12:1 ◊ Mark 8:15

[1]Meanwhile, a crowd of many thousands had thronged together and were trampling each other.

He began to speak first to his disciples:

1 d "Guard against the leaven of the Pharisees,

which is to say, their hypocrisy.

☆ **John 6:32–35**

[32]Jesus responded to them: "I swear to God, it was not Moses who gave you bread from heaven to eat; rather, it is my Father who gives you real bread from heaven. [33]I mean this: God's bread comes down from heaven and gives life to the world."

[34]"Sir," they said to him, "give us this bread every time."

[35]Jesus explained to them: "I am the bread of life. Anyone who comes to me will never be hungry again, and anyone who believes in me will never again be thirsty."

Jer 5:21 (LXX) ◊ Mark 8:18

[21]Pay attention to these things, you foolish and senseless people, who have eyes but do not see, who have ears, but do not hear.

Ezek 12:2 (LXX) ◊ Mark 8:18

[2]O son of Adam, you live in the midst of wrongdoers, those who have eyes to see but don't see; who have ears to hear but don't hear.

cf. Mark 6:35–44 ◊ Mark 8:19

cf. Mark 8:1–10 ◊ Mark 8:20

Mark	Matt	Luke
	1612a Then they understood	

1612a Then they understood
 b that he was not talking about
   guarding against the leaven in bread
 c but against the teaching of the
   Pharisees and Sadducees.

K40: Jesus Cures a Blind Man

Mark 8:22–26	**Matt**	**Luke**

8 22a They come to Bethsaida,
  b and they bring him a blind person,
  c and plead with him to touch him.
 23a He took the blind man by the hand
  b and led him out of the village.
  c And he spat into his eyes,
  d and placed his hands on him,
  e and started questioning him:
  f "Do you see anything?"
 24a When his sight began to come back,
  b the first thing he said was:
  c "I see human figures,
  d as though they were trees walking
   around."
 25a Then he put his hands over his eyes a
   second time.
  b And he opened his eyes,
  c and his sight was restored,
  d and he saw everything clearly.
 26a And he sent him home,
  b saying,
  c "Don't bother to go back to the
   village!"

K40: Jesus Cures a Blind Man

△ **John 9:1–7**

[1]As he was leaving, he saw a man who had been blind from birth. [2]His disciples asked him, "Rabbi, was it this man's wrongdoing or his parents' that caused him to be born blind?"

[3]Jesus responded, "This fellow did nothing wrong, nor did his parents. Rather, ⟨he was born blind⟩ so God could display his work through him. [4]We must carry out the work of the one who sent me while the light lasts. Nighttime is coming and then no one will be able to undertake any work. [5]So long as I am in the world I am the light of the world."

[6]With that he spat on the ground, made mud with his spit and treated the man's eyes with the mud. [7]Then ⟨Jesus⟩ said to him, "Go, rinse off in the pool of Siloam" (the name means "Emissary"). So he went over, rinsed ⟨his eyes⟩ off and came back with his sight restored.

VILLAGES OF CAESAREA PHILIPPI

K41: Who Do People Say I Am?

Mark 8:27–30

8 27a Jesus and his disciples set out for the villages of Caesarea Philippi.

b On the road he started questioning his disciples,
c asking them,
d "What are people saying about me?"

28a In response they said to him,
b "⟨Some say, 'You are⟩ John the Baptist,'
c and others, 'Elijah,'
d but others, 'One of the prophets.'"

29a But he continued to press them,
b "What about you, who do you say I am?"
c Peter responds to him,
d "You are the Anointed!"

30a And he warned them
b not to tell anyone about him.

Matt 16:13–20

16 13a When Jesus came to the region of Caesarea Philippi,

b he started questioning his disciples,
c asking,
d "What are people saying about the son of Adam?"

14a They said,
b "Some ⟨say, 'He is⟩ John the Baptist,'
c but others, 'Elijah,'
d and others, 'Jeremiah or one of the prophets.'"

15a He says to them,
b "What about you, who do you say I am?"

16a And Simon Peter responded,
b "You are the Anointed,
c the son of the living God!"

17a And in response Jesus said to him,
b "You are to be congratulated, Simon son of Jonah,
c because flesh and blood did not reveal this to you
d but my Father who is in heaven.

18a Let me tell you,
b You are Peter, 'the Rock,'
c and on this very rock I will build my congregation,
d and the gates of Hades will not be able to overpower it.

19a I shall give you the keys of Heaven's domain,
b and whatever you bind on earth
c will be considered bound in heaven
d and whatever you release on earth
e will be considered released in heaven."

20a Then he ordered the disciples
b not to tell anyone that he was the Anointed.

Luke 9:18–21

9 18a And on one occasion
b when Jesus was praying alone
c the disciples were with him;
d and he questioned them

e asking:
f "What are the crowds saying about me?"

19a They said in response,
b "⟨Some say, 'You are⟩ John the Baptist,'
c while others, 'Elijah,'
d and still others, 'One of the ancient prophets has come back to life.'"

20a And he said to them,
b "What about you, who do you say I am?"
c And Peter responded,
d "God's Anointed!"

21a Then he warned them,
b and forbade them to tell this to anyone,

K41: Who Do People Say I Am?

△ **Thom 13:1–8**

[1]Jesus said to his disciples, "Compare me to something and tell me what I am like."

[2]Simon Peter said to him, "You are like a just angel."

[3]Matthew said to him, "You are like a wise philosopher."

[4]Thomas said to him, "Teacher, my mouth is utterly unable to say what you are like."

[5]Jesus said, "I am not your teacher. Because you have drunk, you have become intoxicated from the bubbling spring that I have tended."

[6]And he took him, and withdrew, and spoke three sayings to him.

[7]When Thomas came back to his friends, they asked him, "What did Jesus say to you?"

[8]Thomas said to them, "If I tell you one of the sayings he spoke to me, you will pick up rocks and stone me, and fire will come from the rocks and devour you."

✩ **John 1:49** ◊ Mark 8:29

[49]Nathanael responded to him, "Rabbi, you are God's son! You are King of Israel!"

✩ **John 6:68–69** ◊ Mark 8:29

[68]Simon Peter replied to him, "Lord, is there anyone else we can turn to? You have the words of real life! [69]We have become believers and are certain that you are God's holy one."

✩ **John 11:27** ◊ Mark 8:29

[27]"Yes, Master," she says, I believe that you are the Anointed, God's son, who is to come to earth."

K42: Son of Adam Must Suffer

Mark 8:31–33	**Matt 16:21–23**	**Luke 9:22**
	16 21 a From that time on	9 22 a adding,
8 31 a He started teaching them	b Jesus started to make it clear to his disciples	
	c that he was destined to go to Jerusalem,	
b that the son of Adam was destined to suffer a great deal,	d and suffer a great deal	b "The son of Adam is destined to suffer a great deal,
c and be rejected by the elders and the ranking priests and the scholars,	e at the hands of the elders and ranking priests and scholars,	c be rejected by the elders and ranking priests and scholars,
d and be killed,	f and be killed	d and be killed
e and after three days rise.	g and, on the third day, be raised.	e and, on the third day, be raised."
32 a And he would say this openly.		
b And Peter took him aside	22 a And Peter took him aside	
c and began to lecture him.	b and began to lecture him,	
	c saying,	
	d "May God spare you, master;	
	e this surely can't happen to you."	
33 a But he turned,	23 a But he turned	
b noticed his disciples,		
c and reprimanded Peter verbally:	b and said to Peter,	
d "Get out of my sight, you Satan, you,	c "Get out of my sight, you Satan, you.	
	d You are dangerous to me	
e because you're not thinking in God's terms,	e because you are not thinking in God's terms,	
f but in human terms."	f but in human terms."	

K43: Saving One's Life

Mark 8:34–9:1	**Matt 16:24–28**	**Luke 9:23–27**
8 34 a After he called the crowd together with his disciples,		
b he said to them,	16 24 a Then Jesus said to his disciples,	9 23 a He would say to everyone,
c "If any of you wants to come after me,	b "If any of you wants to come after me,	b "If any of you wants to come after me,
d you should deny yourself,	c you should deny yourself,	c you should deny yourself,
e pick up your cross,	d pick up your cross,	d pick up your cross every day,
f and follow me!	e and follow me!	e and follow me!
35 a Remember, by trying to save your own life	25 a Remember, by trying to save your own life,	24 a Remember, by trying to save your own life,
b you're going to lose it,	b you are going to lose it,	b you're going to lose it,
c but by losing your life for the sake of the good news,	c but by losing your own life for my sake,	c but by losing your life for my sake,
d you're going to save it.	d you are going to find it.	d you're going to save it.
36 a After all, what good does it do you	26 a After all, what good will it do	25 a After all, what good does it do you
b to acquire the whole world	b if you acquire the whole world	b to acquire the whole world
c and pay for it with life?	c but forfeit your life?	c and lose or forfeit yourself?

8:35c Most mss add: *for my sake and* (except 𝔓⁴⁵ D *pc*).

K42: Son of Adam Must Suffer

Mark 9:30–32

[30]They left there and started going through Galilee, and he did not want anyone to know. [31]Remember, he was instructing his disciples and telling them: "The son of Adam is being turned over to his enemies, and they will end up killing him. And three days after he is killed he will rise!" [32]But they never understood this remark, and always dreaded to ask him ⟨about it⟩.

Mark 10:32–34

[32]On the road going up to Jerusalem, Jesus was leading the way, they were apprehensive, and others who were following were frightened. Once again he took the twelve aside and started telling them what was going to happen to him:

[33]"Listen, we're going up to Jerusalem, and the son of Adam will be turned over to the ranking priests and the scholars, and they will sentence him to death, and turn him over to foreigners, [34]and they will make fun of him, and spit on him, and flog him, and put ⟨him⟩ to death. Yet after three days he will rise!"

Matt 17:22–23

[22]And when had they been reunited in Galilee, Jesus said to them, "The son of Adam is about to be turned over to his enemies, [23]and they will end up killing him, and on the third day he'll be raised." And they were very sad.

Matt 20:17–19

[17]On the way up to Jerusalem Jesus took the twelve aside privately and said to them as they walked along: [18]"Listen, we're going up to Jerusalem, and the son of Adam will be turned over to the ranking priests and scholars, and they will sentence him to death, [19]and turn him over to the foreigners to make fun of, and flog, and crucify. Yet on the third day he will be raised."

△ SecJas 4:10–5:6

[10]". . . you should scorn death and be concerned about life. [11]Remember my cross and my death, and you will live!"

5 [1]And I answered him, "Lord, don't proclaim the cross and death to us, for they are far from you."

[2]The Lord replied, "I swear to you, none will be saved unless they believe in my cross; [for] God's domain belongs to those who have believed in my cross. [3]Become seekers of death, therefore, like the dead who are seeking life, for what they seek is manifest to them. So what can be of concern to them? [4]When you inquire

Luke 9:43b–45

[43]. . . While they all were marveling at everything he was doing, he said to his disciples, [44]"Mark well these words: the son of Adam is about to be turned over to his enemies."

[45]But they never understood this remark. It was couched in veiled language, so they would not get its meaning. And they always dreaded to ask him about this remark.

Luke 18:31–34

[31]⟨Jesus⟩ took the twelve aside and instructed them: "Listen, we're going up to Jerusalem, and everything written by the prophets about the son of Adam will come true. [32]For he will be turned over to the foreigners, and will be made fun of and insulted. They will spit on him, [33]and flog him, and put him to death. Yet after three days he will rise." [34]But they did not understand any of this; this remark was obscure to them, and they never did figure out what it meant.

into the subject of death, it will teach you about election. [5]I swear to you, none will be saved who are afraid of death; for ⟨God's⟩ domain belongs to those are dead. [6]Become better than I; be like the son of the holy spirit!"

K43: Saving One's Life

Matt 10:38–39 ◊ Mark 8:34–35

[38]"Unless you take your cross and come along with me, you're not worthy of me. [39]By finding your life, you'll lose it, and by losing your life for my sake, you'll find it."

Luke 14:27 ◊ Mark 8:34

[27]"Unless you carry your own cross and come along with me—you're no disciple of mine."

Thom 55:1–2 ◊ Mark 8:34

[1]Jesus said, "Whoever does not hate father and mother cannot be my disciple, [2]and whoever does not hate brothers and sisters, and carry the cross as I do, will not be worthy of me."

Luke 17:33 ◊ Mark 8:35

[33]"Whoever tries to hang on to life will forfeit it, but whoever forfeits life will preserve it."

Thom 101:1–3 ◊ Mark 8:34

[1]"Whoever does not hate [father] and mother as I do cannot be my [disciple], [2]and whoever does [not] love [father and] mother as I do cannot be my [disciple]. [3]For my mother [. . .], but my true [mother] gave me life."

John 12:25 ◊ Mark 8:35

[25]"Those who love life lose it, but those who hate life in this world will preserve it for unending, real life."

Mark	Matt	Luke
8 37 Or, what would you give in exchange for life?	**16**26 d Or what will you give in exchange for your life?	
38 a Moreover, if any of you are ashamed of me and my message		**9** 26 a Moreover, if any of you are ashamed of me and of my message,
b in this adulterous and sinful generation,		
c of you the son of Adam will likewise be ashamed		b of you will the son of Adam be ashamed
d when he comes in his Father's glory	27 a Remember, the son of Adam is going to come in the glory of his Father	c when he comes in his glory
		d and the glory of the Father
e accompanied by holy angels!"	b with his messengers,	e and of the holy messengers.
	c and then he will reward everyone according to their deeds.	
9 1 a And he used to tell them,		
b "I swear to you:	28 a I swear to you:	27 a I swear to you,
c Some of those standing here won't ever taste death	b Some of those standing here won't ever taste death	b some of those standing here won't ever taste death
d before they see God's imperial rule set in with power!"	c before they see the son of Adam's imperial rule arriving."	c before they see God's imperial rule."

Matt 10:33 ◊ Mark 8:38

[33]"But the one who disowns me in public, I too will disown before my Father in the heavens."

Luke 12:9 ◊ Mark 8:38

[9]"But whoever disowns me in public will be disowned in the presence of God's messengers."

Table 6

Aphoristic Compounds and Clusters

		Mark
1.	Patches and Wineskins	2:21–22
2.	Adam Over the Sabbath	2:27–28
3.	Satan Against Satan	3:23c–26
4.	Powerful Man's House	3:27
5.	Blasphemies	3:28–29
6.	Placing the Lamp	4:21–25
7.	What Comes Out Defiles	7:14–23
8.	Saving One's Life	8:34–9:1
9.	Number One Is Last	9:33–50
10.	Mountains Into the Sea	11:23–25
11.	Scholars in Long Robes	12:38–40
12.	Signs of the Final Agonies	13:3–37

ROMAN AND JEWISH COINS

The copper *as* depicts the emperor Antoninus Pius (138–161 C.E.). The obverse reads ANTONINVS AVG PIVS P P. The reverse records his titles, TR POT COS III. The coin shown here depicts Mars, holding a spear and shield, descending through the air to the sleeping Rhea Silvia, a vestal virgin of royal lineage who, through this nocturnal violation, became the mother of Romulus and Remus.

The gold *aureus* depicts Faustina Junior, the wife of the Roman emperor Marcus Aurelius (161–180 C.E.). The reverse features the great mother goddess Cybele (MATRI MAGNAE) seated on a throne flanked by two sacred lions. Goddess of nature and mistress of wild beasts, her cult festival involved ecstatic dancing and self-emasculation. Phrygian in origin, she was introduced at Rome in 204 B.C.E. to aid in Hannibal's defeat. The conservative Romans did not easily adjust to her cult. Roman citizens were forbidden to participate in her services on the Palatine, and she did not become an acceptable subject for Roman coinage until the 2nd century C.E.

The silver *shekel* depicts the facade of the Temple at Jerusalem with the Ark of the Covenant in its interior. The name Simon appears in Hebrew characters. The coin was struck over a "pagan" tetradrachm during the Second Jewish Revolt against Rome (132–135 C.E.). Led by Simon bar Kochba, this nationalistic movement included in its programs the reconstruction of the Jewish Temple destroyed by Titus during the First Revolt in 70 C.E. The reverse depicts the lulav, a bundle of myrtle, palm, and willow branches, and an etrog or citron fruit, both used in the Temple ritual. The inscription translates "Year Two of the Freedom of Israel."

Photographs and descriptions courtesy of Numismatics Fine Arts, Inc., Los Angeles, and the Institute for Antiquity and Christianity, Claremont, CA.

K44.1: Jesus Transformed

Mark 9:2–8	**Matt 17:1–8**	**Luke 9:28–36**
9 2a Six days later,	17 1a Six days later,	9 28a About eight days after these sayings,
b Jesus takes Peter and James and John along	b Jesus takes Peter and James and his brother John along	b Jesus happened to take Peter and John and James along with him
c and leads them off by themselves to a lofty mountain.	c and he leads them off by themselves to a lofty mountain.	c and climbed up the mountain to pray.
		29a And it so happened as he was praying
d He was transformed in front of them,	2a He was transformed in front of them	
	b and his face shone like the sun,	b that his face took on a strange appearance,
3a and his clothes became an intensely brilliant white,	c and his clothes turned as white as light.	c and his clothing turned dazzling white.
b whiter than any laundry on earth could make them.		
4a Elijah appeared to them, with Moses,	3a The next thing you know, Moses and Elijah appeared to them	30 The next thing you know, two figures were talking with him, Moses and Elijah,
b and they were conversing with Jesus.	b and were conversing with Jesus.	
		31a who appeared in glory
		b and were discussing his departure,
		c which he was destined to carry out in Jerusalem.
		32a Now Peter and those with him were half asleep at the time.
		b But they came wide awake
		c when they saw his glory
		d and the two men standing next to him.
		33a And it so happened
		b as the men were leaving him
5a Peter responds by saying to Jesus,	4a Then Peter responded by saying to Jesus,	c that Peter said to Jesus,
b "Rabbi, it's a good thing we're here.	b "Master, it's a good thing we're here.	d "Master, it's a good thing we're here.
	c If you want,	
c In fact, why not set up three tents,	d I'll set up three tents here,	e In fact, why not set up three tents here,
d one for you,	e one for you,	f one for you,
e and one for Moses,	f one for Moses,	g one for Moses,
f and one for Elijah!"	g and one for Elijah!"	h and one for Elijah!"
6a (You see, he didn't know how else to respond,		i (He didn't know what he was saying).
b since they were terrified.)		
7a And a cloud moved in	5a While he was speaking,	34a While he was still speaking,
b and cast a shadow over them,	b there was a bright cloud	b a cloud moved in
	c that cast a shadow over them.	c and cast a shadow over them.
		d And their fear increased
		e as they entered the cloud.

145

Mark	**Matt**	**Luke**
9 7c and a voice came out of the cloud:	**17** 5d and just then a voice spoke from the cloud:	**9** 35a And out of the cloud a voice spoke:
d "This is my favored son,	e "This is my favored son	b "This is my son, my chosen one.
e listen to him!"	f of whom I fully approve.	
	g Listen to him!"	c Listen to him!"
	6a And as the disciples listened,	
	b they prostrated themselves,	
	c and were frightened out of their wits.	
	7a And Jesus came	
	b and touched them and said:	
	c "Get up;	
	d don't be afraid."	
		36a When the voice had spoken,
8a Suddenly, as they looked around,	8a Looking up	
b they saw no one,	b they saw no one	b Jesus was perceived to be alone.
c but were alone with Jesus.	c except Jesus by himself.	c And they were speechless
		d and told no one back then anything of what they had seen.

K44.2: Elijah Must Come

Mark 9:9–13	**Matt 17:9–13**	**Luke**
9 9a And as they were walking down the mountain	**17** 9a And as they came down from the mountain,	
b he instructed them	b Jesus ordered them:	
c not to describe what they had seen to anyone,	c "Don't tell anyone about this vision	
d until the son of Adam rise from the dead.	d until the son of Adam has been raised from the dead."	
10a And they kept it to themselves,		
b puzzling over what this could mean, this 'rising from the dead.'		
11a And they started questioning him:	10a And the disciples questioned him:	
b "The scholars claim,	b "Why, in the light of this, do the scholars claim	
c don't they,		
d that Elijah must come first?"	c that Elijah must come first?"	
12a He would respond to them,	11a In response he said,	
b "Of course Elijah comes first	b "Elijah does indeed come	
c to restore everything.	c and will restore everything.	
d So, how does scripture claim that the son of Adam will suffer greatly	12e So the son of Adam is also going to suffer at their hands."	
e and be the object of scorn?		
13a On the other hand, I tell you	a But I tell you	
b that Elijah in fact has come,	b that Elijah has already come,	
	c and they did not recognize him	
c and they had their way with him,	d but had their way with him.	
d just as the scriptures indicate."		
	13a Then the disciples understood	
	b that he had been talking to them about John the Baptist.	

☆ **Mark 1:10–11** ◊ Mark 9:7

[10]And just as he got up out of the water, he saw the skies torn open and the spirit coming down toward him like a dove. [11]There was also a voice from the skies: "You are my favored son—I fully approve of you."

☆ **Matt 3:16–17** ◊ Mark 9:7

[16]After Jesus had been baptized, he got right up out of the water, and—amazingly—the skies opened up, he saw God's spirit coming down on him like a dove, perching on him, [17]and—listen!—there was a voice from the skies, which said, "This is my favored son—I fully approve of him!"

☆ **Luke 3:22** ◊ Mark 9:7

[22]and the holy spirit came down on him in bodily form like a dove, and a voice came from the sky, "You are my son; today I have become your father."

Ps 2:7 (LXX) ◊ Mark 9:7

[7]I will tell of the decree of the Lord: He said to me, "You are my son, today have I conceived you."

Isa 42:1 (LXX) ◊ Mark 9:7

[1]Here is my servant, whom I uphold,
    my chosen, in whom my soul delights;
I have put my spirit on him,
    he will produce justice for the nations.

K44.2: Elijah Must Come

☆ **Thom 51:1–2** ◊ Mark 9:13

[1]His disciples said to him, "When will the rest for the dead take place, and when will the new world come?"
[2]He said to them, "What you are looking forward to has come, but you don't know it."

Mal 4:5–6 (LXX) ◊ Mark 9:11–12

[5]"Look out! I am sending you Elijah the Tishbite before that great and remarkable day of the Lord comes. [6]He will redirect the heart of the father towards the son and the hearts of everyone towards their neighbor, so I won't have to come and give the earth a devastating blow."

1 Kgs 19:1–3, 9–10 (LXX) ◊ Mark 9:13

[1]And Ahab reported to Jezebel, his wife, everything Elijah had done—how he had killed the prophets with a sword. [2]Then Jezebel sent word to Elijah and said, "If you are Elijah and I am Jezebel, may God do the same thing to me and then some, unless by this time tomorrow I take your life just like the life of one of them." [3]And Elijah was afraid, so he got up and ran for his life. He came to Beersheba, in Judah, and left his servant there. . . . [9]And he found a cave there and took up residence in it.
    And then the word of the Lord ⟨came⟩ to him: "What are you doing here, Elijah?" [10]And Elijah replied, "I have been extremely zealous for the Lord God Almighty because the people of Israel have forsaken you, have razed your altars, and have put the prophets to the sword. I alone am left of them, and they now seek to take my life."

K45: The Man with the Mute Spirit

Mark 9:14–29	**Matt 17:14–20**	**Luke 9:37–43**
		9 37a On the following day, 　b when they came down from the mountain, 　c a huge crowd happened to meet him.
9 14a When they rejoined the disciples, 　b they saw a huge crowd surrounding them 　c and scholars arguing with them. 15a And all of a sudden, when the whole crowd caught sight of him, 　b they were alarmed 　c and rushed up to meet him. 16a He asked them, 　b "Why are you bothering to argue with them?"	**17**14a And when they rejoined the crowd,	
	b a person approached 　c and knelt before him	
17a And one person from the crowd answered him, 　b "Teacher, I brought my son to you, 　c because he has a mute spirit.	15a and said, 　b "Master, have mercy on my son, 　c because he is epileptic 　d and suffers great ⟨pain⟩. 　e For instance, he often falls into the fire 　f and just as often into the water.	38a Suddenly a man from the crowd shouted, 　b "Teacher, I beg you to take a look at my son, 　c for he is my only child.
18a Whenever it takes him over, 　b it knocks him down, 　c and he foams at the mouth 　d and grinds his teeth 　e and stiffens up.		39a Without warning a spirit gets hold of him, 　b and all of a sudden he screams; 　c it throws him into convulsions, 　d causing him to foam at the mouth; 　e and it leaves him 　f only after abusing him.
f I asked your disciples to drive it out, 　g but they couldn't." 19a In response he says, 　b "You distrustful lot, 　c how long must I associate with you? 　d How long must I put up with you? 　e Bring him over to me!" 20a And they brought him over to him. 　b And when the spirit noticed him,	16a So I brought him to your disciples 　b but they couldn't heal him." 17a In response Jesus said, 　b "You distrustful and perverted lot, 　c how long must I associate with you? 　d How long must I put up with you? 　e Bring him here to me!"	40a I begged your disciples to drive it out, 　b but they couldn't." 41a In response Jesus said, 　b "You distrustful and perverted lot, 　c how long must I associate with you 　d and put up with you? 　e Bring your son here."
c right away it threw him into convulsions, 　d and he fell to the ground, 　e and kept rolling around, 　f foaming at the mouth.		42a But as the boy approached, 　b the demon knocked him down 　c and threw him into convulsions.

Mark	Matt	Luke
9 21a And ⟨Jesus⟩ asked his father,		
b "How long has he been like this?"		
c He replied,		
d "Ever since he was a child.		
22a Frequently it has thrown him into fire	**17**15e For instance, he often falls into the fire	
b and into water to destroy him.	f and just as often into the water.	
c So if you can do anything,		
d take pity on us		
e and help us!"		
23a Jesus said to him,		
b "What do you mean, 'If you can'?		
c All things are possible for the one who trusts."		
24a Right away the father of the child cried out		
b and said,		
c "I do trust!		
d Help my lack of trust!"		
25a When Jesus saw that the crowd was about to mob them,		
b he rebuked the unclean spirit,	18a And Jesus rebuked him	**9** 42d Jesus rebuked the unclean spirit,
c and commands it,		
d "Deaf and mute spirit,		
e I command you,		
f get out of him		
g and don't ever go back inside him!"		
26a And after he shrieked		
b and went into a series of convulsions,		
c it came out.	b and the demon came out of him	
d And he took on the appearance of a corpse,		
e so that the rumor went around that he had died.		
27a But Jesus took hold of his hand		
b and raised him,		
c and there he stood.		
	c and the child was healed at that precise moment.	e healed the boy,
		f and gave him back to his father.
		43a And everybody was astounded at the majesty of God.
28a And when he had gone home,	19a Later the disciples came to Jesus privately	
b his disciples started questioning him privately:	b and asked,	
c "Why couldn't we drive it out?"	c "Why couldn't we drive it out?"	
29a He said to them,	20a So he says to them,	
b "The only thing that can drive this kind out is prayer."		

9:21a Greek: *he.*
9:29b Some mss add: *and fasting.*

Mark	**Matt**	**Luke**

	17 20b "Because of your lack of trust.	
	c I swear to you,	
	d even if you have trust no larger than a mustard seed,	
	e you will say to this mountain,	
	f 'Move from here to there,'	
	g and it will move.	
	h And nothing will be beyond you."	

K46: Son of Adam Will Die and Rise

Mark 9:30–32	**Matt 17:22–23**	**Luke 9:43–45**
9 30a They left there		
b and started going through Galilee,	**17** 22a And when they had been reunited in Galilee,	
		9 43b While they all were marveling at everything he was doing,
c and he did not want anyone to know.		
31a Remember, he was instructing his disciples		
b and telling them:	b Jesus said to them,	c he said to his disciples,
		44a "Mark well these words:
c "The son of Adam is being turned over to his enemies,	c "The son of Adam is about to be turned over to his enemies,	b the son of Adam is about to be turned over to his enemies."
d and they will end up killing him.	23a and they will end up killing him,	
e And three days after he is killed	b and on the third day he'll be raised."	
f he will rise!"		
32a But they never understood this remark,		45a But they never understood this remark.
		b It was couched in veiled language,
		c so they would not get its meaning.
b and always dreaded to ask him ⟨about it⟩.		d And they always dreaded to ask him about this remark.
	c And they were very sad.	

K47: Number One Is Last

Mark 9:33–37	**Matt 18:1–5**	**Luke 9:46–48**
9 33a And they came to Capernaum.		
b When he got home,		
c he started questioning them,		
d "What were you arguing about on the road?"		
34a They fell completely silent,		
	18 1a At that moment	
	b the disciples approached Jesus	
	c with the question:	
		9 46a Now an argument broke out among them
b because on the road they had been bickering		b over which of them was greatest.
c about who was greatest.	d "Who is greatest in Heaven's domain?"	

K46: Son of Adam Will Die and Rise

Mark 8:31–33

[31]He started teaching them that the son of Adam was destined to suffer a great deal, and be rejected by the elders and the ranking priests and the scholars, and be killed, and after three days rise. [32]And he would say this openly. And Peter took him aside and began to lecture him. [33]But he turned, noticed his disciples, and reprimanded Peter verbally: "Get out of my sight, you Satan, you, because you're not thinking in God's terms, but in human terms."

Mark 10:32–34

[32]On the road going up to Jerusalem, Jesus was leading the way, they were apprehensive, and others who were following were frightened. Once again he took the twelve aside and started telling them what was going to happen to him:
[33]"Listen, we're going up to Jerusalem, and the son of Adam will be turned over to the ranking priests and the scholars, and they will sentence him to death, and turn him over to foreigners, [34]and they will make fun of him, and spit on him, and flog him, and put ⟨him⟩ to death. Yet after three days he will rise!"

Matt 16:21–23

[21]From that time on Jesus started to make it clear to his disciples that he was destined to go to Jerusalem, and suffer a great deal at the hands of the elders and ranking priests and scholars, and be killed and, on the third day, be raised.
[22]And Peter took him aside and began to lecture him, saying, "May God spare you, master; this surely can't happen to you."
[23]But he turned and said to Peter, "Get out of my sight, you Satan, you. You are dangerous to me because you are not thinking in God's terms, but in human terms."

Matt 20:17–19

[17]On the way up to Jerusalem Jesus took the twelve aside privately and said to them as they walked along: [18]"Listen, we're going up to Jerusalem, and the son of Adam will be turned over to the ranking priests and scholars, and they will sentence him to death, [19]and turn him over to foreigners to make fun of, and flog, and crucify. Yet on the third day he will be raised."

John 7:1 ◊ Mark 9:30

[1]After this, Jesus moved around in Galilee; he decided not to go into Judea, because the Judeans were looking for a chance to kill him.

Luke 9:18–22

[18]And on one occasion when Jesus was praying alone the disciples were with him; and he questioned them: "What are the crowds saying about me?"
[19]They said in response, "⟨Some say, 'You are⟩ John the Baptist,' while others, 'Elijah,' and still others, 'One of the ancient prophets has come back to life.'"
[20]Then he said to them, "What about you, who do you say I am?"
And Peter responded, "God's Anointed!"
[21]Then he warned them, and forbade them to tell this to anyone, [22]adding, "The son of Adam is destined to suffer a great deal, be rejected by the elders and ranking priests and scholars, and be killed and, on the third day, be raised."

Luke 18:31–34

[31]⟨Jesus⟩ took the twelve aside and instructed them: "Listen, we're going up to Jerusalem, and everything written by the prophets about the son of Adam will come true. [32]For he will be turned over to the foreigners, and will be made fun of and insulted. They will spit on him, [33]and flog him, and put him to death. Yet after three days he will rise." [34]But they did not understand any of this; this remark was obscure to them, and they never did figure out what it meant.

K47: Number One Is Last

✩ Thom 12:1–2 ◊ Mark 9:34

[1]The disciples said to Jesus, "We know that you are going to leave us. Who will be our leader?"
[2]Jesus said to them, "No matter where you are, you are to go to James the Just, for whose sake heaven and earth came into being."

Mark	Matt	Luke
9 35a He sat down b and called the twelve c and says to them: d "If any of you wants to be 'number one,' e you have to be last of all f and servant of all!"		
		9 47a But Jesus, knowing what was on their minds, b took a child c and had her stand next to him.
36a And he took a child b and had her stand in front of them, c and he put his arm around her, d and he said to them,	**18** 2a And he called a child over, b had her stand in front of them, 3a and said, b "I swear to you, c if you don't do an about-face d and become like children, e you'll never enter Heaven's domain. 4a Therefore those who put themselves on a level with this child b are greatest in Heaven's domain.	48a He said to them,
37a "Whoever accepts a child like this in my name b is accepting me. c And whoever accepts me d is not so much accepting me e as the one who sent me."	5a And whoever accepts one such child in my name b is accepting me."	b "Whoever accepts this child in my name c is accepting me. d And whoever accepts me e accepts the one who sent me. f Don't forget, the one who has a lower rank among you g is the one who is great."

K48: For and Against

Mark 9:38–41	**Matt 12:30, 10:42**	**Luke 9:49–50**
9 38a John said to him, b "Teacher, we saw someone driving out demons in your name, c so we tried to stop him, d because he wasn't one of our adherents." 39a Jesus responded, b "Don't stop him! c After all, no one who performs a miracle in my name d will turn around the next moment and curse me. 40 In fact, whoever is not against us is on our side.		**9** 49a John said in response, b "Master, we saw someone driving out demons in your name, c and we tried to stop him, d because he isn't one of us." 50a But he said to him, b "Don't stop him;
	12 30a "The one who isn't with me is against me, b and the one who doesn't gather with me scatters."	c in fact, whoever is not against you is on your side."

• **Mark 10:41–45** ◊ Mark 9:35

⁴¹When they learned of it, the ten got annoyed with James and John. ⁴²So, calling them aside, Jesus says to them: "You know how those who supposedly rule over foreigners lord it over them, and how their strong men tyrannize them. ⁴³It's not going to be like that with you! With you, whoever wants to become great must be your servant, ⁴⁴and whoever among you wants to be 'number one' must be everybody's slave. ⁴⁵After all, the son of Adam didn't come to be served, but to serve, even to give his life as a ransom for many."

△ **Matt 20:24–28** ◊ Mark 9:35

²⁴And when they learned of it, the ten became annoyed with the two brothers. ²⁵And calling them aside, Jesus said, "You know how foreign rulers lord it over their subjects, and how their strong men tyrannize them. ²⁶It's not going to be like that with you! With you, whoever wants to become great will be your slave, ²⁷and whoever among you wants to be 'number one' is to be your slave. ²⁸After all, the son of Adam didn't come to be served but to serve, even to give his life as a ransom for many."

☆ **Matt 23:11–12** ◊ Mark 9:35

¹¹"Now whoever is greater than you will be your slave. ¹²Those who promote themselves will be demoted and those who demote themselves will be promoted."

△ **Luke 22:24–30** ◊ Mark 9:35

²⁴Then a feud broke out among them over which of them should be considered the greatest. ²⁵He said to them, "Among the foreigners, it's the kings who lord it over everyone, and those in power are addressed as 'benefactors.' ²⁶But not so with you; rather, the greatest among you must behave as a beginner, and the leader as one who serves. ²⁷Who is the greater, after all: the one reclining at a banquet or the one doing the serving? Isn't it the one who reclines? Among you I am the one doing the serving.

²⁸"You are the ones who have stuck by me in my ordeals. ²⁹And I confer on you the right to rule, just as surely as my Father conferred that right on me, ³⁰so you may eat and drink at my table in my domain, and be seated on thrones and sit in judgment on the twelve tribes of Israel."

• **Mark 10:13–16** ◊ Mark 9:36–37

¹³And they would bring children to him so he could lay hands on them, but the disciples scolded them. ¹⁴Then Jesus grew indignant when he saw this and said to them: "Let the children come to me, don't try to stop them. After all, God's domain belongs to people like that. ¹⁵I swear to you, whoever doesn't accept God's imperial rule the way a child would, certainly won't ever set foot in ⟨his domain⟩!" ¹⁶And he would put his arms around them and bless them, and lay his hands on them.

Luke 18:15–17 ◊ Mark 9:36–37

¹⁵They would even bring him their babies so he could lay hands on them. But when the disciples noticed it, they scolded them. ¹⁶Jesus called for the infants and said, "Let the children come up to me, and don't try to stop them. After all, God's domain belongs to people like that.

¹⁷"I swear to you, whoever doesn't accept God's imperial rule the way a child would, certainly won't ever set foot in ⟨his domain⟩!"

☆ **John 12:44–45** ◊ Mark 9:37

⁴⁴Then Jesus proclaimed aloud: "Those who believe in me do not believe only in me, but in the one who sent me. ⁴⁵And those who see me see the one who sent me."

• **Matt 10:40** ◊ Mark 9:37

⁴⁰"The one who accepts you accepts me, and the one who accepts me accepts the one who sent me."

John 13:20 ◊ Mark 9:37

²⁰"I swear to God, if they welcome the person I send, they welcome me; and if they welcome me, they welcome the one who sent me."

• **Luke 10:16** ◊ Mark 9:37

¹⁶"Whoever hears you hears me, and whoever rejects you rejects me, and whoever rejects me rejects the one who sent me."

• **Luke 11:23** ◊ Mark 9:40

²³"The one who isn't with me is against me, and the one who doesn't gather with me scatters."

K48: For and Against

POxy1224 6:1–2 ◊ Mark 9:40

¹[A]nd p[r]ay for your [ene]mies. For the one who is not [against y]ou is on your side. ²[The one who today i]s at a distance, tomorrow will [b]e [near you,] and in [. . .] of the advers[ary]

Mark	**Matt**	**Luke**
9 41 a By the same token, whoever gives you a cup of water to drink	**10** 42 a "And whoever gives so much as a cup of cool water to one of these little ones,	
b because you carry the name of the Anointed,	b because the little one is a follower of mine,	
c I swear to you,	c I swear to you,	
d such a person certainly won't go unrewarded!	d such a person certainly won't go unrewarded."	

K49: Hand, Foot and Eye

Mark 9:42–50	**Matt 18:6–10, 5:13**	**Luke 17:1–2, 14:34–35**
9 42 a "And any of you who misleads one of these little trusting souls	**18** 6 a "Any of you who misleads one of these little souls who trusts me	**17** 2 a You'd be better off
b would be better off	b would be better off	b if you had a millstone hung around your neck
c if you had a millstone hung around your neck	c to have a millstone hung around your neck	c and were dumped into the sea
d and were thrown into the sea!	d and be drowned in the deepest part of the sea!	
		d than to mislead one of these little ones.
		1 a He said to his disciples,
	7 a Damn the world for the snares it sets!	
	b Even though it's inevitable for snares to be set,	b "It's inevitable that snares will be set;
	c nevertheless, damn the person who sets such snares.	c nevertheless, damn the one who sets them!"
43 a And if your hand gets you into trouble,	8 a If your hand or your foot gets you into trouble,	
b cut it off!	b cut it off	
	c and throw it away!	
c It's better for you to enter life maimed	d It's better for you to enter life maimed or lame	
d than to wind up in Gehenna, in the unquenchable fire, with both hands!	e than to be thrown into the eternal fire with both hands and both feet.	
45 a And if your foot gets you into trouble,		
b cut it off!		
c It's better for you to enter life lame		
d than to be thrown into Gehenna with both feet!		
47 a And if your eye gets you into trouble,	9 a And if your eye gets you into trouble,	
b rip it out!	b rip it out	
	c and throw it away!	
c It's better for you to enter God's domain one-eyed	d After all, it's better for you to enter life one-eyed	
d than to be thrown into Gehenna with both eyes,	e than to be thrown into Gehenna's fire with both eyes.	

9:44 Omit v. 44: ℵ B C L W Δ Ψ *f*¹ 28 *pc*; include v. 44 (identical with v. 48)(cf. Isa 66:24): A D K X Θ Π *f*¹³ *al.*

9:46 Omit v. 46: ℵ B C L W Δ Ψ *f*¹ 28 *pc*; include v. 46 (identical with v. 48)(cf. Isa 66:24): A D K X Θ Π *f*¹³ *al.*

K49: Hand, Foot and Eye

Matt 5:29–30

5 30a "And if your right hand gets you into
        trouble,
     b cut it off
     c and throw it away!
     d For it is more to your advantage to
        lose one of your members,
     e than to have your whole body go to
        Gehenna.

   29a And if your right eye gets you into
        trouble,
     b rip it out
     c and throw it away!
     d For it is more to your advantage to
        lose one of your members,
     e than to have your whole body
        thrown into Gehenna."

Mark	**Matt**	**Luke**
	1810a See that you don't disdain one of these little ones.	
	b For I tell you,	
	c their guardian angels constantly gaze on the face of my Father in heaven."	
9 48a where the worm never dies		
b and the fire never goes out!		
49 As you know, everyone there is salted by fire.		
50a Salt is good ⟨and salty⟩	**5** 13a "You are the salt of the earth.	**14**34a "Salt is good ⟨and salty⟩.
b —if salt becomes bland,	b But if salt loses its zing,	b But if salt loses its zing,
c with what will you renew it?	c how will it be made salty?	c how will it be renewed?
d Maintain 'salt' among yourselves		
e and be at peace with one another."	d It then has no further use	35a It's no good for either earth
		b or manure.
	e than to be thrown out	c It just gets thrown away.
	f and stomped on."	
		d Anyone here with two good ears had better listen."

9:49 Some mss add: *and every sacrifice will be salted with salt* (A C K X Θ Π Ψ 28ᶜ *pm*); text: ℵ B L W Δ *f*¹ *f*¹³ 28* *pc.*

Isa 66:24 (LXX) ◊ Mark 9:48

24And they shall go out and view the limbs of the people who have rebelled against me. There the maggots never die, the fire is never extinguished, and they will be a spectacle for the whole world.

Lev 2:13 (LXX) ◊ Mark 9:49

13You are to salt every sacrificial offering with salt. You are not to withhold the salt of the covenant with your Lord from your burnt offerings. You are to offer salt to the Lord your God with every offering.

Table 7

Collections and Complexes

1. One Day at Capernaum
   Mark 1:21–39

2. A Sequence of Controversy Stories
   Mark 2:1–3:6

3. Jesus' Relatives and the Beelzebul Controversy
   Mark 3:20–35

4. Teaching in Parables
   Mark 4:1–34

5. Didactic Scenes
   Mark 4:3–20
   Mark 7:14–23
   Mark 8:11–21
   Mark 9:14–29
   Mark 10:1–12

6. Intercalations
   Mark 2:1–5b/5c–10b/10c–12
   Mark 3:1–3/4–5c/5d–6
   Mark 3:20–21/22–30/31–35
   Mark 5:1–24a/24b–34/35–43
   Mark 6:7–13/14–29/30–34
   Mark 11:12–14/15–19/20–25
   Mark 14:53–54/55–65/66–72
   Mark 15:1–15/16–20/21–32

7. Chains of Miracle Stories
1a. Mark 4:35–42	1b. Mark 6:47–52
2a. Mark 5:1–20	2b. Mark 8:22–26
3a. Mark 5:21–24a, 35–43	3b. Mark 7:24b–30
4a. Mark 5:24b–34	4b. Mark 7:31–37

1a. Mark 2:1–2	1b. John 5:1–8
2a. Mark 6:35–44	2b. John 6:1–15
3a. Mark 6:45–52	3b. John 6:16–21
4a. Mark 8:22–26	4b. John 9:1–7
5a. SecMk 1:1–10	5b. John 11:1–44

8. Death of John the Baptist
   Mark 6:14–29

9. Passion Narrative
   Mark 14:1–15:47

JOURNEY TO JERUSALEM

K50: Jesus Goes to Judea

Mark 10:1   **Matt 19:1–2**   **Luke**

19 1 a And so
  b when Jesus finished this instruction,
  c he took leave of Galilee

10 1 a And from there he gets up
  b and goes to the territory of Judea and across the Jordan,   d and went to the territory of Judea across the Jordan.
  c and once again crowds gather around him.   2 a And large crowds followed him
  d As usual,
  e he started teaching them.

        b and he healed them there.

K51.1: Is Divorce Permitted?

Mark 10:2–9   **Matt 19:3–8**   **Luke**

10 2 a And Pharisees approach him   **19** 3 a And the Pharisees approached him
  b and, to test him,   b and, to test him,
  c they ask   c they ask,
  d whether a husband is permitted to divorce his wife.   d "Is ⟨a husband⟩ permitted to divorce his wife
                    e for any reason?

  3 a In response he puts a question to them: 4 a In response he puts a question to them:
  b "What did Moses command you?"
  4 a They replied,   *cf. Matt 19:7b*
  b "Moses allowed one to prepare a written decree
  c and thus to divorce the other party."
  5 a Jesus said to them,
  b "He gave you this injunction because you are obstinate.   *cf. Matt 19:8b*

  6 a However, in the beginning, at the creation,   b "Have you not read
  b 'God made them male and female.'   c that in the beginning

        d the Creator 'made them male and female,'
        5 a and that further on it says,

10:1b Omit: C²D W △ Θ f¹ f¹³ *al.*
10:2a Omit: D it.
10:6b Omit: D W *pc* it.

K51.1: Is Divorce Permitted?

Matt 5:31

Deut 24:1–4 (LXX) ◊ Mark 10:4

[1]If anyone takes a wife and lives with her, and if she does not meet with his approval because he has found some disgrace in her, he will prepare a writ of abandonment and give it to her and then send her out of his house. [2]And if she goes out and becomes another man's wife, [3]and that man comes to despise her, and he gives her a writ of abandonment and gives it to her and sends her out of his house; or, if the second husband dies, [4]the first man, who divorced her, cannot again take her as his wife after she has been defiled, for that would be an abomination to the Lord your God. Do not defile the earth, which the Lord your God gives you as an inheritance.

☆ **1 Cor 7:10–11** ◊ Mark 10:6

[10]To the married I give charge, not I but the Lord, that the wife should not separate from her husband [11](but if she does, let her remain single or else be reconciled to her husband)—and that the husband should not divorce his wife.

Gen 1:27 (LXX) ◊ Mark 10:6

[27]And God created human beings. God created them in accordance with his own image. God created both male and female.

5 31 a "We once were told,
   c should give her a written decree.'

   b 'Whoever divorces his wife,

Mark	Matt	Luke

10 7a 'For this reason, a man will leave his father and mother
  b and be united with his wife,
 8a and the two will become one body,'
  b so they are no longer two individuals but 'one body.'
 9a Therefore those God has coupled together,
  b no one else should separate."

19 5b 'for this reason, a man will leave his father and mother
  c and be united with his wife,
 6a and the two will be one body?'
  b Consequently, from then on they are one body instead of two.
  c Therefore those whom God has coupled together,
  d no one else should separate."
 7a They say to him,
  b "Then why did Moses order 'a written decree of dissolution?'"
 8a He says to them,
  b "Because you are obstinate Moses permitted you to divorce your wives,
  c but it wasn't like that originally.

K51.2: The Disciples Question Jesus

Mark 10:10–12	Matt 19:9	Luke 16:18

10 10a And once again, as usual,
  b when they got home,
  c the disciples questioned him about this.
 11a And he says to them,
  b "Whoever divorces his wife

  c and marries another
  d commits adultery against her;
 12a and if she divorces her husband
  b and marries another,
  c she commits adultery."

19 9a Now I say to you,
  b whoever divorces his wife,
  c except for infidelity,
  d and marries another
  e commits adultery."

16 18a "Everyone who divorces his wife

  b and marries another
  c commits adultery;

  d and the one who marries a woman
  e divorced from her husband
  f commits adultery."

K52: Let the Children Come

Mark 10:13–16	Matt 19:13–15	Luke 18:15–17

10 13a And they would bring children to him
  b so he could lay hands on them,

  c but the disciples scolded them.

19 13a Then little children were brought to him
  b so he could lay his hands on them
  c and pray,
  d but the disciples scolded them.

18 15a They would even bring their babies to him
  b so he could lay hands on them.

  c But when the disciples noticed it,
  d they scolded them.

10:7b Probably a harmonizing addition inspired by Matt 19:5; omit: A B 892 *pc.*

Gen 2:24 (LXX) ◊ Mark 10:7–8a

²⁴For this reason a man will leave his father and mother and be united with his wife, and the two will become one person.

K51.2: The Disciples Question Jesus

Matt 5:32

5 32a But I say to you,
    b everyone who divorces his wife,
    c except for a matter of infidelity,

    d makes her the victim of adultery;
    e and whoever marries a divorced
      woman
    f commits adultery.”

K52: Let the Children Come

inner, and the upper like the lower, ⁵and when you make male and female into a single one, so that the male will not be male nor the female be female, ⁶when you make eyes in place of an eye, a hand in place of a hand, a foot in place of a foot, an image in place of an image, ⁷then you will enter [the ⟨Father's⟩ domain].”

Mark	Matt	Luke

1014a Then Jesus grew indignant
   b when he saw this

   c and said to them:

   d "Let the children come up to me,
   e don't try to stop them.
   f After all, God's domain belongs to people like that.
 15a I swear to you,
   b whoever doesn't accept God's imperial rule the way a child would,
   c certainly won't ever set foot in ⟨his domain⟩!"
 16a And he would put his arms around them
   b and bless them,
   c and lay his hands on them.

1914a Now Jesus said,
   b "Let the children alone.
   d from coming up to me.
   c Don't try to stop them
   e After all, Heaven's domain belongs to people like that."

 15a And he laid his hands on them
   b and left that place.

1816a Jesus called for the infants
   b and said,

   c "Let the children come up to me,
   d and don't try to stop them.
   e After all, God's domain belongs to people like that.
 17a I swear to you,
   b whoever doesn't accept God's imperial rule the way a child would,
   c certainly won't ever seet foot in ⟨his domain⟩!"

K53.1: The Man with Money

Mark 10:17–22	Matt 19:16–22	Luke 18:18–23

1017a As he was traveling along the road,
   b someone ran up,
   c knelt before him,
   d and started questioning him:

   e "Good teacher, what do I have to do to inherit eternal life?"
 18a Jesus said to him,
   b "Why do you call me good?
   c No one is good except for God alone.

 19a You know the commandments:

   b 'You must not murder,
   c you are not to commit adultery,
   d you are not to steal,
   e you are not to give false testimony,

   f you are not to defraud,
   g and you are to honor your father and mother.'"

 20a He said to him,
   b "Teacher, I have observed all these things since I was a child!"

1916a And just then someone came

   b and asked him,
   c "Teacher, what good do I have to do to have eternal life?"
 17a He said to him,
   b "Why do you ask me about the good?
   c There is only One who is good.
   d If you want to enter life,
   e observe the commandments."
 18a He says to him,
   b "Which ones?"
   c Jesus replied,
   d "You must not murder,
   e you are not to commit adultery,
   f you are not to steal,
   g you are not to give false testimony,

 19a you are to honor your father and mother,
   b and you are to love your neighbor as yourself."
 20a The young man says to him,
   b "I have observed all these;

   c what am I missing?"

1818a Someone from the ruling class asked him,
   b "Good teacher, what do I have to do to inherit eternal life?"
 19a Jesus said to him,
   b "Why do you call me good?
   c No one is good except for God alone.

 20a You know the commandments:

   c you must not murder,
   b 'You are not to commit adultery;
   d or steal,
   e and you are not to give false testimony;

   f you are to honor your father and mother.'"

 21a And he said,
   b "I have observed all these since I was a child."

☆ **Matt 18:3** ◊ Mark 10:15

[3]. . . and said, "I swear to you, if you don't do an about-face and become like children, you'll never enter Heaven's domain."

☆ **John 3:3–5** ◊ Mark 10:15

[3]Jesus replied to him, "As God is my witness: No one can experience God's imperial rule without being reborn from above."

[4]Nicodemus says to him, "How can an adult be reborn? Can you reenter your mother's womb and be born a second time?"

[5]Jesus replied, "As God is my witness: no one can enter God's domain without being born of water and spirit."

K53.1: The Man with Money

GNaz 6 ◊ Mark 10:17–22

It is written in a certain gospel called the "Gospel of the Hebrews" —if anyone will accet it, not as authoritative, but to shed light on the question at hand:

[1]The second rich man said to him, 'Teacher, what good do I have to live?'

[2]He said to him, 'Mister, follow the Law and the Prophets.'

He answered, 'I've done that.'

He said to him, 'Go sell everything you own and give it away to the poor and then come follow me.'

[3]But the rich man didn't want to hear this and began to scratch his head. And the Lord said to him, 'How can you say that you follow the Law and the Prophets? In the Law it says: "Love your neighbor as yourself." [4]Look around you: many of your brothers and sisters, sons and daughters of Abraham, are living in filth and dying of hunger. Your house is full of good things and not a thing of yours manages to get out to them.' [5]Turning to his disciple Simon who was sitting with him, he said, 'Simon, son of Jonah, it's easier for a camel to squeeze through a needle's eye than for a wealthy person to get into heaven's domain.'"

(Ps.) Origen, *In Matteum* 15.14

Exod 20:12–16 (LXX) ◊ Mark 10:19

[12]Honor your father and mother so things will go well for you and so you will have a long life on the good land that the Lord your God gives you.

[13]Do not commit adultery.

[14]Do not steal.

[15]Do not kill.

[16]Do not give false testimony against your neighbor.

Deut 5:16–20 (LXX) ◊ Mark 10:19

[16]Honor your father and mother as the Lord your God commanded you, so things may go well with you and so you may have a long life on the land the Lord your God gives you.

[17]Do not commit adultery.

[18]Do not kill.

[19]Do not steal.

[20]Do not give false testimony against your neighbor.

Mark	**Matt**	**Luke**
10 21 a Jesus loved him		18 22 a When Jesus heard this,
b at first sight		
c and said to him,	19 21 a Jesus said to him,	b he said to him,
d "You are missing one thing:		c "You are still short one thing.
	b "If you wish to be perfect,	
e make your move,	c make your move,	
f sell whatever you have	d sell your belongings	d Sell everything you have
g and give ⟨the proceeds⟩ to the poor,	e and give ⟨the proceeds⟩ to the poor	e and distribute ⟨the proceeds⟩ among the poor,
h and you will have treasure in heaven.	f and you will have treasure in heaven.	f and you will have treasure in heaven.
i And then come,	g And then come,	g And then come,
j follow me!"	h follow me!"	h follow me!"
22 a But stunned by this advice,	22 a When the young man heard this advice,	23 a But when he heard this,
b he went away dejected,	b he went away dejected	b he became very sad,
c since he possessed a fortune.	c since he possessed a fortune.	c for he was extremely rich.

K53.2: The Needle's Eye

Mark 10:23–31	**Matt 19:23–30**	**Luke 18:24–30**
10 23 a After looking around,		18 24 a When Jesus observed
		b that he had become very sad,
b Jesus says to his disciples,	19 23 a Jesus said to his disciples,	c he said,
	b "I swear to you,	
c "How difficult it is for those who have money to enter God's domain!"	c it's very difficult for the rich to enter Heaven's domain.	d "How difficult it is for those with real money to enter God's domain!
24 a The disciples were amazed at his words.		
b In response Jesus repeats what he had said,		
c "Children, how difficult it is to enter God's domain!		
25 a It's easier for a camel to squeeze through a needle's eye,	24 a And again I tell you,	25 a It's easier for a camel to squeeze through a needle's eye,
b than for a wealthy person to get into God's domain!"	b it's easier for a camel to squeeze through a needle's eye,	b than for a wealthy person to get into God's domain."
	c than for a wealthy person to get into God's domain."	
	25 a When the disciples heard this,	
26 a And they were very perplexed,	b they were quite perplexed	26 a Those who heard this spoke up:
b wondering to themselves,	c and said,	b "Well then, who can be saved?"
c "Well then, who can be saved?"	d "Well then, who can be saved?"	
27 a Jesus looks them in the eye,	26 a Jesus looked them in the eye,	27 a But he said,
b and says,	b and said to them,	b "What's humanly impossible
c "For mortals it's impossible,	c "For mortals this is impossible;	
d but not for God;		c is perfectly possible for God."
e after all, everything's possible for God."	d for God everything's possible."	

K53.2: The Needle's Eye

✩ **Thom 81:1–2** ◊ Mark 10:23

[1]Jesus said, "The one who has become wealthy should reign, [2]and the one who has power should renounce ⟨it⟩."

Mark	Matt	Luke
1028a Peter started lecturing him:	**19**27a In response Peter said to him,	**18**28a Then Peter said,
b "Look at us, we left everything	b "Look at us, we left everything	b "Look at us! We have left what we had
c to follow you!"	c to follow you!	c to follow you!"
	d What do we get out of it?"	
29a Jesus said,	28a Jesus told them,	29a And he told them,
b "I swear to you,	b "I swear to you,	b "I swear to you,
	c you who have followed me,	
	d when the son of Adam is seated on his throne of glory in the renewal ⟨of creation⟩,	
	e you also will be seated on twelve thrones	
	f and sit in judgment on the twelve tribes of Israel.	
c there is no one who has left home,	29a And everyone who has left homes	c there is no one who has left home,
		d or wife,
d or brothers,	b or brothers	e or brothers,
e or sisters,	c or sisters	
f or mother,	**e** or mother	f or parents,
g or father,	d or father	
h or children,	f or children	g or children,
i or farms	g or farms,	
j on my account	h on my account,	
k and on account of the good news,		h for the sake of God's imperial rule,
30a who won't receive a hundred times as much now,	i will receive a hundred times as much	30a who won't receive many times as much
b in the present time,		b in the present age,
c homes,		
d and brothers,		
e and sisters,		
f and mothers,		
g and children,		
h and farms		
i —including persecutions—		
j and in the age to come, eternal life.	j and inherit eternal life.	c and in the age to come, eternal life."
31a Many of the first will be last,	30a Many of the first will be last,	
b and of the last many will be first."	b and of the last many will be first."	

☆ **SecJas 4:1–3** ◊ Mark 10:28–30

¹And I responded, "Lord, we can obey you if you wish, for we have forsaken our fathers and our mothers and our villages and have followed you. ²Give us the means, [then], not to be tempted by the evil devil."

³The Lord replied, "If you do the Father's will, what credit is that to you—unless he gives you, as part of his gift, your being tempted by Satan?"

Matt 20:16 ◊ Mark 10:31

16a "The last will be first ◊ 10:31a
   b and the first last." ◊ 10:31b

POxy654 4:2–3 ◊ Mark 10:31

2   "For many of the [first] will be [last, and] the last first, ◊ 10:31a
³and [will become one]."

Luke 13:30 ◊ Mark 10:31

³⁰"And remember,
   30b Those who will be first are last,
      ◊ 10:31a
      c and those who will be last are first."
         ◊ 10:31b

Thom 4:2–3 ◊ Mark 10:31

2   "For many of the first will be last,
      ◊ 10:31a
³and will become a single one."

Table 8

Narrator Asides

The author of Mark frequently explains matters to the listener (reader) by filling in missing narrative information or by supplying knowledge the readers do not necessarily possess. These asides are marked in Greek by the word γάρ (literally, *for*). In the Scholars Version these asides are often, but not always, put in parentheses.

1. 2:15c–d	12. 6:52
2. 3:10	13. 7:3–4
3. 3:21c	14. 9:6
4. 5:8	15. 9:31–32
5. 5:28	16. 9:49
6. 5:42	17. 11:13h
7. 6:14b	18. 11:18c–d
8. 6:17	19. 11:32c
9. 6:18	20. 12:23b
10. 6:20	21. 14:2
11. 6:31d–e	22. 16:4c

ON THE ROAD TO JERUSALEM

K54: Son of Adam Will Die and Rise

Mark 10:32–34	Matt 20:17–19	Luke 18:31–34
10 32 a On the road going up to Jerusalem,	20 17 a On the way up to Jerusalem	
b Jesus was leading the way,		
c they were apprehensive,		
d and others who were following were frightened.		
e Once again he took the twelve aside	b Jesus took the twelve aside privately	18 31 a ⟨Jesus⟩ took the twelve aside
f and started telling them	c and said to them as they walked along:	b and instructed them:
g what was going to happen to him:		
33 a "Listen, we're going up to Jerusalem,	18 a "Listen, we're going up to Jerusalem,	c "Listen, we're going up to Jerusalem,
		d and everything written by the prophets about the son of Adam will come true.
b and the son of Adam will be turned over to the ranking priests and the scholars,	b and the son of Adam will be turned over to the ranking priests and scholars,	
c and they will sentence him to death,	c and they will sentence him to death,	
d and turn him over to the foreigners,	19 a and turn him over to foreigners	32 a For he will be turned over to the foreigners,
34 a and they will make fun of him,	b to make fun of,	b and will be made fun of
		c and insulted.
		d They will spit on him,
b and spit on him,		
c and flog him,	c and flog,	33 a and flog him,
d and put ⟨him⟩ to death.	d and crucify.	b and put him to death.
e Yet after three days he will rise!"	e Yet on the third day he will be raised."	c Yet after three days he will rise."
		34 a But they did not understand any of this;
		b this remark was obscure to them,
		c and they never did figure out what it meant.

K55.1: Jesus' Cup and Baptism

Mark 10:35–40	Matt 20:20–23	Luke
10 35 a Then James and John, the sons of Zebedee, come up to him,	20 20 a Then the mother of the sons of Zebedee came up to him with her sons,	
b and say to him,	b bowed down before him,	
	c and asked him for a favor.	
c "Teacher, we want you to do for us whatever we ask!"		
36 a He said to them,	21 a He said to her,	
b "What do you want me to do for you?"	b "What do you want?"	

K54: Son of Adam Will Die and Rise

Mark 8:31–33

[31]He started teaching them that the son of Adam was destined to suffer a great deal, and be rejected by the elders and the ranking priests and the scholars, and be killed, and after three days rise. [32]And he would say this openly. And Peter took him aside and began to lecture him. [33]But he turned, noticed his disciples, and reprimanded Peter verbally: "Get out of my sight, you Satan, you, because you're not thinking in God's terms, but in human terms."

Mark 9:30–32

[30]They left there and started going through Galilee, and he did not want anyone to know. [31]Remember, he was instructing his disciples and telling them: "The son of Adam is being turned over to his enemies, and they will end up killing him. And three days after he is killed he will rise!" [32]But they never understood this remark, and always dreaded to ask him ⟨about it⟩.

Matt 16:21–23

[21]From that time on Jesus started to make it clear to his disciples that he was destined to go to Jerusalem, and suffer a great deal at the hands of the elders and ranking priests and scholars, and be killed and, on the third day, be raised.

[22]And Peter took him aside and began to lecture him, saying, "May God spare you, master; this surely can't happen to you."

[23]But he turned and said to Peter, "Get out of my sight, you Satan, you. You are dangerous to me because you are not thinking in God's terms, but in human terms."

Matt 17:22–23

[22]And when they had been reunited in Galilee, Jesus said to them, "The son of Adam is about to be turned over to his enemies, [23]and they will end up killing him, and on the third day he'll be raised." And they were very sad.

Luke 9:18–22

[18]And on one occasion when Jesus was praying alone the disciples were with him; and he questioned them asking: "What are the crowds saying about me?"

[19]They said in response, "⟨Some say, 'You are⟩ John the Baptist,' while others, 'Elijah,' and still others, 'One of the ancient prophets has come back to life.'"

[20]Then he said to them, "What about you, who do you say I am?"

And Peter responded, "God's Anointed!"

[21]Then he warned them, and forbade them to tell this to anyone, [22]adding, "The son of Adam is destined to suffer a great deal, be rejected by the elders and ranking priests and scholars, and be killed and, on the third day, be raised."

Luke 9:43b–45

[43]. . . While they all were marveling at everything he was doing, he said to his disciples, [44]"Mark well these words: the son of Adam is about to be turned over to his enemies."

[45]But they never understood this remark. It was couched in veiled language, so they would never get its meaning. And they always dreaded to ask him about this remark.

SecMk 1:1–13 ◊ follows on Mark 10:34

[1]And they came to Bethany, and this woman was there whose brother had died. [2]She knelt down in front of Jesus and says to him, "Son of David, have mercy on me." [3]But the disciples rebuked her. [4]And Jesus got angry and went with her into the garden where the tomb was. [5]Just then a loud voice was heard from inside the tomb. [6]Then Jesus went up and rolled the stone away from the entrance to the tomb. [7]He went right in where the young man was, stuck out his hand, grabbed him by the hand, and raised him up. [8]The young man looked at Jesus, loved him, and began to beg him to be with him. [9]Then they left the tomb and went into the young man's house. (Incidentally, he was rich.) [10]Six days later Jesus gave him an order; [11]and when evening had come, the young man went to him, dressed only in a linen cloth. [12]He spent that night with him, because Jesus taught him the mystery of God's domain. [13]From there ⟨Jesus⟩ got up and returned to the other side of the Jordan.

K55.1: Jesus' Cup and Baptism

Mark	Matt	Luke
1037a They reply to him,	**20**21c She said to him,	
	d "Give me your word that these two sons of mine	
b "In your glory,		
c let one of us sit at your right hand,	e may sit one at your right hand	
d and the other at your left."	f and one at your left	
	g in your domain."	
38a Jesus said to them,	22a In response Jesus said,	
b "You have no idea what you're asking for.	b "You have no idea what you're asking for.	
c Can you drink the cup that I'm drinking,	c Can you drink the cup that I am about to drink?"	
d or undergo the baptism I'm undergoing?"		
39a They said to him,	d They said to him,	
b "We can!"	e "We can!"	
c Jesus said to them,	23a He says to them,	
d "The cup I'm drinking you'll be drinking,	b "You'll be drinking my cup	
e and the baptism I'm undergoing you'll be undergoing,		
40a but as for sitting at my right or my left,	c but as for sitting at my right or my left,	
b that's not mine to grant,	d that's not mine to grant,	
c but belongs to those for whom it has been reserved."	e but belongs to those for whom it's been reserved by my Father."	

K55.2: Number One Is Slave

Mark 10:41–45	Matt 20:24–28	Luke 22:24–27
1041a When they learned of it,	**20**24a And when they learned of it,	
b the ten got annoyed with James and John.	b the ten became annoyed with the two brothers.	
		2224 Then a feud broke out among them over which of them should be considered the greatest.
42a So, calling them aside,	25a And calling them aside,	25a He said to them,
b Jesus says to them:	b Jesus said,	b "Among the foreigners it's the kings
c "You know how those who supposedly rule over foreigners	c "You know how foreign rulers	c who lord it over everyone,
d lord it over them,	d lord it over their subjects,	
e and how their strong men tyrannize them.	e and how their strong men tyrannize them.	d and those in power are addressed as 'benefactors.'
43a It's not going to be like that with you!	26a It's not going to be like that with you!	26a But not so with you;
b With you, whoever wants to become great	b With you, whoever wants to become great,	b rather, the greatest among you
c must be your servant,	c will be your slave,	c must behave as a beginner,
44a and whoever among you wants to be 'number one'	27a and whoever among you wants to be 'number one'	d and the leader
b must be everybody's slave.	b is to be your slave.	e as one who serves.

☆ **Luke 12:49–53** ◊ Mark 10:38–40

⁴⁹"I came to set the earth on fire, and how I wish it were already ablaze! ⁵⁰I have a baptism to be baptized with, and what pressure I'm under until it's over! ⁵¹Do you supposed I came here to bring peace on earth? No, I tell you, on the contrary: conflict. ⁵²As a result, from now on in any given house there will be five in conflict, three against two and two against three. ⁵³Father will be pitted against son and son against father, mother against daughter and daughter against mother, mother-in-law against daughter-in-law and daughter-in-law against mother-in-law."

K55.2: Number One Is Slave

• **Mark 9:33–37** ◊ Mark 10:41–45

³³And they came to Capernaum. When he got home, he started questioning them, "What were you arguing about on the road?" ³⁴They fell completely silent, because on the road they had been bickering about who was greatest.

³⁵He sat down and called the twelve and says to them, "If any of you wants to be 'number one,' you have to be last of all and servant of all!"

³⁶And he took a child and had her stand in front of them, and he put his arm around her, and he said to them, ³⁷"Whoever accepts a child like this in my name is accepting me. And whoever accepts me is not so much accepting me as the one who sent me."

△ **Matt 18:1–4** ◊ Mark 10:41–45

¹At that moment the disciples approached Jesus with a question: "Who is greatest in Heaven's domain?"

²And he called a child over, had her stand in front of them, ³and said, "I swear to you, if you don't do an about-face and become like children, you'll never enter Heaven's domain. ⁴Therefore those who put themselves on a level with this child are greatest in Heaven's domain."

△ **Matt 23:11** ◊ Mark 10:41–45

¹¹Now whoever is greater than you will be your slave.

△ **Luke 9:46–50** ◊ Mark 10:41–45

⁴⁶Now an argument broke out among them over which of them was greatest. ⁴⁷But Jesus, knowing what was on their minds, took a child and had her stand next to him. ⁴⁸He said to them, "Whoever accepts this child in my name is accepting me. And whoever accepts me accepts the one who sent me. Don't forget, the one who has lower rank among you is the one who is great."

⁴⁹John said in response, "Master, we saw someone driving out demons in your name, and we tried to stop him, because he isn't one of us."

⁵⁰But he said to him, "Don't stop him; in fact, whoever is not against you is on your side."

Mark	Matt	Luke

Mark   **Matt**   **Luke**

Luke

22 27 a Who is the greater, after all:
     b the one reclining at a banquet
     c or the one doing the serving?
     d Isn't it the one who reclines?
     e Among you I am the one

Mark

10 45 a After all, the son of Adam didn't come to be served,
     b but to serve,
     c even to give his life as a ransom for many."

Matt

20 28 a After all, the son of Adam didn't come to be served
     b but to serve,
     c even to give his life as a ransom for many."

     f doing the serving."

K56: Jesus Cures Blind Bartimaeus

Mark 10:46–52   **Matt 20:29–34**   **Luke 18:35–43**

Mark 10:46–52

10 46 a Then they come to Jericho.

     b As he was leaving Jericho with his disciples
     c and a sizable crowd,
     d Bartimaeus, a blind beggar, the son of Timaeus, was sitting alongside the road.

47 a When he learned that it was Jesus the Nazarene,
     b he began to shout:
     c "You son of David, Jesus, have mercy on me!"
48 a And many kept yelling at him to shut up,
     b but he shouted all the louder,
     c "You son of David, have mercy on me!"
49 a Jesus paused
     b and said,
     c "Tell him to come over here!"

     d They called to the blind man,
     e "Be brave,
     f get up,
     g he's calling you!"
50 a So he threw off his cloak,
     b and jumped to his feet,
     c and went over to Jesus.

51 a In response Jesus said,
     b "What do you want me to do for you?"
     c The blind man said to him,
     d "Rabbi, I want to see again!"

Matt 20:29–34

20 29 a And as they were leaving Jericho,

     b a huge crowd followed him.
30 a There were two blind men sitting beside the road.

     b When they learned that Jesus was going by,
     c they shouted,
     d "Have mercy on us, Master, you son of David."
31 a The crowd yelled at them to shut up,

     b but they shouted all the louder,
     c "Have mercy on us, Master, you son of David."
32 a Jesus paused
     b and called out to them,

     c "What do you want me to do for you?"
33 a They said to him,
     b "Master, open our eyes!"

Luke 18:35–43

18 35 a One day as he was coming into Jericho,

     b this blind man was sitting along the roadside begging.

36 a Hearing a crowd passing through,
     b he asked what was going on.
37 a They told him,
     b "Jesus the Nazarene is going by."

38 a Then he shouted,
     b "Jesus, you son of David, have mercy on me!"
39 a Those in the lead kept yelling at him to shut up,
     b but he kept shouting all the louder,
     c "You son of David, have mercy on me!"
40 a Jesus paused

     b and ordered them to guide the man over.

     c When he came near,
     d ⟨Jesus⟩ asked him,
41 a "What do you want me to do for you?"
     b He said,
     c "Master, I want to see again."

K56: Jesus Cures Blind Bartimaeus

| ‡ Matt 9:27–31 | SecMk 2:1–2 ◊ follows on Mark 10:46a | △ John 9:1–7 |

‡ Matt 9:27–31

27And when Jesus left there, two blind men followed him,
27c crying out, ◊ 10:47b
  d "Have mercy on us, son of David."
  ◊ 10:47c
28When ⟨Jesus⟩ arrived home, the blind men came to him. Jesus says to them, "Do you trust that I can do this?"
  They reply to him, "Yes, master."
29a Then he touched their eyes, saying,
29c "Your trust will be the measure of your cure." ◊ 10:52c
30And their eyes were opened. Then Jesus scolded them, saying, "See that no one finds out about it." 31But they went out and spread the news of him throughout that whole territory.

SecMk 2:1–2 ◊ follows on Mark 10:46a

1The sister of the young man whom Jesus loved was there, along with his mother and Salome, 2but Jesus refused to see them.

△ John 9:1–7

1As he was leaving he saw a man who had been blind from birth. 2His disciples asked him, "Rabbi, was it this man's wrongdoing or his parents' that cause him to be born blind?"
3Jesus responded, "This fellow did nothing wrong, nor did his parents. Rather, ⟨he was born blind⟩ so God could display his work through him. 4We must carry out the work of the one who sent me while the light lasts. Nighttime is coming and then no one will be able to undertake any work. 5So long as I am in the world I am the light of the world."
6With that he spat on the ground, made mud with his spit and treated the man's eyes with the mud. 7Then ⟨Jesus⟩ said to him, "Go, rinse off in the pool of Siloam" (the name means "Emissary"). So he went over, rinsed ⟨his eyes⟩ off, and came back with his sight restored.

| Mark | Matt | Luke |

Mark

Matt

Luke

2034a Then Jesus took pity on them,
   b touched their eyes,

1052a And Jesus said to him,
   b "Be on your way,

   c your trust has cured you."
   d And right away he regained his sight,

   e and he started following him on the road.

1842a Jesus said to him,

   b "Then use your eyes;
   c your trust has cured you."
43a And right then and there he regained his sight,
   b and began to follow him,

   c and right away they regained their sight
   d and followed him.

   c praising God all the while. And everyone who saw it gave God the praise.

K57: Jesus Enters Jerusalem

Mark 11:1–11	**Matt 21:1–11**	**Luke 19:28–40**

Luke 19:28–40

19 28 a When he had finished the parable,
b he walked on ahead,
c on his way up to Jerusalem.
29 a And it so happened
b as he got close to Bethphage and Bethany,
c at the mountain called Olives,

Mark 11:1–11

11 1 a When they get close to Jerusalem,

b near Bethphage and Bethany at the Mount of Olives,
c he sends off two of his disciples
2 a with these instructions:
b "Go into the village across the way,
c and right after you enter it,
d you'll find a colt tied up,
e one that has never been ridden.

f Untie it
g and bring it here.
3 a If anyone questions you,
b 'Why are you doing this?'
c tell them,
d 'Its master has need of it
e and he will send it back here right away.'"

Matt 21:1–11

21 1 a When they got close to Jerusalem,

b and came to Bethphage at the Mount of Olives,
c then Jesus sent off two disciples
2 a with these instructions:
b "Go into the village across the way,
c and right away
d you will find a donkey tied up,

e and a colt alongside her.
f Untie ⟨them⟩
g and bring ⟨them⟩ to me.
3 a And if anyone says anything to you,

b you are to say,
c 'Their master has need of them
d and he will send them back right away.'"
4 a This happened
b so the word spoken through the prophet would come true:
5 a "Tell the daughter of Zion,
b Look, your king comes to you in all modesty
c and mounted on a donkey and on a colt,
d the foal of a pack animal."
6 a Then the disciples went

b and did as Jesus instructed them,

d that he sent off two of the disciples,
30 a with these instructions:
b "Go into the village across the way.
c As you enter it,
d you will find a colt tied there,
e one that has never been ridden.

f Untie it
g and bring it here.
31 a If anyone asks you,
b 'Why are you untying it?'
c Just tell them:
d 'Its master has need of it.'"

Mark 11:1–11

4 a They set out

b and found a colt tied up at the door out on the street,
c and they untie it.
5 a Some of the people standing around started saying to them,
b "What do you think you're doing,
c untying that colt?"

Luke 19:28–40

32 a So those designated went off

b and found it exactly as he had described.
33 a Just as they were untying the colt,
b its owners challenged them:

c "What are you doing
d untying that colt?"

11:3d Greek (κύριος): *master* or *owner* or *lord*.

Mark	Matt	Luke
11 6a But they said just what Jesus had told them to say, b so they left them alone. 7a So they bring the colt to Jesus, b and they throw their cloaks over it; c then he got on it.		**19** 34a So they said, b "Its master needs it."
	21 7a and brought the donkey and colt b and they placed their cloaks on them,	35a So they brought it to Jesus. b They threw their cloaks on the colt c and helped Jesus mount it. 36a And as he rode along, b people would spread their cloaks on the road.
8a And many people spread their cloaks on the road, b while others cut leafy branches from the fields.	8a The enormous crowd spread their cloaks on the road, b and others cut branches from the trees c and spread them on the road.	
		37a As he approached the slope of the Mount of Olives, b the entire throng of his disciples began to cheer c and shout praise to God for all the miracles they had seen. 38a They kept repeating,
9a Those leading the way and those following kept shouting, b "'Hosanna! c Blessed is the one d who comes in the name of the Lord!' 10a Blessed is the coming kingdom of our father David! b 'Hosanna' in the highest!" 11a And he went into Jerusalem to the temple area b and took stock of everything, c but, since the hour was already late, d he returned to Bethany with the twelve.	9a The crowds leading the way and those following kept shouting, b "'Hosanna' to the son of David! c Blessed is the one d who comes in the name of the Lord!' e 'Hosanna' in the highest." 10a And when he entered into Jerusalem b the whole city trembled, saying, c "Who is this?" 11a The crowds said, b "This is the prophet Jesus c from Nazareth, Galilee!"	b "Blessed is the king c who comes in the name of the Lord! d Peace in heaven e and glory in the highest!"
		39a But some of the Pharisees, also in the crowd, said to him, b "Teacher, restrain your followers." 40a But he responded, b "I tell you, c if these folks were to keep quiet, d these stones would break into cheers."

176

John 12:12–19

[12]The next day the huge crowd that had come for the celebration heard that Jesus was coming into Jerusalem. [13]They got palm fronds and went out to meet him. They began to shout,

13d "Hosanna! ◊ 11:9b
  e Blessed is the one who comes in the name of the Lord! ◊ 11:9c–d
  f ⟨Blessed is⟩ the King of Israel!"
  ◊ 11:10a

[14]Then Jesus found a young donkey and rode on it, as scripture puts it,

[15]"Calm your fears, daughter of Zion.
Look, your king comes
riding on a donkey's colt!"

([16]His disciples didn't understand these matters at the time, but when Jesus had been glorified, they then recalled that what had happened to him matched the things written about him.)

[17]The people who were with ⟨Jesus⟩ when he had summoned Lazarus from his tomb and brought him back from the dead kept repeating ⟨this story⟩. ([18]That's why the crowd went out to meet him: they heard that he had performed this miracle.)

[19]So the Pharisees remarked under their breath, "You see, you can't win; look, the world has gone over to him."

Zech 9:9 (LXX) ◊ Mark 11:2, 7, 8

[9]Rejoice with all your heart, daughter of Zion!
Shout out, daughter of Jerusalem!
Look, your King comes to you in innocence and as a savior,
humble and mounted on a beast of burden and a young colt.

Ps 117:26 (LXX; MT 118:26)
◊ Mark 11:9–10

[26]Blessed is the one who comes in the name of the Lord.
We bless you from the house of the Lord.

K58.1: The Fig Tree Without Figs

Mark 11:12–14	**Matt 21:18–22**	**Luke**

11 12a On the next day,
   b as they were leaving Bethany,
   c he got hungry.
  13a So when he spotted a fig tree in the distance
   b with some leaves on it,
   c he went up to it
   d expecting to find something on it.
   e But when he got right up to it,
   f he found nothing on it
   g except some leaves.
   h (You see, it wasn't 'time' for figs.)
  14a And he reacted by saying:
   b "May no one so much as taste your fruit again!"

   c And his disciples were listening.

21 18a Early in the morning,
   b as he was returning to the city,
   c he got hungry.
  19a And so when he spotted a single fig tree on the way,

   b he went up to it,

   c and found nothing on it
   d except some leaves,

   e and he says to it,
   f "You are never to bear fruit again!"

   g And the fig tree withered instantly.

  20a And when the disciples saw this,
   b they expressed amazement:
   c "How could the fig tree wither up so quickly?"
  21a In response Jesus said to them,
   b "I swear to you,
   c if you have trust
   d and do not doubt,
   e not only can you do this to a fig tree
   f but you can even say to this mountain,
   g 'Up with you and into the sea!'
   h and that's what will happen;
  22a and everything you ask for in prayer
   b you'll get if you trust."

K58.2: The Temple as Hideout

Mark 11:15–19	**Matt 21:12–17**	**Luke 19:45–48**

11 15a They come to Jerusalem.
   b And he went into the temple
   c and began chasing the vendors and shoppers out of the temple area,
   d and he turned the bankers' tables upside down,
   e along with the chairs of the pigeon merchants,
  16 and he wouldn't even let anyone carry a container through the temple area.

21 12a And Jesus went into God's temple
   b and chased all the vendors and shoppers out of the temple area
   c and he turned the bankers' tables upside down,
   d along with the chairs of the pigeon merchants.

19 45a Then he entered the temple area
   b and began chasing the vendors out.

K58.1: The Fig Tree Without Figs

‡ Luke 13:6–9

[6]Then he told this parable: "A man had a fig tree growing in his vineyard; he came looking for fruit on it but didn't find any.

[7]"So he said to the vinekeeper, 'See here, for three years in a row I have come looking for fruit on this tree, and haven't found any. Cut it down. Why should it suck the nutrients out of the soil?'

[8]"In response he says to him, 'Let it stand, sir, one more year, until I get a chance to dig around it and work in some manure. [9]Maybe it will produce next year; but if it doesn't, we can go ahead and cut it down.'"

Note: Mark 11:12–14 is continued in Mark 11:20–21.

☆ InThom 3:1–4

[1]The son of Annas the scholar, standing there with Jesus, took a willow branch and drained the water Jesus had collected. [2]Jesus, however, saw what had happened and became angry, saying to him, "Damn you, you irreverent fool! What harm did the ponds of water do to you? From this moment you, too, will dry up like a tree, and you'll never produce leaves or root or bear fruit."

[3]In an instant the boy had completely withered away. Then Jesus departed and left for the house of Joseph. [4]The parents of the boy who had withered away picked him up and were carrying him out, sad because he was so young. And they came to Joseph and accused him: "It's your fault—your boy did all this."

☆ InThom 4:1–4

[1]Later he was going through the village again when a boy ran by and bumped him on the shoulder. Jesus got angry and said to him, "You won't continue your journey." [2]And all of a sudden he fell down and died.

[3]Some people saw what had happened and said, "Where has this boy come from? Everything he says happens instantly!"

[4]The parents of the dead boy came to Joseph and blamed him, saying, "Because you have such a boy, you can't live with us in the village, or else teach him to bless and not curse. He's killing our children!"

K58.2: The Temple as Hideout

‡ John 2:13–22

[13]It was almost time for the Jewish Passover celebration, so Jesus went up to Jerusalem. [14]In the temple precincts he came upon people selling oxen and sheep and doves, and bankers were doing business there too. [15]He made a whip out of rope and drove them all out of the temple area, sheep, oxen, and all;

15d Then he knocked over the bankers' tables, ◊ 11:15d

and sent their coins flying. [16]And to the dove merchants he said, "Get these birds out of here! How dare you use my Father's house as a public market."

([17]His disciples were reminded of the words of scripture: "Zeal for your house is eating me alive.")

[18]To this the Judeans responded, "What miracle can you show us ⟨to justify⟩ doing all this?"

[19]Jesus replied, "Destroy this temple and I'll resurrect it in three days." [20]"It has taken forty-six years to build this temple," the Judeans said, "and you can reconstruct it in three days?"

([21]However, he was referring to his body as a temple. [22]When he had been raised from the dead his disciples

remembered that he had made this remark, and so they came to believe both the written word and the word Jesus had spoken.)

Mark	Matt	Luke

Mark

11 17 a Then he started teaching
b and would say to them:
c "Don't the scriptures say,
d 'My house is to be regarded as a house of prayer for all peoples'?
e —but you have turned it into 'a hideout for crooks'!"

18 a And the ranking priests and the scholars heard this

b and kept looking for a way to get rid of him.
c (The truth is that they stood in fear of him,

d and that the whole crowd was astonished at his teaching.)

19 a And when it grew dark,

b they made their way out of the city.

Matt

21 13 a Then he says to them,
b "It is written,
c 'My house is to be regarded as a house of prayer,'
d but you're turning it into 'a hideout for crooks'!"

14 a And some blind and lame people came to him in the temple area
b and he healed them.
15 a Then the ranking priests and scholars saw the remarkable feats
b he performed,
c and the children who kept cheering in the temple area,
d shouting,
e "Hosanna to the son of David,"
f and they were infuriated.
16 a And they said to him,
b "Do you hear what these people are saying?"
c Jesus says to them,
d "Of course. Have you never read
e 'You have produced praise for yourselves out of the mouths of babies and infants at breast'?"

17 a And leaving them behind,
b he went outside the city to Bethany
c and spent the night there.

Luke

19 46 a He says to them,
b "It is written,
c 'My house is to be a house of prayer';

d but you have turned it into a 'hideout for crooks'!"
47 a Every day he would teach in the temple area.
b The ranking priests and the scholars,

c along with the leaders of the people,
d kept looking for some way to get rid of him.

48 a But they never figured out how to do it,
b because all the people hung on his every word.

11:19b Some mss read the singular *he* (cf. Mark 11:11 and Matt 21:17b).

✩ **Mark 12:12** ◊ Mark 11:18

¹²(His opponents) kept looking for some opportunity to seize him, but they were still afraid of the crowd, since they realized that he had aimed the parable at them. So they left him there and went on their way.

✩ **Mark 14:1–2** ◊ Mark 11:18

¹Now it was two days until Passover and the feast of Unleavened Bread. And the ranking priests and the scholars were looking for some way to arrest him by trickery and kill him. ²For their slogan was: "Not during the festival, otherwise the people will riot."

Isa 56:7 (LXX) ◊ Mark 11:17

⁷I will lead them to my sacred mountain and I will make them rejoice in my house of prayer. Their burnt-offerings and sacrifices will be acceptable on my altar. For my house shall be known as a house of prayer for all peoples.

Jer 7:11 (LXX) ◊ Mark 11:17

¹¹"My house, the one that bears my name, hasn't become a hideout for criminals before your very eyes, has it? But I have seen that it has," says the Lord.

K59.1: Mountains Into the Sea

Mark 11:20–25	**Matt 21:20–22**	**Luke**

11 20 a As they were walking along early one morning,

b they saw the fig tree withered from the roots up.

21 a And Peter remembered

b and says to him:

c "Rabbi, look, the fig tree you cursed has withered up!"

21 20 a And when the disciples saw this,

cf Luke 21:20c

b they expressed amazement:

c "How could the fig tree wither up so quickly?"

22 a In response Jesus says to them:

b "Have trust in God.

23 a I swear to you,

b those who say to this mountain,

c 'Up with you and into the sea!'

d and do not waver in their conviction,

e but trust that what they say will happen,

f that's the way it will be.

24 a This is why I keep telling you,

b trust that you will receive

c everything you pray and ask for,

d and that's the way it will turn out.

25 a And when you stand up to pray,

b if you are holding anything against anyone,

c forgive them,

d so your Father in heaven may forgive your misdeeds."

21 a In response Jesus said to them,

cf Luke 21:21c

b "I swear to you,

c if you have trust

d and do not doubt,

e not only can you do this to a fig tree

f but you can even say to this mountain,

g 'Up with you and into the sea!'

h and that's what will happen;

22 **b** you'll get if you trust."

a and everything you ask for in prayer,

K59.2: Who Gave You the Authority?

Mark 11:27–33	**Matt 21:23–27**	**Luke 20:1–8**

11 27 a Once again they come to Jerusalem.

b As he walks around in the temple area,

c the ranking priests and scholars and elders come up to him

21 23 a And when he came to the temple area,

b the ranking priests and elders of the people approached him

c while he was teaching,

20 1 a One day

b as he was teaching the people in the temple area

c and speaking of the good news,

d the ranking priests and the scholars approached him along with the elders,

---

11:26 Important mss omit v. 26 (ℵ B L W Δ Ψ *al*); other mss have (cf. Matt 6:15): *If you don't practice forgiveness, your Father in heaven won't forgive your misdeeds.*

K59.1: Mountains Into the Sea

‡ Luke 13:6–9 ◊ Mark 11:20–21

⁶Then he told this parable: "A man had a fig tree growing in his vineyard; he came looking for fruit on it but didn't find any.

⁷"So he said to the vinekeeper, 'See here, for three years in a row I have come looking for fruit on this tree, and haven't found any. Cut it down. Why should it suck the nutrients out of the soil?'

⁸"In response he says to him, 'Let it stand, sir, one more year, until I get a chance to dig around it and work in some manure. ⁹Maybe it will produce next year; but if it doesn't, we can go ahead and cut it down.'"

Luke 17:5–6 ◊ Mark 11:22–23

⁵The apostles said to the Lord, "Make our trust grow!"

⁶And the Lord said, "If you had trust no larger than a mustard seed, you could tell this mulberry tree, 'Uproot yourself and plant yourself in the sea,' and it would obey you."

• Matt 17:19–20 ◊ Mark 11:22–23

¹⁹Later the disciples came to Jesus privately and asked, "Why couldn't we drive it out?"

²⁰So he says to them, "Because of your lack of trust. I swear to you, even if you have trust no larger than a mustard seed, you will say to this mountain, 'Move from here to there,' and it will move. And nothing will be beyond you."

☆ Mark 9:28–29 ◊ Mark 11:24

²⁸And when he had gone home, his disciples started questioning him privately: "Why couldn't we drive it out?"

²⁹He said to them, "The only thing that can drive this kind out is prayer."

☆ Matt 18:19 ◊ Mark 11:24

¹⁹"Again I assure you, if two of you on earth agree on anything you ask for, it will be done for you by my Father in heaven."

☆ Matt 6:14 ◊ Mark 11:25

¹⁴"For if you forgive others their failures and offenses, your heavenly Father will also forgive yours."

Note: The first part of the narrative in Mark 11:20–21 is found in Mark 11:12–14.

• Thom 48 ◊ Mark 11:22–23

Jesus said, "If two make peace with each other in a single house, they will say to the mountain, 'Move from here!' and it will move."

• Thom 106:1–2 ◊ Mark 11:22–23

¹Jesus said, "When you make the two into one, you will become children of Adam, ²and when you say, 'Mountain, move from here!' it will move."

☆ John 14:13–14 ◊ Mark 11:24

¹³"In addition, I'll do whatever you request in my name, so the Father can be honored by means of the son. ¹⁴If you request anything using my name, I'll do it."

☆ John 15:7 ◊ Mark 11:24

⁷"If you stay attached to me and my words lodge in you, ask whatever you want and it will happen to you."

☆ John 16:23 ◊ Mark 11:24

²³"When that time comes you'll ask nothing of me. I swear to God, if you ask the Father for anything using my name, he will grant it to you."

K59.2: Who Gave You the Authority?

	Mark		**Matt**		**Luke**

Mark

11 28 a and start questioning him:

b "By what right are you doing these things?"
c or, "Who gave you the authority to do these things?"
29 a But Jesus said to them:
b "I have one question for you.

c If you answer me,
d then I will tell you by what authority I do these things.
30 a Tell me, was the baptism of John

b heaven-sent
c or was it of human origin?
d Answer me that."
31 a And they conferred among themselves,
b saying,
c "If we say 'heaven-sent,'
d he'll say,
e 'Then why didn't you trust him?'
32 a But if we say 'Of human origin . . . !'"

b They were afraid of the crowd.
c (You see, everybody considered John a genuine prophet.)
33 a So they answered Jesus by saying,
b "We can't tell."

c And Jesus says to them:
d "I'm not going to tell you by what authority I do these things either!"

Matt

21 23 d and asked,

e "By what right are you doing these things?"
f and "Who gave you this authority?"

24 a In response Jesus said to them,
b "I also have one question for you.

c If you answer me,
d I will tell you by what authority I do these things.
25 a The baptism of John, what was its origin?
b Was it heaven-sent
c or was it of human origin?"

d And they conferred among themselves,
e saying,
f "If we say 'heaven-sent,'
g he'll say to us,
h 'Why didn't you trust him?'
26 a And if we say 'Of human origin . . . !'

b We are afraid of the crowd."
c (Remember, everybody considered John a prophet.)
27 a So they answered Jesus by saying,
b "We can't tell."

c He replied to them in kind:
d "I'm not going to tell you by what authority I do these things either!"

Luke

20 2 a and put this question to him,
b "Tell us,
c by what right are you doing these things?
d Who gave you this authority?"

3 a In response Jesus said to them,
b "I also have a question for you:
c tell me,

4 a was John's baptism

b heaven-sent
c or was it of human origin?"

5 a And they started conferring among themselves,
b reasoning as follows:
c "If we say, 'heaven-sent,'
d he'll say,
e 'Why didn't you trust him?'
6 a But if we say, 'Of human origin,'
b the people will all stone us."

c Remember, ⟨the people⟩ were convinced John was a prophet.
7 a So they answered
b that they couldn't tell where it came from.
8 a And Jesus said to them,
b "Neither am I going to tell you by what authority I do these things!"

K59.3: Parable of the Leased Vineyard

Mark 12:1–12	**Matt 21:33–46**	**Luke 20:9–19**

Mark 12:1–12

12 1 a And he began to speak to them in parables:

b "Someone planted a vineyard,

c put a hedge around it,
d dug a winepress,
e built a tower,
f leased it out to some farmers,
g and went abroad.

Matt 21:33–46

21 33 a "Listen to another parable:

b There once was a landlord
c who 'planted a vineyard,

d put a hedge around it,
e dug a winepress in it,
f built a tower,'
g leased it out to some farmers,
h and went abroad.

Luke 20:9–19

20 9 a Then he began to tell the people this parable:

b "Someone planted a vineyard,

c leased it out to some farmers,
d and went abroad for an extended time.

✫ **POxy840 2:1–9**

¹And taking ⟨the disciples⟩ along, he led them into the inner sanctuary itself, and began walking about in the temple precinct.

²This Pharisee, a leading priest, Levi by name, also entered, ran into them, and said to the Savior, "Who gave you permission to wander around in this inner sanctuary and lay eyes on these sacred vessels, when you have not performed your ritual bath, and your disciples have not even washed their feet? ³Yet in a defiled state you have invaded this sacred place, which is ritually clean. No one walks about in here, or dares lay eyes on these vessels, unless they have bathed themselves and changed clothes."

⁴And the Savior stood up immediately, with his disciples, and replied, "Since you are here in the temple, I take it you are clean."

⁵He replies to ⟨the Savior⟩, "I am clean. I bathed in the pool of David, you know, by descending into it by one set of steps and coming up out of it by another. ⁶I also changed to white and ritually clean clothes. Only then did I come here and lay eyes on these sacred vessels."

⁷In response the Savior said to him: "Damn the blind who won't see. You bathe in these stagnant waters where dogs and pigs wallow day and night. ⁸And you wash and scrub the outer layer of skin, just like prostitutes and dance-hall girls, who wash and scrub and perfume and paint themselves to entice men, while inwardly they are crawling with scorpions and filled with all sorts of corruption. ⁹But my disciples and I—you say we are unbathed —have bathed in lively, life-giving water that comes down from [. . .] But damn those [. . .]"

✫ **John 2:18** ◊ Mark 11:28

¹⁸To this the Judeans responded, "What miracle can you show us ⟨to justify⟩ doing all this?"

K59.3: Parable of the Leased Vineyard

Thom 65–66

65 1 a He said,

 b "A [. . .] person owned a vineyard

 c and leased it to some farmers,

 d so they could work it
 e and he could collect its crop from
  them.

Isa 5:1–2 (LXX) ◊ Mark 12:1

¹I'll sing for my beloved a love song about
 my vineyard.
My beloved had a vineyard on a small hill
 with rich soil.
²And he built a wall around it—fortified
 it—and planted a vineyard.
He built a tower in the middle of it and
 dug a winepress in it.
I waited for it to produce grapes, but it
 produced thorns.

Mark	Matt	Luke
12 2a In due time he sent a slave to the farmers b to collect his share of the vineyard's crop from them. 3a But they grabbed him, b beat him, c and sent him away empty-handed.	**21**34a Now when it was about harvest time, b he sent his slaves to the farmers to collect his crop. 35a And the farmers grabbed his slaves, b and one they beat c and another they killed, d and another they stoned.	**20**10a In due course he sent a slave to the farmers, b so they could pay him his share of the vineyard's crop. c But the farmers beat him d and sent him away empty-handed.
4a So once again he sent another slave to them, b but they attacked him c and abused him. 5a Then he sent another, b and this one they killed; c many others followed, d some of whom they beat, e others of whom they killed.	36a Again he sent other slaves, b more than the first group, c and they did the same thing to them.	11a He repeated his action by sending another slave; b but they beat him up too, c and humiliated him, d and sent him away empty-handed. 12a And he sent yet a third slave; b but they injured him c and threw him out. 13a Then the owner of the vineyard asked himself, b 'What should I do now? c I know, I will send my son, the apple of my eye.
6a He still had one more, a son who was the apple of his eye. b This one he finally sent to them, c with the thought, d 'They will show this son of mine some respect.' 7a But those farmers said to one another, b 'This fellow's the heir! c Come on, let's kill him d and the inheritance will be ours!' 8a So they grabbed him, b and killed him, c and threw him outside the vineyard.	37a Then finally he sent his son to them, b with the thought, c 'They will show this son of mine some respect.' 38a But when the farmers recognized the son b they said to one another, c 'This fellow's the heir! d Come on, let's kill him e and we'll have his inheritance!' 39a And they grabbed him, **c** and killed him. b dragged him outside the vineyard,	d Perhaps they will show him some respect.' 14a But when the farmers recognized him, b they talked it over, and concluded: c 'This fellow's the heir! d Let's kill him e so the inheritance will be ours!' 15**b** and killed him. a So they dragged him outside the vineyard

Thom

65 2a He sent his slave

   b so the farmers would give him the
     vineyard's crop.
   3a They grabbed him,
    b beat him,

    c and almost killed him,
    d and the slave returned
    e and told his master.
   4a His master said,
    b 'Perhaps he didn't know them.'
   5a He sent another slave,

    b and the farmers beat that one as well.

6a Then the master sent his son

   b and said,
   c 'Perhaps they'll show my son some
    respect.'

7a Because the farmers knew that he
    was the heir to the vineyard,

   b they grabbed him
   c and killed him.

Mark	Matt	Luke
	2140a When the owner of the vineyard comes,	
12 9a What will the owner of the vineyard do?	b what will he do to those farmers then?"	**20**15c What will the owner of the vineyard do to them as a consequence?
	41a They say to him,	
b He will come in person,		16a He will come in person,
c and do away with those farmers,	b "He'll get rid of these wicked villains	b do away with those farmers,
d and give the vineyard to someone else.	c and lease the vineyard out to other farmers	c and give the vineyard to someone else."
	d who will deliver their produce to him at the proper time."	
		d When they heard this,
		e they said,
		f "God forbid!"
		17a But ⟨Jesus⟩ looked them straight in the eye
		b and said,
10a Haven't you read this scripture,	42a Jesus says to them,	c "What can this scripture possibly mean:
	b "Haven't you read in the scriptures,	
b 'A stone that the builders rejected	c 'A stone that the builders rejected	d 'A stone that the builders rejected
c has ended up as the keystone.	d has ended up the keystone.	e has ended up as the keystone'?
11a It was the Lord's doing	e It was the Lord's doing	
b and is something you admire'?"	f and is something you admire?'	
		18a Everyone who falls over that stone will be smashed to bits,
		b and anyone on whom it falls will be crushed."
	43a Therefore I say to you,	
	b God's domain will be taken away from you	
	c and given to a people that bears its fruit."	
	45a And when the ranking priests and Pharisees heard his parable,	
12a ⟨His opponents⟩ kept looking for some opportunity to seize him,	46a They wanted to seize him,	19a The scholars and the ranking priests wanted to lay hands on him then and there,
b but they were still afraid of the crowd,	b but were afraid of the crowds,	b but they were afraid of the people,
c since they realized that he had aimed the parable at them.	45b they realized that he was talking about them.	c since they realized he had aimed this parable at them.
	46c because everyone regarded him as a prophet.	
d So they left him there		
e and went on their way.		

12:9a Greek (κύριος): or *master* or *lord*.

Thom   **Ps 118:22–23** (LXX) ◊ Mark 12:10

22A stone that the builders rejected,
this has become the keystone.
23It was the Lord's doing and is admired in
        our eyes.

65 8 Anyone here with two ears had
      better listen!"

66 1 a Jesus said,
     b "Show me the stone that the builders
       rejected:
     c that is the keystone."

K59.4: Is It Permissible to Pay the Tax?

Mark 12:13–17	Matt 22:15–22	Luke 20:19–26
		20 19a The scholars and the ranking priests wanted to lay hands on him then and there,
		b but they were afraid of the people,
		c since they realized he had aimed this parable at them.
		20a So they kept him under surveillance,
	22 15a Then the Pharisees went	
	b and conferred on how to entrap him	
12 13a And they send some of the Pharisees and the Herodians to him	16a And they send their disciples to him along with the Herodians	b and sent spies,
		c who feigned sincerity,
b to trap him		d so they could twist something he said
c with a riddle.	15c with a riddle.	
		e and turn him over to the authority and jurisdiction of the governor.
14a They come		21a They asked him,
b and say to him,	16b to say,	b "Teacher, we know that what you speak and teach is correct,
c "Teacher, we know that you are honest	c "Teacher, we know that you are honest	
d and impartial,	e and are impartial,	c that you show no favoritism,
e because you pay no attention to appearances,	f because you pay no attention to appearances.	
f but instead you teach God's way forthrightly.	d and that you teach God's way forthrightly,	d but instead teach God's way forthrightly.
	17a So tell us what you think:	
g Is it permissible to pay the poll tax to the Roman emperor or not?	b Is it permissible to pay the poll tax to the Roman emperor or not?"	22 Is it permissible for us to pay taxes to the Roman emperor or not?"
h Should we pay		
i or should we not pay?"		
15a But he saw through their trap,	18a Jesus knew how devious they were,	23a But he saw through their duplicity,
b and said to them,	b and said,	b and said to them,
c "Why do you provoke me like this?	c "Why do you provoke me, you pious frauds?	
d Let me have a look at a coin."	19a Let me see the coin used to pay the poll tax."	24a "Show me a coin.
	b And they handed him a silver coin.	
16a They handed him a silver coin,	20a And he says to them,	
b and he says to them,	b "Whose picture is this?	b Whose likeness does it bear?
c "Whose picture is this?	c Whose name is on it?"	c And whose name is on it?"
d Whose name is on it?"	21a They say to him,	d They said,
e They replied,	b "The emperor's."	e "The emperor's."
f "The emperor's."		

12:15d denarius: see the note on Mark 6:37e.

K59.4: Is It Permissible to Pay the Tax?

Thom 100:1–4	‡ GEger 3:1–6	John 3:1–2 ◊ Mark 12:14
	[1]They come to him and interrogate him as a way of putting him to the test. [2]They ask, "Teacher, Jesus, we know that you are [from God], since the things you do put you above all the prophets. [3]Tell us, then, is it permissible to pay to rulers what is due them? Should we pay them or not?" [4]Jesus knew what they were up to, and became indignant. [5]Then he said to them, "Why do you pay me lip service as a teacher, but not [do] what I say? [6]How accurately Isaiah prophesied about you when he said, 'This people honors me with their lips, but their heart stays far away from me; their worship of me is empty, [because they insist on teachings that are human] commandments [. . .]'"	[1]A Pharisee named Nicodemus, a Judean leader, [2]came to ⟨Jesus⟩ during the night and said, "Rabbi, we know that you've come as a teacher from God; after all, nobody can perform the miracles you do unless God is with him."

100 1 a They showed Jesus a gold coin
b and said to him,
c "The Roman emperor's people demand taxes from us."

Mark	Matt	Luke
12 17 a Jesus said to them: b "Pay the emperor what belongs to the emperor, c and God what belongs to God!"	**22** 21 c Then he says to them, d "Pay the emperor what belongs to the emperor, e and God what belongs to God!"	**20** 25 a So he said to them, b "Then pay the emperor what belongs to the emperor, c and God what belongs to God!"
		26 a And so they were unable to catch him in anything he said in front of the people;
d And they were dumbfounded at him.	22 a Upon hearing his reply, b they were dumbfounded.	b they were dumbfounded at his answer c and fell silent.
	c And they withdrew from him d and went away.	

K59.5: Whose Wife Will She Be?

Mark 12:18–27	Matt 22:23–33	Luke 20:27–40
12 18 a And some Sadducees b —those who maintain there is no resurrection— c come up to him d and they start questioning him. 19 a "Teacher," b they said, c "Moses wrote for our benefit, d 'If someone's brother dies e and leaves his widow childless, f his brother is obligated to take the widow as his wife g and produce offspring for his brother.' 20 a There were seven brothers; b now the first took a wife c but left no children d when he died. 21 a So the second married her b but died without leaving offspring, c and the third likewise. 22 a In fact, all seven ⟨married her but⟩ left no offspring. b Finally, the wife died too. 23 a In the resurrection, after they rise, whose wife will she be?" b (Remember, all seven had her as wife.)	**22** 23 a That same day, b some Sadducees c —who maintain there is no resurrection— d came up to him e and questioned him. 24 a "Teacher," b they said, c "Moses said, d 'If someone dies e without children, f his brother is obligated to marry the widow g and produce offspring for his brother.' 25 a There were seven brothers we knew; b now the first married **d** And since he left no children, c and died. e he left his widow to his brother. 26 a The second brother did the same thing, b and the third, c and so on, d through the seventh brother. 27 Finally the wife died. 28 a So then, in the resurrection whose wife, of the seven, will she be?" b (Remember, they had all married her.)	**20** 27 a Some of the Sadducees b —those who argue there is no resurrection— c came up to him 28 a and put a question to him. b "Teacher," c they said, d "Moses wrote for our benefit, e 'If someone's brother dies, f leaving behind a wife but no children, g his brother is obligated to take the widow as his wife h and produce offspring for his brother.' 29 a Now let's say there were seven brothers; b the first took a wife, c and died childless. 30 Then the second 31 a and the third married her, b and so on. c All seven ⟨married her but⟩ left no children when they died. 32 Finally, the wife died too. 33 a So then, in the 'resurrection' whose wife will the woman be?" b (Remember, all seven had her as wife.)

Thom

100 2 a He said to them,
    b "Give the emperor what belongs to
    the emperor,
   3 give God what belongs to God,
   4 and give me what is mine."

K59.5: Whose Wife Will She Be?

Gen 38:8 (Lxx) ◊ Mark 12:19

[8]Judah said to Onan, "Go to your brother's wife, and you take her as your wife, and produce heirs for your brother."

Deut 25:5–6 (Lxx) ◊ Mark 12:19

[5]If two brothers live together and if one of them dies without an heir, his wife is not to be given to an heir as next of kin. The brother of her husband should go to her and take her as his wife and live with her. [6]And her child, if she bears one, is to be given the name of her deceased husband, so his name will not die out in Israel.

Mark	Matt	Luke

Mark

12 24 a Jesus said to them:
 b "You've missed the point again,
  haven't you,
 c all because you underestimate both
  the scriptures and the power of God.

25 a After all, when men and women rise
  from the dead,

 b they do not marry,

 c but resemble heaven's messengers.

26 a As for whether or not the dead are
  raised,
 b haven't you read in the book of
  Moses in the passage about the bush,
 c how God spoke to him:

 d 'I am the God of Abraham and the
  God of Isaac and the God of Jacob'?
27 a This is not the God of the dead,
 b only of the living

 c —you're constantly missing the
  point!"

Matt

22 29 a In response Jesus said to them,
 b "You have missed the point again,

 c all because you underestimate both
  the scriptures and the power of God.

30 a After all, at the resurrection

 b people do not marry,

 c but resemble heaven's messengers.

31 a As for the resurrection of the dead,

 b haven't you read God's word to you:

32 a 'I am the God of Abraham and the
  God of Isaac and the God of Jacob.'
 b This is not the God of the dead,
 c only of the living."

33 a And when the crowd heard,
 b they were stunned by his teaching.

Luke

20 34 a And Jesus said to them,

 b "The children of this age marry and
  are given in marriage;
35 a but those who are considered worthy
  of participating in the coming age,
 b which means, 'in the resurrection
  from the dead,'
 c do not marry.
36 a They can no longer die,
 b since they are the equivalent of
  heavenly messengers;
 c they are children of God
 d and children of the resurrection.
37 a That the dead are raised,

 b Moses demonstrates
 c in the passage about the bush:

 d he calls the Lord
 e 'the God of Abraham, the God of
  Isaac, and the God of Jacob.'
38 a So this is not the God of the dead,
 b only of the living,
 c since to him they are all alive."

39 a And some of the scholars answered,
 b "Well put, Teacher."
40 You see, they no longer dared to ask
  him about anything else.

K59.6: Which Commandment?

Mark 12:28–34	Matt 22:34–40	Luke

Mark 12:28–34

12 28 a And one of the scholars approached
 b when he heard them arguing,
 c and because he saw how skillfully
  Jesus answered them,

 d he asked him,
 e "Of all the commandments, which is
  the most important?"

Matt 22:34–40

22 34 a When the Pharisees learned
 b that he had silenced the Sadducees,
 c they conspired against him.
35 a And one of them, a legal expert,
 b put him to the test:
36 "Teacher, which commandment in
  the Law is the greatest?"

Luke

Exod 3:6 ◊ Mark 12:26
⁶Then he said to him, "I am God your
Father, the God of Abraham, the God of
Isaac, the God of Jacob."

K59.6: Which Commandment?

Mark	Matt	Luke
12 29 a Jesus answered:	22 37 a He replied to him,	
b "The first is,'Hear, Israel, the Lord your God is one Lord,		
30 a and you are to love the Lord your God	b "'You are to love the Lord your God	
b with all your heart	c with all your heart	
c and all your soul	d and all your soul	
d and all your mind	e and all your mind.'	
e and with all your energy.'		
	38 This commandment is first and foremost.	
31 a The second is this:	39 a And the second is like it:	
b 'You are to love your neighbor as yourself.'	b 'You are to love your neighbor as yourself.'	
c There is no other commandment greater than these."		
	40 On these two commandments hangs everything in the Law and the Prophets."	
32 a And the scholar said to him,		
b "That's a fine answer, Teacher.		
c You have correctly said that God is one		
d and there is no other beside him.		
33 a And 'to love him with all one's heart		
b and with all one's mind		
c and with all one's energy'		
d and 'to love one's neighbor as oneself'		
e is greater than all the burnt offerings and sacrifices put together."		
34 a And when Jesus saw that he answered him sensibly,		
b he said to him,		
c "You are not far from God's domain."		
d And from then on no one dared question him.		

K59.7: Whose Son Is the Anointed?

Mark 12:35–37	Matt 22:41–46	Luke 20:41–44
12 35 a And during the time Jesus was teaching in the temple area,		
b he would pose this question:		20 41 a Then he asked them,
	22 41 a When the Pharisees gathered around,	
	b Jesus asked them,	

12:30d A few mss omit the phrase (D *pc* c d);
most mss have it, but they are probably
influenced by Matt 22:37e.

‡ **Luke 10:25–29**

²⁵On one occasion, a legal expert stood up to put him to the test with a question: "Teacher, what do I have to do to inherit eternal life?"

²⁶He said to him, "How do you read what is written in the Law?"

²⁷And he answered, "You are to love the Lord your God with all your heart, with all your soul, with all your energy, and with all your mind; and your neighbor as yourself."

²⁸Jesus said to him, "You have given the correct answer; do this and you will have life."

²⁹But with a view to justifying himself, he said to Jesus, "But who is my neighbor?"

☆ **Luke 20:39** ◊ Mark 12:32

³⁹And some of the scholars answered, "Well put, Teacher."

☆ **Luke 20:40** ◊ Mark 12:34

⁴⁰You see, they no longer dared to ask him about anything else.

‡ **Did 1:2** ◊ Mark 12:30–31

¹This is the way of life: "First, you are to love the God who made you, second, ⟨you are to love⟩ your neighbor as you do yourself. Further, don't do to someone else what you don't want done to yourself."

☆ **Thom 25:1–2** ◊ Mark 12:31

¹Jesus said, "Love your friends like your own soul, ²protect them like the pupil of your eye."

△ **Barn 19:5** ◊ Mark 12:31

⁵You must not be of two minds whether this is so or not. You must not take the name of the Lord in vain. You are to love your neighbor as yourself. You are not to kill a child by abortion, nor again are you to put an infant to death. You must not withhold your hand from son or daughter, but teach them the fear of God from their youth.

☆ **Thom 82:1–2** ◊ Mark 12:34

¹Jesus said, "Whoever is near me is near the fire, ²and whoever is far from me is far from the ⟨Father's⟩ domain."

☆ **InThom 15:7** ◊ Mark 12:34

⁷When the child heard this, he immediately smiled at him and said, "Because you have spoken and testified rightly, that other teacher who was struck down will be healed." And right away he was. Joseph took his child and went home.

Deut 6:4–5 (LXX) ◊ Mark 12:29–30

⁴Hear, Israel, the Lord your God is one Lord, ⁵and you are to love the Lord your God with all your heart, and all your soul, and all your mind, and with all your energy.

Lev 19:18 (LXX) ◊ Mark 12:31

¹⁸You are to love your neighbor as yourself.

1 Sam 15:22 (LXX) ◊ Mark 12:33

²²And Samuel said, "Does the Lord prefer burnt-offerings and sacrifices to obedience to his voice? Listen, full obedience is better than sacrifice and compliance is better than the fat of rams."

K59.7: Whose Son Is the Anointed?

Mark	Matt	Luke
12 35c "How can the scholars claim that the Anointed is the son of David?	22 42a "What do you think about the Anointed? b Whose son is he?" c They said to him, d "David's." 43a He said to them, b "Then how can David call him 'lord,' c while speaking under the influence of the spirit:	20 41b "How can they say that the Anointed is the son of David?
36a David himself said under the influence of the holy spirit, b 'The Lord said to my lord, c "Sit here at my right, d until I make your enemies grovel at your feet."' 37a David himself calls him 'lord,' b so how can he be his son?" c And a huge crowd would listen to him with delight.	44a 'The Lord said to my lord, b "Sit here at my right, c until I make your enemies grovel at your feet"'? 45a If David actually called him 'lord,' b how can he be his son?"	42a Remember, David himself says in the book of Psalms, b 'The Lord said to my lord, c "Sit here at my right, 43 until I make your enemies grovel at your feet."' 44a Since David calls him 'lord,' b how can he be his son?"
	46a And no one could come up with an answer to his riddle. b And from that day on no one dared ask him a question.	

K59.8: Scholars in Long Robes

Mark 12:38–40	Matt 23:6	Luke 20:45–47
		20 45a Within earshot of the people b Jesus said to the disciples,
12 38a During the course of his teaching he would say: b "Look out for the scholars c who like to parade around in long robes, d and insist on being addressed properly in the marketplaces,		46a "Be on guard against the scholars b who like to parade around in long robes, c and who love to be addressed properly in the marketplaces,
39a and prefer important seats in the synagogues b and the best couches at banquets.	23 6b and prominent seats in synagogues. a They love the best couches at banquets	d and who prefer important seats in the synagogues e and the best couches at banquets.
40a They are the ones who prey on widows and their families, b and recite long prayers just to put on airs. c These people will get a stiff sentence!"		47a They are the ones who prey on widows and their families, b and recite long prayers just to put on airs. c These people will get a stiff sentence!"

12:36b The first *Lord* refers to Yahweh, the second to the or a ruling king, or to the messiah. Greek in both instances is κύριος.

☆ **John 7:40–44**

⁴⁰When they heard this declaration, some in the crowd said, "This man has to be the Prophet." ⁴¹"The Anointed!" others said. Still others objected: "Is the Anointed to come from Galilee? ⁴²Doesn't scripture teach that the Anointed is to be descended from David and come from the village of Bethlehem, where David lived?" (⁴³As you can see, the crowd was split over who he was.)

⁴⁴Some were in favor of arresting him, but no one laid a hand on him.

☆ **1 Cor 15:20–28**

²⁰But in fact Christ has been raised from the dead, the first fruits of those who have fallen asleep. ²¹For as by a man came death, by a man has come also the resurrection of the dead. ²²For as in Adam all die, so also in Christ shall all be made alive. ²³But each in his own order: Christ the first fruits, then at his coming those who belong to Christ. ²⁴Then comes the end, when he delivers the kingdom to God the Father after destroying every rule and every authority and power. ²⁵For he must reign until he has put all his enemies under his feet. ²⁶The last enemy to be destroyed is death. ²⁷"For God has put all things in subjection under his feet." But when it says, "All things are put in subjection under him," it is plain that he is excepted who put all things under him. ²⁸When all things are subjected to him, then the Son himself will also be subjected to him who put all things under him, that God may be everything to every one.

Ps 109:1 (LXX; MT 110:1) ◊ Mark 12:36

¹The Lord said to my lord,
"Sit here on my right until I make your
    enemies grovel at your feet."

K59.8: Scholars in Long Robes

‡ **Luke 11:37–44**

³⁷While he was speaking, a Pharisee invites him to dinner at his house. So he came and reclined at the table. ³⁸The Pharisee was astonished that he did not first wash before the meal.

³⁹But the Lord said to him, "You Pharisees clean the outside of cups and dishes, but inside you are full of greed and evil. ⁴⁰You fools! Did not the one who made the outside also make the inside? ⁴¹Still, donate what is inside to charity, and then you'll see how everything comes clean for you.

⁴²"Damn you, Pharisees! You pay tithes on mint and rue and every herb, but neglect justice and the love of God. You should have attended to the last without neglecting the first.

⁴³"Damn you, Pharisees! You're so fond of the prominent seat in synagogues and respectful greetings in marketplaces. ⁴⁴Damn you! You are like unmarked graves that people walk on without realizing it."

☆ **Luke 14:7–11**

⁷Or would tell a parable for those who had been invited, when he noticed how they were choosing the places of honor.

He said to them, ⁸"When someone invites you to a wedding banquet, don't take the place of honor, in case someone more important than you has been invited. ⁹Then the one who invited you both will come and say to you, 'Make room for this person,' and you'll be embarrassed to have to take the lowest place. ¹⁰Instead, when you are invited, go take the lowest place, so when the host comes he'll say to you, 'Friend, come up higher.' Then you'll be honored in front of all those reclining around the table with you.

¹¹"Those who promote themselves will be demoted, and those who demote themselves will be promoted."

K59.9: The Widow's Pittance

Mark 12:41–44	**Matt**	**Luke 21:1–4**
12 41 a And he would sit across from the treasury		
b and observe the crowd dropping money into the collection box.		**21** 1 a He looked up b and observed the rich dropping their donations into the collection box.
c And many wealthy people would drop large amounts in.		
42 a Then one poor widow came		
b and put in two small coins,		2　Then he noticed that a needy widow put in two small coins,
c which is a pittance.		
43 a And he motioned his disciples over		
b and said to them:		3 a and he observed:
c "I swear to you,		b "I swear to you,
d this poor widow has contributed more than all those who dropped something into the collection box!		c this poor widow has contributed more than all of them!
44 a After all, they were all donating out of their surplus,		4 a After all, they all made donations out of their surplus,
b whereas she, out of her poverty, was contributing		b whereas she, out of her poverty, was contributing
c all she had,		**d** which was everything she had."
d her entire livelihood!"		c her entire livelihood,

K60.1: What Wonderful Buildings!

Mark 13:1–2	**Matt 24:1–2**	**Luke 21:5–6**
13 1 a And as he was going out of the temple area,	**24** 1 a And Jesus was leaving the temple area b on his way out,	
b one of his disciples remarks to him,	c when his disciples came to him	**21** 5 a When some were remarking about b how the temple was adorned with fine masonry
c "Teacher, look, what magnificent masonry!		
d What wonderful buildings!"	d and called his attention to the sacred buildings.	c and ornamentation, d he said,
2 a And Jesus replied to him,	2 a In response he said to them,	6 a "As for these things that you now admire,
b "Take a good look at these monumental buildings!	b "Yes, take a good look at all this!	
	c I swear to you,	b the time will come
c You may be sure not one stone will be left on top of another!	d you may be sure not one stone will be left here on top of another!	c when not one stone will be left on top of another!
d Every last one will certainly be knocked down!"	e Every last one will certainly be knocked down!"	d Every last one will be knocked down!"

13:2c Most mss (except A K *pm* it and versions in part) add the word *here,* perhaps under the influence of Matt 24:2d.

K60.1: What Wonderful Buildings!

☆ **Luke 19:44b** ◊ Mark 13:2

[44]"They will not leave one stone upon another within you, because you failed to recognize the time of your visitation."

K60.2: Signs of the Final Agonies

Mark 13:3–13	Matt 24:3–9, 13–14	Luke 21:5–19
		21 5a When some were remarking about
		b how the temple was adorned with fine masonry
		c and ornamentation,
		d he said,
		6a "As for these things that you now admire,
		b the time will come
		c when not one stone will be left on top of another!
		d Every last one will be knocked down!"
13 3a And as he was sitting on the Mount of Olives across from the temple,	24 3a As he was sitting on the Mount of Olives,	
b Peter would ask him privately,	b the disciples came to him privately,	7a And they asked him,
c as would James and John and Andrew:		
	c and said,	
4a "Tell us,	d "Tell us,	
b when are these things going to happen,	e when are these things going to happen,	b "Teacher, when are these things going to happen?
c and what will be the sign	f and what will be the sign of your coming	c What sort of portent will signal
d to indicate when all these things are about to take place?"	g and the end of the age?"	d when these things are about to occur?"
5a And Jesus would say to them,	4a And in response Jesus said to them:	8a He said,
b "Stay alert,	b "Stay alert,	b "Stay alert!
c otherwise someone might just delude you!	c otherwise someone might just delude you!	c Don't be deluded.
6a You know, many will come using my name	5a You know, many will come using my name,	d You know, many will come in my name
b and claim,	b and claim,	e and claim,
c 'I'm the one!'	c 'I am the Anointed!'	f 'I'm the one!'
		g and 'The time is near!'
d and they will delude many people.	d and they will delude many people.	h Don't go running after them!
7a When you hear of wars and rumors of wars,	6a You are going to hear about wars and rumors of wars.	9a And when you hear of wars and insurrections,
b don't be afraid.	b See that you are not afraid.	b don't panic.
c These are inevitable,	c For these are inevitable,	c After all, it's inevitable that these things take place first,
d but it is not yet the end.	d but it is not yet the end.	d but it doesn't mean the end is about to come."
		10a Then he went on to tell them,
8a For nation will rise up against nation	7a For nation will rise up against nation	b "Nation will rise up against nation,
b and empire against empire;	b and empire against empire;	c and empire against empire;
c there will be earthquakes everywhere;	d and earthquakes everywhere.	11a there will be major earthquakes,
d there will be famines.	c and there will be famines	b and famines and plagues all over the place;
		c there will be dreadful events
		d and impressive portents from heaven.
e These things mark the beginning of the final agonies.	8 Now all these things mark the beginning of the final agonies.	

K60.2: Signs of the Final Agonies

✩ Mark 13:21–23 ◊ Mark 13:6

[21]"And then if someone says to you, 'Look, here is the Anointed,' or 'Look, there he is!' don't count on it! [22]After all, counterfeit messiahs and phony prophets will show up, and they will provide portents and miracles so as to delude, if possible, even the chosen people. [23]But you be on your guard! Notice how I always warn you about these things in advance."

✩ Matt 24:23–26 ◊ Mark 13:6

[23]"Then if someone says to you, 'Look, here is the Anointed,' or 'over here,' don't count on it! [24]After all, counterfeit messiahs and phony prophets will show up, and they'll offer great portents and miracles to delude, if possible, even the chosen people. [25]Look, I have warned you in advance. [26]In fact, if they should say to you, 'Look, he's in the wilderness,' don't go out there; 'Look, he's in one of the secret rooms,' don't count on it."

✩ Luke 17:23 ◊ Mark 13:6

[23]"And they'll be telling you, 'Look, there it is!' or 'Look, here it is!' Don't rush off; don't pursue it."

Dan 2:28 (LXX) ◊ Mark 13:7

[28]But there is a God in heaven who reveals secrets, and who has revealed to King Nebuchanezzer the things that are ordained ⟨to take place⟩ at the end of time.

2 Chr 15:6 (LXX) ◊ Mark 13:8

[6]And nation will make war against nation, and city against city, for God has confounded them with every kind of distress.

cf. Isa 19:2 ◊ Mark 13:8

Mark	Matt	Luke
13 9a But you look out for yourselves!		21 12a But before all these things ⟨take place⟩,
b They will turn you over to councils,	24 9a At that time they will turn you over for torture,	b they will manhandle you,
c and beat you in synagogues,		c and persecute you, d and turn you over to synagogues
d and haul you up before governors and kings, e on my account, f so you can make your case to them.	14b so you can make your case to all peoples. a And this good news of Heaven's imperial rule will have been proclaimed in the whole inhabited world, c And then the end will come.	e and deliver you to prisons, f and you will be hauled up before kings and governors g on account of my name. 13 This will give you a chance to make your case.
10 Yet the good news must first be announced to all peoples.		
11a And when they arrest you to lock you up,		
b don't be worried about what you should say. c Instead, whatever occurs to you at the moment, d say that. e For it is not you who are speaking f but the holy spirit.		14a So make up your minds b not to rehearse your defense in advance,
		15a for I will give you the wit and wisdom b which none of your adversaries will be able to resist or refute.
12a And one brother will turn in another b to be put to death,		16a You will be turned in, b even by parents and brothers c and relatives and friends;
c and a father his child, d and children will turn against their parents e and kill them.	9b and will kill you,	d and they will put some of you to death.
13a And you will be universally hated because of me.	c and you will be universally hated because of me.	17 And you will be universally hated because of me. 18 Yet not a single hair on your head will be harmed. 19a By your perseverance b you will secure your lives.
b Those who hold out to the end c will be saved!	13a Those who hold out to the end b will be saved!	

Matt 10:17–22

10 17a "And beware of people,

    b for they will turn you over to the Council

    c and in the synagogues they will scourge you.

18a And you will be hauled up before governors and even kings
    b on my account
    c so you can make your case to them and to the nations.

19a And when they lock you up,

    b don't worry about how you should speak or what you should say.

20**a** For it is not you who are speaking
   b but your Father's spirit speaking through you.
19c It will occur to you at that moment what to say.

21a One brother will turn in another
    b to be put to death,

    c and a father his child,
    d and children will turn against their parents
    e and kill them.

22a And you will be universally hated because of me.

    b But those who hold out to the end
    c will be saved."

Luke 12:11–12 ◊ Mark 13:11

11"And when they make you appear in synagogues and haul you up before rulers and authorities, don't worry about how or in what way you should defend yourself or what you should say. 12The holy spirit will teach you at that very moment what you ought to say."

Matt 10:35–36 ◊ Mark 13:12

35"After all, I have come to pit a man against his father, a daughter against her mother, and a daughter-in-law against her mother-in-law. 36Your enemies live under your own roof."

☆ **John 14:26** ◊ Mark 13:11

26"Yet the advocate, the holy spirit the Father will send in my stead, will teach you everything and remind you of everything I told you."

☆ **John 16:2** ◊ Mark 13:12

2"They are going to expel you from the synagogue. But the time is coming when those who kill you will think they are doing God a service."

☆ **John 15:18–21** ◊ Mark 13:13

18"If the world hates you, don't forget that it hated me first. 19If you were at home in the world, the world would befriend ⟨you as⟩ its own. But you are not at home in the world; on the contrary, I have separated you from the world; that's why the world hates you. 20Recall what I told you: 'Slaves are never better than their masters.' If they persecute me, they'll surely persecute you. If they observe my teaching, they'll also observe yours. 21Yet they are going to do all these things to you because of me, since they don't recognize the one who sent me."

cf. Mic 7:6 ◊ Mark 13:12

K60.3: Days of Distress

Mark 13:14–23	**Matt 24:15–28**	**Luke 21:20–24**
13 14a "When you see the 'devastating desecration'	24 15a "So when you see the 'devastating desecration'	
	b (as described by Daniel the prophet)	
b standing where it should not	c standing 'in the holy place'	
c (the reader had better figure out what this means),	d (the reader had better figure out what this means),	
		21 20a "When you see Jerusalem surrounded by armies,
		b know then that its destruction is just around the corner.
d then the people in Judea should head for the hills;	16 then the people in Judea should head for the hills;	21a Then the people in Judea should head for the hills,
		b and those inside the city flee,
		c and those out in the countryside not re-enter.
		22a For these are days of retribution,
		b when everything that was predicted will come true.
15a no one on the roof should go downstairs;	17a no one on the roof should go downstairs	
b no one should enter the house to retrieve anything;	b to retrieve anything;	
16 and no one in the field should turn back to get a coat.	18 and no one in the field should turn back to get a coat.	
17a It'll be too bad for pregnant women	19a It'll be too bad for pregnant women,	23a It'll be too bad for pregnant women
b and nursing mothers in those days!	b and nursing mothers in those days!	b and nursing mothers in those days!
18 Pray that none of this happens in winter!	20a Pray that you don't have to flee during the winter	
	b or on the sabbath day.	
19a For those days will see distress	21a For there will be great distress,	c For there will be utter misery throughout the land
		d and wrath ⟨will fall⟩ upon this people.
b the likes of which has not occurred since God created the world	b the likes of which has not occurred since the world began,	
c until now,	c until now,	
d and will never occur again.	d and will never occur again.	
20a And if the Lord had not cut short the days,	22a And if those days had not been cut short,	
b no human being would have survived!	b no human being would have survived.	
c But he did shorten the days,	**d** those days will be cut short.	
d for the sake of the chosen people	c But for the sake of the chosen people,	
e whom he selected.		

13:14b Or: *he.*

13:20a Greek (κύριος): or *God.*

K60.3: Days of Distress

Luke 17:31

Dan 9:27 (LXX) ◊ Mark 13:14

[27]And he will make a strong covenant with many for one week. And for half of the week he will remove sacrifices and drink offerings. And upon the temple a devastating desecration ⟨will come⟩ until an end is put to the devastation.

Dan 11:31 (LXX) ◊ Mark 13:14

[31]Soldiers commanded by him will desecrate the sanctuary and the citadel. They will abolish the regular offerings and will erect 'the devastating desecration.'

Dan 12:11 (LXX) ◊ Mark 13:14

[11]From the time the regular offering is abolished and 'the devastating desecration' set up, it will be one thousand two hundred and ninety days.

1731 a "On that day,

b if anyone is on the roof
c and their things are in the house,
d they had better not go down to fetch them.
e The same goes for those in the field:
f they had better not turn back for anything left behind."

1 Macc 1:54 (LXX) ◊ Mark 13:14

[54]On the fifteenth day of Chislev, in the one hundred and forty-fifth year, he erected a devastating desecration on the altar of burnt offering. And they also built altars in the neighboring cities of Judah.

cf. Ezek 7:16 ◊ Mark 13:14

✩ **Thom 79:1–3** ◊ Mark 13:17

[1]A woman in the crowd said to him, "Lucky are the womb that bore you and the breasts that fed you."
[2]He said to [her], "Lucky are those who have heard the word of the Father and have truly kept it. [3]For there will be days when you will say, 'Lucky are the womb that has not conceived and the breasts that have not given milk.'"

Dan 12:1 (LXX) ◊ Mark 13:19

[1]At that time, Michael, the great leader and protector of your fellow-countrymen, will appear. There will be a period of anguish, the likes of which has never been known since the nation came into being, until that moment. At that time your people will be delivered, everyone whose name is inscribed in the book.

Mark	Matt	Luke
		21 24 a They will fall by the edge of the sword,
		b and be taken prisoner ⟨and scattered⟩ in all the foreign countries,
		c and Jerusalem will be overrun by pagans,
		d until the period allotted to the pagans has run its course.
13 21 a And then if someone says to you,	24 23 a Then if someone says to you,	
b 'Look, here is the Anointed,'	b 'Look, here is the Anointed,'	
c or 'Look, there he is!'	c or 'over here,'	
d don't count on it!	d don't count on it!	
22 a After all, counterfeit messiahs and phony prophets will show up,	24 a After all, counterfeit messiahs and phony prophets will show up,	
b and they will provide portents and miracles	b and they'll offer great portents and miracles	
c so as to delude, if possible, even the chosen people.	c to delude, if possible, even the chosen people.	
23 a But you be on your guard!	25 a Look,	
b Notice how I always warn you about these things in advance.	b I have warned you in advance.	
	26 a In fact, if they should say to you,	
	b 'Look, he's in the wilderness,'	
	c don't go out there;	
	d 'Look, he's in one of the secret rooms,'	
	e don't count on it.	
	27 a For just as lightning	
	b comes out of the east and is visible all the way to the west,	
	c that's what the coming of the son of Adam will be like.	
	28 a For wherever there's a corpse,	
	b that's where vultures gather.	

K60.4: Son of Adam Comes on Clouds

Mark 13:24–31	Matt 24:29–35	Luke 21:25–33
13 24 a "But in those days,	24 29 a "Immediately	
b after that tribulation,	b after the tribulation of those days	
c the sun will be darkened,	c 'the sun will be darkened,	
d and the moon will not give off her glow,	d and the moon will not give off her glow,	
		21 25 a "And there will be portents in the sun and moon and stars,
		b and on the earth nations will be dismayed
		c in their confusion at the roar of the surging sea.
		26 a People will faint from terror
		b at the prospect of what is coming over the civilized world,
25 a and the stars will fall from the sky,	e and the stars will fall from the sky,	
b and the heavenly forces will be shaken!	f and the heavenly forces will be shaken!'	c for the heavenly forces will be shaken!

Luke 17:23–24, 37

Thom 113:1–4 ◊ Mark 13:21

[1]His disciples said to him, "When will the ⟨Father's⟩ imperial rule come?"
[2]"It will not come by watching for it. [3]It will not be said, 'Look, here!' or 'Look, there!' [4]Rather, the Father's imperial rule is spread out upon the earth, and people don't see it."

Deut 13:2–4 (LXX) ◊ Mark 13:22

[2]If a prophet or a visionary turns up among you and speaks to you of a sign or portent [3]and the sign or portent comes ⟨true⟩—the one he promised you when he said, "Let's go and worship other gods unfamiliar to us"—[4]don't pay any attention to the advice of that prophet or that visionary. God is putting you to the test to see whether you love the Lord your God with all your heart and all your mind.

1723a And they'll be telling you,
　　b 'Look, there it is!'

　　c or, 'Look, here it is!'

　　d Don't rush off; don't pursue it.
　24a For just as lightning
　　b flashes and lights up the sky from one end to the other,
　　c that's what the son of Adam will be like in his day.
　37**b** wherever there's a carcass."
　　a "Vultures collect

K60.4: Son of Adam Comes on Clouds

Isa 13:10 (LXX) ◊ Mark 13:24

[10]For the stars of the heaven and Orion and all the constellations of the heavens will not give their light, and the sun will be dark when it comes up, and the moon will not give off her glow.

Isa 34:4 (LXX) ◊ Mark 13:24

[4]And the sky will roll up like a scroll, and all the stars will fall like leaves from a vine, and like leaves from a fig tree.

Mark	Matt	Luke
	24 30 a And then the son of Adam's sign will appear in the sky, b and every tribe of the earth will lament, c and they'll see the son of Adam coming on clouds of the sky d with great power and splendor.	
13 26 a And then they will see the son of Adam coming on the clouds b with great power and splendor.	c and they'll see the son of Adam coming on clouds of the sky d with great power and splendor.	**21** 27 a And then they will see the son of Adam coming on clouds b with great power and splendor. 28 a Now when these things begin to happen, b stand tall c and hold your heads high, d because your deliverance is just around the corner!"
27 a And then he will send out messengers b and will gather the chosen people c from the four winds, d from the ends of the earth to the edge of the sky!	31 a And he'll send out his messengers b with a blast on the trumpet, c and they'll gather his chosen people d from the four winds, e from one end of the sky to the other!	
28 a "Take a cue from the fig tree. b When its branch is already in bud c and leaves come out, d you know that summer is near. 29 a So, b when you see these things take place, c you ought to realize that he is near, just outside your door. 30 a I swear to you, b this generation certainly won't pass into oblivion c before all these things take place! 31 a The earth will pass into oblivion and so will the sky, b but my words will never be obliterated!"	32 a "Take a cue from the fig tree. b When its branch is already in bud c and leaves come out, d you know that summer is near. 33 a So, b when you see all these things, c you ought to realize that he is near, just outside your door. 34 a I swear to God, b this generation certainly won't pass into oblivion c before all these things take place! 35 a The earth will pass into oblivion and so will the sky, b but my words will never be obliterated!"	29 a Then he told them a parable: b "Observe the fig tree, c or any tree, for that matter. 30 a Once it puts out foliage, b you can see for yourselves c that summer is at hand. 31 a So, b when you see these things happening, c you ought to realize that God's imperial rule is near. 32 a I swear to you, b this generation certainly won't pass into oblivion c before it all takes place! 33 a The earth will pass into oblivion and so will the sky, b but my words will never be obliterated!"

13:27b Most mss (except D L W *f*¹ *pc* it) read *his chosen people,* perhaps under the influence of Matt 24:31c.

☆ **Mark 14:62** ◊ Mark 13:26

[62]Jesus replied, "I am! And you will see the son of Adam sitting at the right hand of Power and coming with the clouds of the sky!"

☆ **Mark 9:1** ◊ Mark 13:30

[1]And he used to tell them, "I swear to you: Some of those standing here won't ever taste death before they see God's imperial rule set in with power!"

☆ **Matt 16:28** ◊ Mark 13:30

[28]"I swear to you: Some of those standing here won't ever taste death before they see the son of Adam's imperial rule arriving."

☆ **Luke 9:27** ◊ Mark 13:30

[27]"I swear to you, some of those standing here won't ever taste death before they see God's imperial rule."

☆ **1 Thess 4:15–16** ◊ Mark 13:26–27

[15]For this we declare to you by the word of the Lord, that we who are alive, who are left until the coming of the Lord, shall not precede those who have fallen asleep. [16]For the Lord himself will descend from heaven with a cry of command, with the archangel's call, and with the sound of the trumpet of God. And the dead in Christ will rise first.

☆ **Rev 1:7** ◊ Mark 13:26

[7]Look! He is coming with clouds!
Every eye will see him,
Even those who killed him,
All the clans of the earth will mourn him.
So be it.

☆ **4 Ezra 13:1–3** ◊ Mark 13:26

[1]And after seven days it happened that at night I saw a vision. [2]Then suddenly a wind was rising from the sea so as to stir up all its waves. [3]And I looked and, surprisingly, that wind raised up from the heart of the sea one like a human being. I looked again and, to my astonishment, that son of Adam was flying with the clouds of heaven. And wherever he turned his face to look, all that he saw before him trembled.

☆ **1 Enoch 46:1–5** ◊ Mark 13:26

[1]And there I saw one who was like the head of time and his head was like wool. And there was another with him who appeared like a human being. His face was full of grace like one of the angels. [2]And I asked the angel who went with me and showed me all the hidden things: "Who is this son of Adam and where is he from? And why does he accompany the head of time?" [3]And he told me in reply: "This is the son of Adam who is just. And justice dwells with him. And he reveals all the treasures of what is hidden because the Lord of Spirits has chosen him. And before the Lord of Spirits his lot is first in justice forever. [4]This son of Adam whom you have seen shall raise up the kings and strongmen from their seats. And he will loosen the reins of the strong and break the teeth of sinners . . . [5]For they do not extol and praise nor humbly acknowledge by whom they were given kingship."

☆ **Dan 7:13–14** (MT) ◊ Mark 13:26–27

[13]As I looked on, in a night vision, one like a human being came with the clouds of heaven; he reached the Ancient of Days and was presented to him. [14]Dominion, glory and kingship were given to him; all peoples and nations of every language must serve him. His dominion is an everlasting dominion that shall not pass away, and his kingship one that shall not be destroyed.

☆ **Deut 30:3–4** (LXX) ◊ Mark 13:27

[3]. . . and the Lord will heal all your faults, have mercy on you, and gather you again from among the heathen, where they once dispersed you. [4]Even if you are dispersed from one end of the skies to the other, the Lord your God will collect you from there; from there the Lord your God will fetch you.

☆ **Zech 2:10** (LXX; RSV 2:6) ◊ Mark 13:27

[10]"O! O! Flee from the northland," says the Lord, "because I will gather you from the four winds of heaven," says the Lord.

K60.5: No One Knows the Day or Hour

Mark 13:32–37	**Matt 24:36, 42**	**Luke**

Mark 13:32–37

13 32 a "As for that exact day or minute: no one knows,
  b not even heaven's messengers,
  c nor even the son,
  d no one, except the Father.
33 a Be on guard!
  b Stay alert!
  c For you never know what time it is.
34 a It's like a person who takes a trip
  b and puts slaves in charge,
  c each with a task,
  d and enjoins the doorkeeper to be alert.
35 a Therefore, stay alert!
  b For you never know when the landlord returns,
  c maybe at dusk,
  d or at midnight,
  e or when the rooster crows,
  f or maybe early in the morning.
36 a He may return suddenly
  b and find you asleep.
37 a What I'm telling you,
  b I say to everyone:
  c Stay alert!"

Matt 24:36, 42

24 36 a "As for that exact day and minute:
    no one knows,
  b not even heaven's messengers,
  c nor even the son—
  d no one, except the Father alone."

42 a So stay alert!
  b You never know on what day your lord returns.

13:35b Greek (κύριος): or *lord* or *master*.

K60.5: No One Knows the Day or Hour

† Matt 24:37–51

[37]"The son of Adam's coming will be just like the days of Noah. [38]This is how people behaved then before the flood came: they ate and drank, married and were given in marriage, until the day 'Noah boarded the ark,' [39]and they were oblivious until the flood came and swept them all away. This is how it will be when the son of Adam comes. [40]Then two men will be in the field; one will be taken and one will be left. [41]Two women will be grinding at the mill; one will be taken and one left.

42a So, stay alert!
  b You never know on what day your
     lord returns.

[43]"Mark this well: if the homeowner had known when the burglar was coming, he would have been on guard and not have allowed anyone to break into his house . [44]By the same token, you too should be prepared. Remember, the son of Adam is coming when you least expect it.

[45]"Who then is the reliable and shrewd slave to whom the master assigns responsibility for his household, to provide them with food at the right time? [46]Congratulations to the slave who's on the job when his master arrives. [47]I swear to you, he'll put him in charge of all his property. [48]But suppose that worthless slave says to himself, 'My master's taking his time,' [49]and begins to beat his fellow slaves, and starts eating and drinking with drunkards, [50]that slave's master will show up on a day he least expects and at an hour he doesn't suspect. [51]He'll cut him to pieces, and assign him a fate fit for the other impostors. ⟨Those who share this fate⟩ will moan and grind their teeth."

† Luke 21:34–36

34a "So guard yourselves ◊ 33a
so your minds won't be dulled by hangovers and drunkenness and the worries of everyday life, and so that day won't spring upon you suddenly like some trap you weren't expecting. [35]It will descend for sure on all who inhabit the earth.
36a Stay alert! ◊ 33b
Pray constantly that you may have the strength to escape all these things that are about to occur and stand before the son of Adam."

△ Luke 12:35–40

[35]"Keep your belts fastened and your lamps lighted. [36]Imitate those who are waiting for their master to come home from a wedding, ready to open the door for him as soon as he arrives and knocks. [37]Those slaves the master finds alert when he arrives are to be congratulated. I swear to you, he will put on an apron, have them recline at the table, and proceed to wait on them. [38]If he gets home around midnight, or even around 3 a.m., and finds them so, they are to be congratulated! [39]Mark this well: if the homeowner had known what time the burglar was coming, he would not have let anyone break into his house. [40]You too should be prepared. Remember, the son of Adam is coming when you least expect it."

✩ Did 16:1

[1]You should guard your life. Your lamps should not be snuffed out, and your thighs should not be ungirded. Rather, be prepared since you don't know the time our Lord is to come.

✩ Matt 25:13 ◊ Mark 13:32, 35

[13]"So stay alert because you don't know either the day or the hour."

THE PASSION NARRATIVE

K61.1: Some Way to Kill Jesus

Mark 14:1–2	Matt 26:1–5	Luke 22:1–2
	26 1 a And so	
	b when Jesus had concluded his discourse,	
	c he told his disciples,	
14 1 a Now it was two days until Passover and the feast of Unleavened Bread.	2 a "You know that Passover comes in two days,	**22** 1 a The feast of Unleavened Bread,
		b known as Passover,
		c was approaching.
	b and the son of Adam will be turned over to be crucified."	
	3 a Then the ranking priests and elders of the people gathered	
	b in the courtyard of the high priest,	
	c whose name was Caiaphas,	
b And the ranking priests and the scholars were looking for some way to arrest him by trickery	4 a and they conspired to seize Jesus by trickery	2 a The ranking priests and the scholars were still looking for some way to get rid of Jesus.
c and kill him.	b and kill him.	
2 a For their slogan was:	5 a Their slogan was:	
b "Not during the festival,	b "Not during the festival,	
c otherwise the people will riot."	c so there won't be a riot among the people."	b But remember, they feared the people.

K61.2: A Woman Anoints Jesus

Mark 14:3–9	Matt 26:6–13	Luke
14 3 a When he was in Bethany at the house of Simon the leper,	**26** 6 While Jesus was in Bethany at the house of Simon the leper,	
b he was just reclining there,	7 **d** while he was reclining ⟨at table⟩.	
c and a woman came in carrying an alabaster jar of myrrh,	a a woman who had an alabaster jar of very expensive myrrh	
	b came up to him	
d of pure and expensive nard.		
e She broke the jar		
f and poured ⟨the myrrh⟩ on his head.	c and poured it over his head	
	8 a When they saw this,	
4 a Now some were annoyed	b the disciples were annoyed,	
b ⟨and thought⟩ to themselves:	c and said,	
c "What good purpose is served by this waste of myrrh?	d "What good purpose is served by this waste?	

K61.1: Some Way to Kill Jesus

† John 11:45–53

⁴⁵As a result, many of the Judeans who had come to Mary and had observed what Jesus had done came to believe in him. ⁴⁶But some of them went to the Pharisees and reported what Jesus had done.

⁴⁷So the ranking priests and Pharisees called the Council together and posed this question to them: "What are we going to do now that this fellow performs many miracles? ⁴⁸If we let him go on like this, everybody will come to believe in him. Then the Romans will come and destroy our ⟨holy⟩ place and our nation."

⁴⁹Then one of them, Caiaphas, that year's high priest, addressed them as follows: "Don't you know anything? ⁵⁰Don't you realize that it's to your advantage to have one person die for the people and not have the whole nation wiped out?"

(⁵¹He didn't say this on his own authority, but since he was that year's high priest he could foresee that Jesus would die for the nation. ⁵²In fact, ⟨he would die⟩ not only for the nation, but to gather together all God's dispersed children and make them one ⟨people⟩.)

⁵³So from that day on they began plotting how to kill him.

† Luke 7:36–50

³⁶One of the Pharisees invited him to dinner; he entered the Pharisee's house, and reclined at the table. ³⁷A local woman who was a sinner, found out that he was having dinner at the Pharisee's house. She suddenly showed up with an alabaster jar of myrrh, ³⁸and stood there behind him weeping at his feet. Her tears wet his feet, and she wiped them dry with her hair; she kissed his feet, and anointed them with the myrrh.

³⁹The Pharisee who had invited him saw this and said to himself, "If this man were a prophet, he would know who this is and what kind of woman is touching him, since she is a sinner."

† John 11:54

⁵⁴As a consequence, Jesus no longer moved openly among the Judeans publicly, but withdrew to a region bordering the wilderness, to a town called Ephraim, and there he stayed with the disciples.

† John 11:55–57

⁵⁵It was almost time for the Jewish Passover, and many of the country people went up to Jerusalem before Passover to purify themselves. ⁵⁶They were on the lookout for Jesus, and as they stood around in the temple area, they were saying to one another, "What do you think? He certainly won't come to the celebration, will he?" (⁵⁷The ranking priests and the Pharisees had given orders that anyone who knew his whereabouts was to report it, so they could arrest him.

☆ Mark 11:18

¹⁸And the ranking priests and the scholars heard this and kept looking for a way to get rid of him. (The truth is that they stood in fear of him, and that the whole crowd was astonished at his teaching.)

K61.2: A Woman Anoints Jesus

⁴⁰And Jesus answered him, "Simon, I have something to tell you."

"Teacher," he said, "Speak up."

⁴¹"This moneylender had two debtors; one owed five hundred silver coins, and the other fifty. ⁴²Since neither of them could pay, he wrote off both debts. Now which of them will love him more?"

⁴³Simon answered, "I would imagine, the one for whom he wrote off the larger debt."

And he said to him, "You're right." ⁴⁴Then turning to the woman, he said to Simon, "Do you see this woman? I walked into your house and you didn't offer me water for my feet; yet she has washed my feet with her tears and dried them with her

☆ Mark 12:12

¹²⟨His opponents⟩ kept looking for some opportunity to seize him, but they were still afraid of the crowd, since they realized that he had aimed the parable at them. So they left him there and went on their way.

☆ Matt 21:45

⁴⁵And when the ranking priests and Pharisees heard his parable, they realized that he was talking about them.

☆ Luke 19:47–48

⁴⁷Every day he would teach in the temple area. The ranking priests and the scholars, along with the leaders of the people, kept looking for some way to get rid of him. ⁴⁸But they never figured out how to do it, because all the people hung on every word.

☆ Luke 20:19

¹⁹The scholars and the ranking priests wanted to lay hands on him then and there, but they were afraid of the people, since they realized he had aimed this parable at them.

hair. ⁴⁵You didn't offer me a kiss, but she hasn't stopped kissing my feet since I arrived. ⁴⁶You didn't anoint my head with oil, but she has anointed my feet with myrrh. ⁴⁷For this reason, I tell you, her sins, many as they are, have been forgiven, as this outpouring of love shows. But the one who is forgiven little shows little love."

⁴⁸And he said to her, "Your sins have been forgiven."

⁴⁹Then those having dinner with him began to mutter to themselves, "Who is this who even forgives sins?"

⁵⁰And he said to the woman, "Your trust has saved you; go in peace."

Mark	**Matt**	**Luke**

14 5 a For she could have sold the myrrh
for more than three hundred silver
coins
b and given ⟨the money⟩ to the poor.”
c And they were angry with her.

6 a Then Jesus said,
b “Let her alone!
c Why are you bothering her?

d She has done me a courtesy.
7 a Remember, there will always be poor
around,
b and whenever you want
c you can do good for them,
d but I you won't always be around.
8 a She did what she could

b —she anticipates in anointing my
body for burial.
9 a So help me,
b wherever the good news is
announced in all the world,
c what she has done will also be told in
memory of her!”

26 9 a After all, she could have sold it for a
good price

b and given ⟨the money⟩ to the poor.”

10 a But Jesus saw through ⟨their
complaint⟩
b and said to them,

c “Why are you bothering this
woman?
d After all, she has done me a courtesy.
11 a Remember, there will always be poor
around;

b but I won't always be around.
12 a After all, by pouring this myrrh on
my body
b she has made me ready for burial.

13 a So help me,
b wherever this good news is
announced in all the world,
c what she has done will be told in
memory of her.”

K61.3: Priests Promise to Pay Judas

Mark 14:10–11	**Matt 26:14–16**	**Luke 22:3–6**

1410 a And Judas Iscariot,
b one of the twelve,
c went off to the ranking priests

d to turn him over to them.

2614 b Judas Iscariot by name,
a Then one of the twelve,
c went to the ranking priests

15 a and said,
b “What are you willing to pay me
c if I turn him over to you?”

22 3 a Then Satan took possession of
Judas,
b the one called Iscariot,
c who was a member of the twelve.
4 a He went off
b to negotiate with the ranking priests
and officers
c on a way to turn Jesus over to them.

11 a When they heard,
b they were delighted,
c and promised to pay him in silver.

d They agreed on thirty silver coins.

5 a They were delighted,
b and consented to pay him in silver.
6 a And Judas accepted the deal,
b and began looking for the right
moment to turn him over to them

d And he started looking for some way
to turn him in at the right moment.

16 And from that moment he started
looking for the right occasion to turn
him in.

c when a crowd was not around.

14:5a See the note on 6:37e.

† John 12:1–8

[1]Six days before Passover Jesus came to Bethany, where Lazarus lived, the one Jesus had brought back from the dead. [2]There they gave a dinner for him; Martha did the serving, and Lazarus was one of those who ate with him. [3]Mary brought in a pound of expensive lotion and anointed Jesus' feet and wiped them with her hair. The house was filled with the lotion's fragrance. [4]Judas Iscariot, the disciple who was going to turn him in, says,

5 a "Why wasn't this lotion sold? It would bring a year's wages, ◊ 14:5a

b and the proceeds could have been given to the poor." ◊ 14:5b

([6]He didn't say this because he cared about the poor, but because he was a thief. He was in charge of the common purse, and now and again would pilfer money put into it.)

7 "Let her alone," Jesus said. ◊ 14:6b "Let her keep it for the time I am to be embalmed.

8 a There will always be poor around; ◊ 14:7a

b but I won't always be around." ◊ 14:7d

K61.3: Priests Promise to Pay Judas

K62: Jesus Celebrates Passover

Mark 14:12–26	Matt 26:17–30	Luke 22:7–23
1412a On the first day of Unleavened Bread, b when they would sacrifice the Passover lamb,	**26**17a On the first ⟨day⟩ of Unleavened Bread	**22** 7a The feast of Unleavened Bread arrived, b when the Passover ⟨lambs⟩ had to be sacrificed. 8a So ⟨Jesus⟩ sent Peter and John, b with these instructions: c "Go d get things ready for us to eat the Passover."
c his disciples say to him, d "Where do you want us to go and get things ready e for you to celebrate Passover?"	b the disciples came to Jesus, c and said, d "Where do you want us to get things ready e for you to celebrate Passover?"	9a They said to him, b "Where do you want us to get things ready?"
13a He sends two of his disciples b and says to them, c "Go into the city, d and someone carrying a waterpot will meet you. e Follow him, 14a and whatever place he enters b say to the head of the house, c 'The teacher asks, d "Where is my guest room	18a He said, b "Go into the city c to so-and-so d and say to him, e 'The teacher says,	10a He said to them, b "Look, when you enter the city, c someone carrying a waterpot will meet you. d Follow him e into the house he enters, 11a and say to the head of the house, b 'The Teacher asks you, c "Where is the guest room
e where I can celebrate Passover with my disciples?'"	f "My time is near, g I will observe Passover at your place with my disciples."'" 19a And the disciples did as Jesus instructed them	d where I can celebrate Passover with my disciples?'"
15a And he'll show you a large upstairs room b that's been arranged. c That's the place you're to get ready for us." 16a And the disciples left, b went into the city, c and found it exactly as he had told them; d and they got things ready for Passover.		12a And he will show you a large upstairs room c that's been arranged; b That's the place you're to get things ready." 13a They set off b and found things exactly as he had told them; c and they got things ready for Passover.
17a When evening comes, b he arrives with the twelve. 18a And as they reclined at table	b and they got things ready for Passover. 20a When it was evening,	14a When the time came,
b and were eating, c Jesus said,	b he was reclining ⟨at table⟩ c with his twelve followers. 21a And as they were eating, b he said,	b he took his place ⟨at table⟩, c and the apostles joined him. 15a He said to them, b "I have looked forward with all my heart to celebrating this Passover with you c before my ordeal begins. 16a For I tell you, b I certainly won't eat it again c until everything comes true in God's domain."

K62: Jesus Celebrates Passover

† John 13:21–30 ◊ Mark 14:17–21

²¹When he had said all this, Jesus became deeply disturbed. He declared: "I swear to God, one of you will turn me in."

²²The disciples stole glances at each other, at a loss to understand who it was. ²³One of them, the disciple Jesus loved most, was sitting at Jesus' right. ²⁴So Simon Peter leans over to ask that disciple who it was ⟨Jesus⟩ was talking about. ²⁵He, in turn, leans over to Jesus and asks him, "Master, who is it?"

²⁶Jesus answers: "I am going to dunk this piece of bread, and the one I give it to is the one." So he dunks the piece of bread and gives it to Judas, Simon Iscariot's son. ²⁷The moment ⟨he had given Judas⟩ the piece of bread, Satan took possession of him. Then Jesus says to him, "Go ahead and do what you're going to do."

²⁸Of course no one at dinner understood why Jesus had made this remark. ²⁹Some had the idea that because Judas kept charge of the funds, Jesus was telling him, "Buy whatever we need for the celebration," or to give something to the poor. ³⁰In any case, as soon as ⟨Judas⟩ had eaten the piece of bread he went out. It was nighttime.

GEbi 7 ◊ Mark 14:12–16

They take it on themselves to obscure the logic of the truth and to alter the saying, as is evident to everyone from the context, and make the disciples say: ¹"Where do you want us to get things ready for you to eat the Passover meal?" And apparently they make him answer: ²"I certainly have not looked forward with all my heart to eating meat with you at this Passover, have I?" Anyone can detect their deceit because the sequence makes it obvious that the *mu* and the *eta* have been added. Instead of saying, "I have looked forward with all my heart" they add the additional word *mē* ("not"). Now in fact he said, "I have looked forward with all my heart to eating the Passover meal with you." However, they deceive themselves by adding the word "meat," and they do evil by saying, "I do not look forward to eating meat with you at this Passover."

Epiphanius, *Haer.* 30.22.4

Mark	Matt	Luke

Mark

14 18 d "So help me,
  e one of you eating with me is going to turn me in!"
19 a They began to fret
  b and to say to him one after another,
  c "I'm not the one, am I?"

20 a But he said to them,
  b "It's one of the twelve,
  c the one who is dipping into the bowl with me.
21 a The son of Adam departs just as the scriptures predict,
  b but damn the one responsible for turning the son of Adam in!
  c It would be better for that man
  d had he never been born!"

22 a And as they were eating,
  b he took a loaf,
  c gave a blessing,
  d broke it into pieces
  e and offered it to them.
  f And he said,
  g "Take some;

  h this is my body!"

23 a He also took a cup,

  b gave thanks
  c and offered it to them,
  d and they all drank from it.
24 a And he said to them:
  b "This is my blood of the covenant,

  c which has been poured out for many!

Matt

26 21 c "So help me,
  d one of you is going to turn me in."
22 a And they were very upset
  b and each one said to him in turn,
  c "I'm not the one, am I, Master?"

23 a In response he said,
  c that's who's going to turn me in!
  b "The one who dips his hand in the bowl with me—
24 a The son of Adam departs just as the scriptures predict,
  b but damn the one responsible for turning the son of Adam in.
  c It would be better for that man
  d had he never been born!"
25 a Judas,
  b who was to turn him in,
  c responded,
  d "You can't mean me, can you, Rabbi?"
  e He says to him,
  f "You said it."
26 a As they were eating,
  b Jesus took a loaf,
  c gave a blessing,
  d and broke it into pieces.
  e And he offered it to the disciples,
  f and said,
  g "Take some
  h and eat,
  i this is my body."

27 a He also took a cup

  b and gave thanks,
  c and offered it to them,
  e "Drink from it, all of you,
  d saying,
28 a for this is my blood of the covenant,

  b which has been poured out for many
  c for the forgiveness of sins.

Luke

22 17 a Then he took a cup,
  b gave thanks,
  c and said,
  d "Take this
  e and share it among yourselves.

23 a And they began to ask one another
  b which of them could possibly attempt such a thing.
21 a Yet look!
  b Here with me at this very table
  c is the one who is going to turn me in.
22 a The son of Adam goes to meet his destiny;
  b yet damn the one responsible for turning him in."

19 a And he took a loaf,
  b gave thanks,
  c broke it into pieces,
  d offered it to them,
  e and said,

  f "This is my body
  g which is offered for you.
  h Do this as my memorial."
20 a And, in the same manner, ⟨he took⟩
  b the cup after dinner,
  c and said,

  d "This cup is the new covenant in my blood,
  e which is poured out for you.

✩ **John 6:48–58** ◊ Mark 14:22–25

[48]"I am the bread of life. [49]Your ancestors ate the manna in the desert, but they still died. [50]This is the bread that comes down from heaven:, anyone who eats it never dies. [51]I am the life-giving bread that came down from heaven. Anyone who eats this bread will live forever. And the bread that I will give for the world's life is my mortal flesh."

[52]At this point the Judeans began quarreling among themselves: "How can this fellow give us his mortal flesh to eat?"

[53]So Jesus told them: "I swear to God, if you don't eat the son of Adam's mortal flesh and drink his blood, you don't possess life. [54]Everyone who feeds on my mortal flesh and drinks my blood possesses real life, and I will resurrect them on the last day. [55]For my mortal flesh is real food, and my blood real drink. [56]Those who feed on my mortal flesh and drink my blood are part of me, and I am part of them. [57]The Father of life sent me, and I have life because of the Father. Just so, anyone who feeds on me will have life because of me. [58]This is the bread that comes down from heaven sky. Unlike your ancestors who ate ⟨manna⟩ and then died, anyone who feeds on this bread will live forever."

✩ **1 Cor 11:23–25** ◊ Mark 14:22–25

[23]For I received from the Lord what I also delivered to you, that the Lord Jesus on the night when he was betrayed took bread, [24]and when he had given thanks, he broke it, and said, "This is my body which is for you. Do this in remembrance of me." [25]In the same way also the cup, after supper, saying, "This cup is the new covenant in my blood. Do this, as often as you drink it, in remembrance of me."

✩ **Did 9:1–5** ◊ Mark 14:22–25

[1]Concerning the eucharist, this is how you are to conduct it: [2]First, concerning the cup, "We thank you, our Father, for the sacred vine of David, your child, whom you made known to us through Jesus, your child. To you be glory forever." [3]Then concerning the fragments ⟨of bread⟩: "We thank you, our Father, for the life and knowledge that you made known to us through Jesus, your child. To you be glory forever. [4]Just as this loaf was scattered upon the mountains but was gathered into a unity, so your church should be gathered from the ends of the earth into your domain. Yours is the glory and the power through Jesus Christ forever." [5]No one is to eat or drink from your eucharist except those baptized in the name of the Lord. Recall what the Lord said about this: "Don't throw what is sacred to the dogs."

Ps 40:10 (LXX; MT 41:10) ◊ Mark 14:18

[10]For my close friend, in whom I placed my hope,
the one who eats bread with me, has magnified my downfall.

✩ **Justin,** *Apology* 1.66.3 ◊ Mark 14:22–25

[3]In their memoirs, which are called gospels, the apostles passed on the instructions given to them, as follows: Jesus took bread, gave thanks, and said, "Do this in remembrance of me; this is my body." In a similar manner, he took the cup, gave thanks, and said, "This is my blood." And he gave it to them alone.

Exod 24:8 (LXX) ◊ Mark 14:24

[8]Moses took blood and sprinkled it on the people. He said, "Look, this is the blood of the covenant which the Lord made with you in relation to all these injunctions."

Jer 38:31 (LXX; MT 31:31) ◊ Mark 14:24

[31]"Look, the time is coming," says the Lord, "when I will make a new covenant with the house of Israel and with the house of Judah."

Zech 9:11 (LXX) ◊ Mark 14:24

[11]And because of the blood of the covenant you have released your prisoners from the dry pit.

Mark	Matt	Luke
1425 a So help me, b I certainly won't drink any of the fruit of the vine again c until that day when I drink it for the first time in God's domain!"	**26**29 a Now I tell you, b I certainly won't drink any of this fruit of the vine from now on, c until that day when I drink it for the first time with you in my Father's domain!"	**22**18 a For I tell you, b I certainly won't drink of the fruit of the vine from now on
26 a And they sang a hymn b and left for the Mount of Olives.	30 a And they sang a hymn, b and left for the Mount of Olives.	

K63.1: Peter Takes an Oath

Mark 14:27–31	Matt 26:31–35	Luke 22:31–34
1427 a And Jesus says to them, b "You will all lose faith. c Remember, scripture says, d 'I will strike the shepherd e and the sheep will be scattered!'	**26**31 a Then Jesus says to them, b "All of you will lose faith in me on this night, c Remember, it is written, d 'I will strike the shepherd e and the sheep of his flock will be scattered!'	
28 a But after I'm raised b I'll go ahead of you to Galilee."	32 a But after I'm raised, b I'll go ahead of you to Galilee."	
		2231 a "Simon, Simon, look out, b Satan is after all of you, c to winnow you like wheat. 32 a But I have prayed for you b that your trust may not give out. c And once you have recovered, d you are to shore up these brothers of yours." 33 a He said to him, b "Master, I'm prepared to follow you not only to prison but all the way to death."
29 a Peter said to him, b "Even if everyone else loses faith, c I won't!"	33 a In response Peter said to him, b "If everyone else loses faith in you, c I never will."	
30 a And Jesus says to him, b "So help me, c tonight before the rooster crows twice d you will disown me three times!"	34 a Jesus said to him, b "So help me, c tonight before the rooster crows d you will disown me three times!"	34 a He said, b "Let me tell you, Peter, c the rooster will not crow tonight d until you disavow three times e that you know me."
31 a But he repeated it with more bluster: b "If they condemn me to die with you, c I will never disown you!" d And they took the same oath—all of them.	35 a Peter says to him, b "Even if they condemn me to die with you, c I will never disown you!" d And all of the disciples took the same oath—all of them.	

† **Luke 22:39** ◊ Mark 14:26

[39]Then he left and walked, as usual, over to the Mount of Olives; and the disciples followed him.

† **John 18:1** ◊ Mark 14:26

[1]When he had said all this, Jesus went out with his disciples across the Kidron valley. There was a garden there where he and his disciples went.

Fayyum Fragment ◊ Mark 14:27, 29–30

. . . while he was going out, he said "This night you will all desert me, as it is written, 'I will strike the shepherd and the sheep will be scattered.'" Then Peter said, "Even if they all do, I will not." Jesus says, "Before the rooster crows twice, you will this day disown me three times."

K63.1: Peter Takes an Oath

☆ **John 16:32** ◊ Mark 14:27

[32]"Look, the time has come for all of you to scatter and return home; you'll abandon me. But I won't be alone, because the Father is with me."

† **John 13:36–38** ◊ Mark 14:29–30

[36]Simon Peter says to him, "Master, where are you going?"

Jesus answered, "For now you can't follow me where I'm going; you'll follow later."

[37]Peter says to him, "Master, why can't I follow you now? I'd give my life for you."

[38]Jesus responded, "You'd give your life for me? I swear to God: the rooster won't crow before you disown me three times."

☆ **John 11:16** ◊ Mark 14:31

[16]Then Thomas, called "the Twin," said to his fellow disciples, "Let's go along too, so we can die with him."

Zech 13:7 (LXX) ◊ Mark 14:27

[7]"O sword! You should be raised against my shepherds, and against my leader," says the Lord Almighty. "Strike my shepherds and scatter my sheep, and I will lift my hand against my shepherds."

223

K63.2: Jesus Prays in Gethsemane

Mark 14:32–42	**Matt 26:36–46**	**Luke 22:39–46**

Luke 22:39–46

b and walked, as usual, over to the Mount of Olives;
c and the disciples followed him.
40 a When he arrived at his usual place

b he said to them,

c "Pray that you won't be put to the test."

Mark 14:32–42

14 32 a And they go to a place
b the name of which was Gethsemane,
c and he says to his disciples,
d "Sit down here
e while I pray."

Matt 26:36–46

26 36 a Then Jesus goes with them to a place
b called Gethsemane,
c and he says to the disciples,
d "Sit down here
e while I go over there and pray."

33 a And he takes Peter and James and John along with him,
b and he grew apprehensive
c and full of anguish.
34 a He says to them,
b "I'm so sad I could die.
c You stay here and be alert!"
35 a And he would move on a little,

b fall on the ground,
c and pray that he might avoid the crisis,
d if possible.

37 a And taking Peter and the two sons of Zebedee,
b he began to feel dejected
c and full of anguish.
38 a He says to them,
b "I'm so sad I could die.
c You stay here with me and be alert!"
39 a And he went a little farther,

b lay facedown,

41 a And he withdrew from them about a stone's throw away,
b fell to his knees
c and began to pray,

36 a And he would say,
b "*Abba* (Father),
c all things are possible for you!
d Take this cup away from me!
e But it's not what I want ⟨that matters⟩,
f but what you want."

c and prayed,
d "My Father,
e if it is possible,
f take this cup away from me!
g Yet it's not what I want ⟨that matters⟩,
h but what you want."

42 a "Father,
b if you so choose,
c take this cup away from me!
d Yet not my will,

e but yours, be done."

37 a And he returns
b and finds them sleeping,

c and says to Peter,
d "Simon, are you sleeping?
e Couldn't you stay awake for one hour?
38 a Be alert
b and pray that you won't be put to the test!
c Though the spirit is willing,
d the flesh is weak."
39 a And once again he went away

b and prayed,
c saying the same thing.

40 a And he returns to the disciples
b and finds them sleeping,

c and says to Peter,

d "Couldn't you stay awake with me for one hour?
41 a Be alert,
b and pray that you are not put to the test!
c Though the spirit is willing,
d the flesh is weak."
42 a Again for a second time he went away
b and prayed,

c "My Father,
d if it is not possible for me to avoid this ⟨cup⟩
e without drinking it,
f your will must prevail!"

45 a And when he got up from his prayer
b and returned to the disciples,
c he found them asleep,
d weary from grief.
46 a He said to them,
b "What are you doing sleeping?

c Get up
d and pray that you won't be put to the test."

K63.2: Jesus Prays in Gethsemane

† John 18:1 ◊ Mark 14:32

[1]When he had said all this, Jesus went out with his disciples across the Kidron valley. There was a garden there where he and his disciples went.

† John 12:27 ◊ Mark 14:34

[27]"Now my life is in turmoil, but should I say, 'Father, rescue me from this moment'? No, it was to face this moment that I came!"

☆ John 18:11 ◊ Mark 14:36

[11]"Put the sword back in its scabbard," Jesus told Peter. "Am I not to drink from the cup my Father has given me?"

Luke 22:43–44 Some manuscripts add here, or after Matt 26:39, vv 43–44:
[43]Heaven's messenger appeared to him and gave him strength. [44]In his anxiety he prayed more fervently, and it so happened that his sweat fell to the ground like great drops of blood.

Mark	**Matt**	**Luke**

14 40 a And once again he came
b and found them sleeping,
c since their eyes had grown very heavy,
d and they didn't know what to say to him.

21 43 a And once again he came
b and found them sleeping,
c since their eyes had grown heavy.

44 a And leaving them again,
b he went away
c and prayed,
d repeating the same words for a third time.

41 a And he comes a third time
b and says to them,
c "You may as well sleep on now
d and get your rest.
e It's all over!
f The time has come!
g Look, the son of Adam is being turned over to foreigners.
42 a Get up,
b let's go!
c See for yourselves!
d Here comes the one who is going to turn me in."

45 a Then he comes to the disciples
b and says to them,
c "Are you still sleeping
d and taking a rest?

e Look, the time is at hand!
f The son of Adam is being turned over to foreigners.
46 a Get up,
b let's go!
c See for yourselves!
d Here comes the one who is going to turn me in."

K63.3: Judas Turns Jesus In

Mark 14:43–52	**Matt 26:47–56**	**Luke 22:47–54**

14 43 a And right away,
b while he was still speaking,
c Judas,
d one of the twelve,
e shows up,
f and with him a crowd,
g dispatched by the ranking priests
h and the scholars
i and the elders,
j wielding swords and clubs.
44 a Now the one who was to turn him in had arranged a signal with them,
b saying,
c "The one I'm going to kiss is the one you want.
d Arrest him
e and escort him safely away!"
45 a And right away he arrives,
b comes up to him,

c and says,
d "Rabbi,"
e and kissed him.

26 47 a And while he was still speaking,
b suddenly Judas,
c one of the twelve,
d arrived
e and with him a great crowd
g dispatched by the ranking priests

h and elders of the people.
f wielding swords and clubs,
48 a Now the one who was to turn him in had arranged a sign with them,
b saying,
c "The one I'm going to kiss is the one you want.
d Arrest him!"

49 a And he came right up to Jesus,

b and said,
c "Hello, Rabbi,"
d and kissed him.
50 a But Jesus said to him,
b "Look friend, what are you doing here?"
c Then they came

22 47 a Suddenly,
b while he was still speaking,
d with the one called Judas,
e one of the twelve,
f leading the way.
c a crowd appeared

g He stepped up to Jesus to give him a kiss.

48 a But Jesus said to him,
b "Judas, would you turn in the son of Adam with a kiss?"

† John 14:31 ◊ Mark 14:42

[31]"However, so the world may know I love the Father, I act exactly as my Father instructed me. Come on, let's get out of here."

K63.3: Judas Turns Jesus In

† John 18:1–11

[1]When he had said all this, Jesus went out with his disciples across the Kidron valley. There was a garden there where he and his disciples went. [2]But because Jesus had often gone there with his disciples, Judas, who was about to turn him in, knew the place too. [3]So it wasn't long before Judas arrives, bringing with him the detachment ⟨of Roman soldiers⟩ and some of the police from the ranking priests and the Pharisees, armed with their lamps and torches.

[4]Jesus, of course, knew just what would happen to him, so he went right up to them and says, "Who is it you're looking for?"

[5]"Jesus the Nazarene," was their reply.

"That's me," says Jesus.

And all the while Judas, who was turning him in, was standing there with them. [6]But as soon as he said, "That's me," they all retreated and fell to the ground.

[7]So Jesus asked them again, "Who are you looking for?"

"Jesus the Nazarene," they said.

[8]"I told you that's me," Jesus answered, "so if it's me you're looking for, let the others go."

([9]This was so the prediction he had made would come true: "I haven't lost one—not one of those you put in my care.")

[10]Simon Peter had brought along a sword, and now he drew it, slashed at the high priest's slave, who was called Malchus, and cut off his right ear.

[11]"Put the sword back in its scabbard," Jesus told Peter. "Am I not to drink from the cup my Father has given me?"

Mark	Matt	Luke
14 46 a And they seized him b and held him fast.	**26** 50 d and seized him e and held him fast.	
		22 49 a And when those around him realized what was coming next, b they said, c "Master, now do we use our swords?
47 a One of those standing around b drew his sword c and struck the high priest's slave d and cut off his ear.	51 a At that moment one of those with Jesus lifted his hand, b drew his sword, c struck the high priest's slave, d and cut off his ear.	50 a And one of them struck the high priest's slave b and cut off his right ear. 51 a But Jesus responded,
	52 a Then Jesus says to him, b "Put your sword back where it belongs. c For everyone who takes up the sword d will be done in by the sword. 53 a Or do you suppose b I am not able to call on my Father, c who would put more than twelve legions of heavenly messengers at my disposal? 54 a How then would the scriptures come true b that say these things are inevitable?"	
		b "Stop! c That will do!" d And he touched his ear e and healed him. 52 a Then Jesus addressed the ranking priests and temple officers and elders b who had come out after him:
48 a In response Jesus said to them, b "Have you come out to take me with swords and clubs as though you were apprehending a rebel? 49 a I was with you in the temple area day after day teaching b and you didn't lift a hand against me. c But the scriptures must come true!"	55 a At that moment Jesus said to the crowds, b "Have you come out to take me with swords and clubs as though you were apprehending a rebel? c I used to sit there in the temple area day after day teaching, d and you didn't lift a hand against me." 56 a All of this happened b so the writings of the prophets would come true.	c "Have you come out with swords and clubs as though you were apprehending a rebel? 53 a When I was with you day after day in the temple area, b you didn't lay a hand on me.
		c But this is your hour, d and the authority darkness confers is yours." 54 a They arrested him b and marched him away c to the house of the high priest.
50 a And they all deserted him b and ran away. 51 a And a young man was following him, b wearing a shroud over his nude body, c and they grab him. 52 a But he dropped the shroud b and ran away naked.	c Then all the disciples deserted him d and ran away.	

† **John 18:20** ◊ Mark 14:49

²⁰"I have talked publicly to anyone and everyone," Jesus replied. "I have also taught in synagogues and in the temple area, in places where all Judeans gather. I've said nothing in secret."

Table 9

Framework Stories

	Mark
1. Voice in the Wilderness	1:1–8
2. John Baptizes Jesus	1:9–11
3. Jesus Is Put to the Test	1:12–13
4. Jesus Proclaims the Good News	1:14–15
5. Who Do People Say I Am?	8:27–30
6. Son of Adam Must Suffer	8:31–33
7. Jesus Transformed	9:2–8
8. Son of Adam Will Die and Rise	9:30–32
9. Son of Adam Will Die and Rise	10:32–34
10. Passion Story	14:1–15:47
11. Empty Tomb	16:1–8

K64.1: Trial Before the Council

Mark 14:53–65	**Matt 26:57–68**	**Luke 22:54–55, 63–71**
1453 a And they brought Jesus before the high priest,	**26**57 a Those who had arrested Jesus	
b and all the ranking priests and elders and scholars assemble.	b brought him before Caiaphas the high priest,	
	c where the scholars and elders had assembled.	
54 a Peter followed him at a distance	58 a But Peter followed him at a distance	**22**54 d Peter followed at a distance.
	b as far as the courtyard of the high priest.	
b until he was inside the courtyard of the high priest,	c He went inside	
		55 a When they had started a fire in the middle of the courtyard
		b and were sitting around it,
c and was sitting with the attendants	d and sat with the attendants	c Peter joined them.
d and keeping warm by the fire.		
	e to see how things would turn out.	
55 a The ranking priests and the whole Council were looking for evidence against Jesus	59 a The ranking priests and the whole Council were looking for false testimony against Jesus	
b in order to issue a death sentence,	b so they might issue a death sentence;	
c but they couldn't find any.	60 a but they couldn't find many perjurers to come forward.	
56 a Although many gave false evidence against him,		
b their stories didn't agree.		
57 a And some people stood up	b Finally, two persons came forward	
b and testified falsely against him:	61 a and said,	
58 a "We have heard him saying,	b "This fellow said,	
b 'I'll destroy this temple made with hands	c 'I'm able to destroy the temple of God	
c and in three days I'll build another,	d and rebuild it within three days.'"	
d not made with hands!'"		
59 Yet even then their stories did not agree.		
60 a And the high priest got up	62 a The high priest got up	
b and questioned Jesus:	b and questioned him:	
c "Don't you have some answer to give?	c "Don't you have something to say?	
d Why do these people testify against you?"	d Why do these people testify against you?"	
61 a But he was silent	63 a But Jesus was silent.	
b and refused to answer.		
c Once again the high priest questioned him		

14:55a *Council* or *Sanhedrin*: the highest Jewish governing body, composed of ranking priests, elders, and scholars.

K64.1: Trial Before the Council

† John 18:13–14 ◊ Mark 14:55–65

¹³They took him first to Annas. (Annas was the father-in-law of that year's high priest, Caiaphas. ¹⁴It was Caiaphas, you'll remember, who had given the Judeans this advice: It's to ⟨your⟩ advantage that one man die for the people.)

† John 18:19–24 ◊ Mark 14:55–65

¹⁹Now the high priest interrogated Jesus about his disciples and about his teaching.

²⁰"I have talked publicly to anyone and everyone," Jesus replied. "I have always taught in the synagogues and in the temple area, in places where all Judeans gather. I've said nothing in secret. ²¹Why are you asking me? Ask those who listened to what I told them—you'll find that they know what I said."

²²No sooner had he said this than one of the police on duty there slapped Jesus. "So this is how you talk back to the high priest!" he said.

²³"If I have said the wrong thing, tell me what's wrong with it," Jesus said in reply. "But if I'm right, why do you hit me?"

²⁴At that Annas sent him, under constraint as before, to the high priest, Caiaphas.

☆ Thom 71 ◊ Mark 14:58

Jesus said, "I will destroy [this] house, and no one will be able to build it [. . .]."

☆ John 2:19 ◊ Mark 14:58

¹⁹Jesus replied, "Destroy this temple and I'll resurrect it in three days."

Mark	Matt	Luke
		22 66 a When day came,
		b the elders of the people convened,
		c along with the ranking priests and scholars.
		d They had him brought before their Council,
14 61 d and says to him,	**26** 63 b And the high priest said to him,	e where they interrogated him:
	c "I adjure you by the living God:	
e "Are you the Anointed,	d Tell us if you are the Anointed,	67 a "If you are the Anointed,
f the son of the Blessed One?"	e the son of God!"	
		b tell us."
62 a Jesus replied,	64 a Jesus says to him,	c But he said to them,
b "I am!	b "If you say so.	d "If I tell you,
		e you certainly won't believe me.
		68 a If I ask you a question,
		b you certainly won't answer.
c And you will see the son of Adam sitting at the right hand of Power	c But I tell you,	69 But from now on the son of Adam will be seated at the right hand of the power of God."
	d from now on you will see the son of Adam sitting at the right hand of Power	
d and coming with the clouds of the sky!"	e and coming on the clouds of the sky."	
cf. Mark 14:61f	*cf. Matt 26:63e*	70 a And they all said,
		b "So you, are you the son of God?"
	cf. Matt 26:64b	c He said to them,
63 a Then the high priest tore his vestments	65 a Then the high priest tore his vestment,	d "You're the ones who say so."
b and says,	b and said,	
c "Why do we still need witnesses?	c "He has blasphemed!	71 a And they said,
64 a You have heard the blasphemy!	d Why do we still need witnesses?	
	e See, now you have heard the blasphemy.	b "Why do we still need witnesses?
b What do you think?"	66 a What do you think?"	c We have heard it ourselves from his own lips."
	b In response they said,	
c And they all concurred in the death penalty.	c "He deserves to die!"	
		63 **a** Then the men who were holding ⟨Jesus⟩ in custody began to make fun of him
65 a And some began to spit on him,	67 a Then they spit in his face,	64 **a** They blindfolded him
b and to put a blindfold on him,		63 **b** and rough him up.
c and punch him,	b and punched him and hit him,	64 **b** and demanded:
d and say to him,	68 a saying,	**c** "Prophesy!
e "Prophesy!"	b "Prophesy for us, you Anointed, you!	
	c Guess who hit you!"	**d** Guess who hit you!"
f And the guards abused him as they took him into custody.		65 And this was only the beginning of their insults.

☆ Mark 13:26 ◊ Mark 14:62

26"And then they will see the son of Adam coming on the clouds with great power and splendor."

☆ Matt 24:30 ◊ Mark 14:62

30"And then the son of Adam's sign will appear in the sky, and every tribe of the earth will lament, and they'll see the son of Adam coming on clouds of the sky with great power and splendor."

† GPet 3:4 ◊ Mark 14:65

4And others standing about would spit in his eyes, and others slapped his face, while others poked him with a rod. Some kept flogging him as they said, "Let's pay proper respect to the son of God."

4 Ezra 13:1–3 ◊ Mark 14:62

1And after seven days it happened that at night I saw a vision. 2Then suddenly a wind was rising from the sea so as to stir up all its waves. 3And I looked and, surprisingly, that wind raised up from the heart of the sea one like a human being. I looked again and, to my astonishment, that son of Adam was flying with the clouds of heaven. And wherever he turned his face to look, all that he saw before him trembled.

1 Enoch 46:1–5 ◊ Mark 14:62

1And there I saw one who was like the head of time and his head was like wool. And there was another with him who appeared like a human being. His face was full of grace like one of the holy messengers. 2And I asked the heavenly messenger who went with me and showed me all the hidden things: "Who is this son of Adam and where is he from? And why does he accompany the head of time?" 3And he told me in reply: "This is the son of Adam who is just. And justice dwells with him. And he reveals all the treasures of what is hidden because the Lord of Spirits has chosen him. And before the Lord of Spirits his lot is first in justice forever. 4This son of Adam whom you have seen shall raise up the kings and strongmen from their seats. And he will loosen the reins of the strong and break the teeth of sinners . . . 5For they do not extol and praise nor humbly acknowledge by whom they were given kingship."

Ps 109:1 (LXX; MT 110:1) ◊ Mark 14:62

1The Lord said to my lord, "Sit here at my right until I make your enemies grovel at your feet."

Dan 7:13–14 (MT) ◊ Mark 14:62

13As I looked on, in a night vision, one like a human being came with the clouds of heaven; he reached the Ancient of Days and was presented to him. 14Dominion, glory and kingship were given to him; all peoples and nations of every language must serve him. His dominion is an everlasting dominion that shall not pass away, and his kingship one that shall not be destroyed.

Lev 24:16 (LXX) ◊ Mark 14:64

16The one who names the name of the Lord shall certainly be executed. The entire congregation of Israel should stone that one with stones. Everyone naming the name of the Lord is to be put to death, whether proselyte or native.

K64.2: Peter Swears and a Rooster Crows

Mark 14:66–72	**Matt 26:69–75**	**Luke 22:56–62**
14 66 a And while Peter was below in the courtyard,	26 69 a Meanwhile Peter was sitting outside in the courtyard,	
b one of the high priest's slave women comes over,	b and one slave woman came up to him,	
67 a and sees Peter warming himself;		22 56 a Then a slave woman noticed him sitting there in the glow of the fire.
b she looks at him closely		b She stared at him,
c and speaks up,	c and said,	c then spoke up,
d "You too were with that Nazarene, Jesus!"	d "You too were with Jesus the Galilean."	d "This fellow was with him, too."
68 a But he denied it,	70 a But he denied it in front of everyone,	57 a He denied it,
b saying,	b saying,	b "My good woman," he said,
c "I haven't the slightest idea	c "I don't know	c I don't know him."
d what you're talking about!"	d what you're talking about!"	
e And he went outside into the forecourt.	71 a After ⟨Peter⟩ went out to the entrance,	
69 a And when the slave woman saw him,	b another slave woman saw him	58 a A little later someone else noticed him
b she once again began to say to those standing nearby,	c and says to those there,	b and said,
c "This fellow is one of them!"	d "This fellow was with Jesus of Nazareth."	c "You are one of them, too."
70 a But once again he denied it.	72 a And again he denied it with an oath:	e Peter replied.
	b "I don't know the man!"	d "Not me, mister,"
b And a little later,	73 a A little later	59 a About an hour went by
c those standing nearby would again say to Peter,	b those standing about came	b and someone else insisted,
	c and said to Peter,	
d "You really are one of them,	d "You really are one of them;	c "No question about it; this fellow was also one of them;
e since you also are a Galilean!"	e even the way you talk gives you away!"	d he's even a Galilean!"
71 a But he began to curse	74 a Then he began to curse	60 a But Peter said,
b and swear,	b and swear:	
c "I don't know the fellow	c "I don't know the fellow."	b "Mister, I don't know
d you're talking about!"		c what you're talking about."
		d And all of a sudden, while he was still speaking,
72 a And just then a rooster crowed a second time,	d And just then a rooster crowed.	e a rooster crowed.
		61 a And the Lord turned
		b and looked straight at Peter.
b and Peter remembered what Jesus had told him:	75 a And Peter remembered what Jesus had said:	c And Peter remembered what the master had told him:
c "Before a rooster crows twice	b "Before the rooster crows	d "Before the rooster crows tonight,
d you will disown me three times!"	c you will disown me three times."	e you will disown me three times."
e And he broke down	d And he went outside	62 a And he went outside
f and started to cry.	e and wept bitterly.	b and wept bitterly.

14:68e Some mss add *and a rooster crowed* (A C D K X Δ Θ Π Ψ^c *f*¹ *f*¹³ 28 33 *al*); Mark 14:72a seems to require it. Other mss omit (ℵ B L W Ψ* *pc*).

K64.2: Peter Swears and a Rooster Crows

† John 18:15–18 ◊ Mark 14:66–68

[15]Simon Peter and another disciple continued to trail along behind Jesus. This other disciple, somehow known to the high priest, went in with Jesus to the high priest's court. [16]Peter was standing outside the door; so this other disciple, the one acquainted with the high priest, went up, had a word with the woman who kept the door, and got Peter in.

[17]The woman who kept watch at the door says to Peter, "You're not one of this man's disciples too, are you?"

"No, I'm not," he replies.

[18]Meanwhile, since it was cold, the slaves and police had made a charcoal fire and were standing around it, trying to keep warm. Peter was standing there too, warming himself.

† John 18:25–27 ◊ Mark 14:69–72

[25]Meanwhile, Simon Peter was still standing outside, keeping warm. The others there said to him, "You're not one of his disciples too, are you?"

He denied it. "No, I'm not," he said.

[26]One of the high priest's slaves, a relative of the one whose ear Peter had cut off, says, "I saw you in the garden with him, didn't I?"

[27]Once again Peter denied it. At that moment a rooster crowed.

K65: Trial Before Pilate

Mark 15:1–15	**Matt 27:1–2, 11–26**	**Luke 23:1–16, 18–25**
15 1 a And right away, at daybreak, b the ranking priests, after consulting with the elders and scholars and the whole Council, c bound Jesus d and led him away e and turned him over to Pilate.	**27** 1 a When morning came, b all the ranking priests and elders of the people plotted against Jesus c to put him to death. 2 a And they bound him b and led him away c and turned him over to Pilate the governor.	**23** 1 a At this point the whole assembly arose b and took him before Pilate.
2 a And Pilate questioned him: b "You are 'the King of the Judeans'?" c And in response he says to him, d "If you say so." 3 And the ranking priests started a long list of accusations against him.	11 a Jesus stood before the governor, b and the governor questioned him: c "You are 'the King of the Judeans'?" d Jesus said, e "If you say so." 12 a And while he was being accused by the ranking priests and elders,	3 **a** Pilate questioned him, **b** "You are the 'King of the Judeans'?" **c** In response he said to him, **d** "If you say so." 2 a They introduced their accusations b by saying, c "We have found this man to be a corrupting influence on our people, d opposing the payment of taxes to the Roman emperor e and claiming that he himself is an anointed king." *cf. Luke 23:9b*
4 a Again Pilate tried questioning him: b "Don't you have some answer to give? c You see what a long list of charges they bring against you!" 5 a But Jesus still did not respond, b so Pilate was baffled.	b he said absolutely nothing. 13 a Then Pilate says to him, b "Don't you have something to say c to the long list of charges they bring against you?" 14 a But he did not respond to him, b not to a single charge, c so the governor was baffled.	
		4 a And Pilate said to the ranking priests and the crowds, b "In my judgment there is no case against this man." 5 a But they persisted, b saying, c "He foments unrest among the people by going around everywhere teaching in Judea, d and as far away as Galilee and everywhere between." 6 a When Pilate heard this, b he asked whether the man were a Galilean. 7 a And once he confirmed that he was from Herod's jurisdiction, b he sent him on to Herod, c who happened to be in Jerusalem at the time.

15:1b *Council* or *Sanhedrin*: the highest Jewish governing body, composed of ranking priests, elders, and scribes (scholars).

K65: Trial Before Pilate

† **John 18:28–19:16** ◊ Mark 15:1–5

[28]They then take Jesus from Caiaphas' place to the governor's residence. By now it was early morning. They didn't actually go into the governor's residence; otherwise they would become unclean, and unable to eat the Passover meal. [29]Then Pilate came out and says to them, "What charge are you bringing against this man?"

[30]"If he hadn't committed a crime," they retorted, "we wouldn't have turned him over to you."

[31]"Deal with him yourselves," Pilate said to them. "Judge him by your own Law."

"But it's illegal for us to execute anyone," the Judeans said to him.

([32]They said this so that Jesus' prediction of how he would die would come true.)

[33]Then Pilate went back into his residence. He summoned Jesus and asked him, "*You* are 'the King of the Judeans'?"

[34]"Is this what you think," Jesus answered, "or what other people have told you about me?"

[35]"Am I a Judean?!" countered Pilate. "It's your own people and the ranking priests who have turned you over to me. What have you done?"

[36]To this Jesus responded, "Mine is not a secular government. If my government were secular my companions would fight to keep me from being turned over to the Judeans. But as it is, my government does not belong to the secular domain."

[37]"So you are a king!" said Pilate.

"You're the one who says I'm a king," responded Jesus. "This is what I was born for, and this is why I came into the world:

to bear witness to the truth. Everyone who belongs to the truth can hear my voice."

[38]"What is the truth?" says Pilate.

When he had said this, he again went out to the Judeans. "In my judgment there is no case against him," he says. [39]"But it's your privilege at Passover to have me free one prisoner for you. So, do you want me to free 'the King of the Judeans' for you?"

[40]At this they shouted out again, "Not him, but Barabbas!"

(Barabbas was a rebel.)

19 [1]Only then did Pilate have Jesus taken away and beaten.

[2]And the soldiers wove a crown out of thorns and put it on his head; they also dressed him up in a purple robe. [3]They began marching up to him: "Greetings, 'King of the Judeans,'" they would say, as they slapped him in the face.

[4]Pilate went outside once more. "See here," he says, "I'm bringing him out to make it clear to you that in my judgment there is no case against him."

[5]Now Jesus came outside, still wearing the crown of thorns and the purple robe.

⟨Pilate⟩ says to them, "See for yourselves: here's the man." [6]When the ranking priests and the police saw him, they screamed, "Crucify him! Crucify him!"

"Deal with him yourselves," Pilate tells them. "You crucify him. I have told you already: I don't find him guilty of any crime."

[7]"We have our Law," the Judeans answered, "and our Law says that he ought to die, because he has made himself out to be God's son."

[8]When Pilate heard their statement he was even more afraid. [9]He went back into his residence.

"Where are you from?" he asks Jesus. But Jesus didn't answer him.

[10]"You won't speak to me?" says Pilate. "Don't you understand? I have the power to free you; and I have the power to crucify you."

[11]"You would have no power of any kind over me," said Jesus, "unless it was given to you from above. That is why the one who turned me in to you has the greater sin."

[12]At this, Pilate began to look for a way to release him. But the Judeans screamed at him, "If you free this man, you're not the emperor's friend! Every self-appointed king is in rebellion against the emperor."

[13]Pilate heard all this, but still he brought Jesus out and sat him on the judge's seat in the place called Stone Pavement (*Gabbatha* in Hebrew). [14]It was now the day of preparation for Passover, about twelve noon. He says to the Judeans, "Look, here's your king."

[15]But they only screamed, "Get him out of here! Crucify him!"

"Am I to supposed to crucify your king?" asks Pilate.

The ranking priests answered him, "The emperor's our king—we have no other!"

[16]And so, in the end ⟨Pilate⟩ turned him over to them, to be crucified.

Mark	Matt	Luke
		23 8 a Now Herod was delighted to see Jesus.
		b In fact, he had been eager to see him for quite some time,
		c since he had heard so much about him,
		d and was hoping to see him perform some sign.
		9 a So ⟨Herod⟩ plied him with questions;
		b but ⟨Jesus⟩ would not answer him at all.
		10 a All this time the ranking priests and the scholars were standing around,
		b hurling accusation after accusation against him.
		11 a Herod and his soldiers treated him with contempt
		b and made fun of him;
		c they put a magnificent robe around him,
		d then sent him back to Pilate.
		12 a That very day Herod and Pilate became fast friends,
		b even though beforehand they had been constantly at odds.
		13 Pilate then called together the ranking priests, the rulers, and the people,
		14 a and addressed them:
		b "You brought me this man
		c as one who has been corrupting the people.
		d Now look,
		e after interrogating him in your presence,
		f I have found in this man no grounds at all for your charges against him.
		15 a Nor has Herod,
		b since he sent him back to us.
		c Indeed, he has done nothing to deserve death.
		16 a So I will teach him a lesson
		b and set him free."
15 6 a At each festival it was the custom for him to set one prisoner free for them,	**27** 15 a At each festival it was the custom for the governor to set one prisoner free for the crowd,	
b whichever one they requested.	b whichever one they wanted.	
7 a And one called Barabbas was being held with the insurgents	16 They were then holding a notorious prisoner named Jesus Barabbas.	
b who had committed murder during the uprising.		
8 a And when the crowd arrived,		
b they began to demand that he do		
c what he usually did for them.		

† **John 18:39** ◊ Mark15:6

³⁹"But it's your privilege at Passover to have me free one prisoner for you. So, do you want me to free 'the King of the Judeans' for you?"

✫ **GNaz 9** ◊ Mark 15:7

In the so-called Gospel of the Hebrews the name of the man who was to be condemned for sedition and murder is interpreted as "son of their teacher."

Jerome, *Comm. in Mattheum* 4

Table 10

Summaries and Transitions

The author of the Gospel of Mark has provided narrative summaries and transitions in linking together pericopes, collections, and complexes to form a connected narrative. These summaries and transitions, insofar as scholars have been able to identify them, end before the passion narrative begins.

1. 1:39	8. 6:6b
2. 1:32–34	9. 6:30
3. 2:13	10. 6:53–56
4. 3:7–12	11. 7:1
5. 4:1	12. 9:14
6. 5:1	13. 9:30
7. 5:21	14. 10:1

Mark	Matt	Luke
15 9a And in response Pilate said to them,	**27**17a When the crowd had gathered,	
	b Pilate said to them,	
	c "Do you want me to set Jesus Barabbas free for you	
b "Do you want me to set 'the King of the Judeans' free for you?"	d or Jesus who is known as 'the Anointed'?"	
10 After all, he realized that the ranking priests had turned him over out of envy.	18 After all, he knew that they had turned him in out of envy.	
	19a While he was sitting on the judgment seat,	
	b his wife sent a message to him:	
	c "Don't have anything to do with that innocent man,	
	d because I have agonized a great deal today in a dream on account of him."	
11 But the ranking priests incited the crowd	20a The ranking priests and the elders induced the crowds	**23**18a But they all cried out in unison,
		b "Do away with this man,
		c and set Barabbas free."
b to get Barabbas set free for them instead.	b to ask for Barabbas	
		19a (This man had been thrown into prison for murder
		b and for an act of sedition carried out in the city.)
		20a But Pilate, who wanted to set Jesus free,
	c but to execute Jesus.	
	21a In response ⟨to their request⟩ the governor said to them,	
	b "Which of the two do you want me to set free for you?"	
	c They said,	
	d "Barabbas!"	
12a But in response ⟨to their request⟩ Pilate would again say to them,	22a Pilate says to them,	b addressed them again,
b "What do you want me to do with the fellow you call 'the King of the Judeans'?"	b "What should I do with Jesus known as 'the Anointed'?"	*cf. Luke 23:20a*
13a And they in turn shouted,	c Everyone responded,	21a but they shouted out,
b "Crucify him!"	d "Have him crucified!"	b "Crucify, crucify him!"
14a Pilate kept saying to them,	23a But he said,	22a For the third time he said to them,
b "Why? What has he done wrong?"	b "Why? What has he done wrong?"	b "Why? What has he done wrong?
		c In my judgment, there is no capital case against him.
		d So, I will teach him a lesson
		e and set him free."
c But they shouted all the louder,	c But they would shout all the louder,	23a But they kept up the pressure,
d "Crucify him!"	d "Have him crucified!"	b demanding with loud cries that he be crucified.
		c And their cries prevailed.

† **John 18:40** ◊ Mark 15:11

⁴⁰At this they shouted out again, "Not him, but Barabbas!"

(Barabbas was a rebel.)

Table 11

Weights and Measures

Measures of Length in the New Testament

Greek	SV	U.S. Measures
pēchus	minute	ca. 1.5 feet
orguia	fathom	ca. 72.44 inches
stadion	the equivalent in miles	ca. 606 feet = .1148 of a mile
milion	mile	ca. 4,879 feet
hodos hemeras	day's journey	ca. 20–25 miles
hodos sabbatou	sabbath day's journey	6 stadia or ca. 3,636 feet

Measures of Capacity in the New Testament

Greek	SV	Equivalence	U.S. Measures
batos	unit	bath (Hebrew)	6.073 gallons
koros	measure	kōr (Hebrew)	60.738 gallons
saton	measure	ṣe'āh (Hebrew)	6.959 dry quarts
metrētēs	measure		8–10 gallons
choinix	quart		0.98 dry quart
modios	bushel	modius (Latin)	7.68 dry quarts
xestēs	jug	sextarius (Latin)	0.96 dry pint = 1.12 fluid pints

Weights in the New Testament

Greek	SV	Equivalence	U.S. Avoirdupois
talenton	talent	talent (Hebrew)	75.558 pounds
mna	pound	mina (Hebrew)	20.148 ounces
litra	pound	libra (Latin)	0.719 pound = 11.504 ounces

U.S. Dry Measures

Bushel	4 pecks
peck	8 quarts
quart	2 pints
pint	.5 quart

Adapted from: *The New Oxford Annotated Bible* (New York: Oxford University Press, 1977), pp. 1546–47 and O. R. Sellers, "Weights and Measures," *Interpreter's Dictionary of the Bible,* ed. G. A. Buttrick, et al. (Nashville: Abingdon Press, 1962), pp. 828–39.

Mark	Matt	Luke

	27 24 a Now when Pilate could see that he was getting nowhere,	
	b but rather that a riot was starting,	
	c he took water	
	d and washed his hands in full view of the crowd,	
	e and said,	
	f "Don't blame me for this fellow's blood.	
	g Now it's your business!"	
	25 a In response all the people said,	
	b "So, smear his blood upon us and upon our children."	
15 15 a And because Pilate was always looking to satisfy the crowd,		23 24 So Pilate ruled that their demand should be carried out.
b he set Barabbas free for them,	26 a Then he set Barabbas free for them,	25 a He set free the man they had asked for,
		b who had been thrown into prison for sedition and murder;
c had Jesus flogged,	b but had Jesus flogged,	
d and then turned him over to be crucified.	c and then turned him over to be crucified.	c but Jesus he turned over to them to do with as they pleased.

K66.1: Soldiers Make Fun of Jesus

Mark 15:16–20	Matt 27:27–31	Luke
15 16 a And the soldiers led him away to the courtyard	27 27 a Then the governor's soldiers took Jesus	
b of the governor's residence,	b into the governor's residence	
c and they called the whole company together.	c and surrounded him with the whole company.	
	28 a They stripped him	
17 a And they dressed him in purple	b and dressed him in a crimson cloak,	
b and crowned him with a garland woven of thorns.	29 a and they wove a crown out of thorns	
	b and put it on his head.	
	c They placed a staff in his right hand,	
	d and bowing down before him,	
	e they made fun of him,	
	f saying, "Greetings, 'King of the Jews'!"	
18 a And they began to salute him:		
b "Greetings,'King of the Judeans'!"		
19 a And they kept striking him on the head with a staff,	30 b they took a staff	
	c and hit him on the head.	
b and spitting on him;	a And spitting on him,	
c and they would get down on their knees	*cf. Matt 27:29d*	
d and bow down to him.		
20 a And when they had made fun of him,	31 a And when they had made fun of him,	
b they stripped off the purple	b they stripped off the cloak	
c and put his own clothes back on him.	c and put his own clothes back on him	
d And they lead him out to crucify him.	d and led him out to crucify him.	

K66.1: Soldiers Make Fun of Jesus

† **John 19:1–3** ◊ Mark 15:16–20

¹Only then did Pilate have Jesus taken away and beaten.

²And soldiers wove a crown out of thorns and put it on his head; they also dressed him up in a purple robe. ³They began marching up to him: "Greetings, 'King of the Judean,'" they would say, as they slapped him in the face.

† **GPet 2:3–3:4** ◊ Mark 15:16–20

³And Herod replied, "Brother Pilate, even if no one had asked for him, we would have buried him, since the sabbath is drawing near. For it is written in the Law, 'The sun must not set upon one who has been executed.'" And he turned him over to the people on the day before the Unleavened Bread, their feast. 3 ¹They took the Lord and kept pushing him along as they ran; and they would say, "Let's drag the son of God along, since we have him in our power." ²And they threw a purple robe around him and sat him upon the judgment seat and said, "Judge justly, king of Israel." ³And one of them brought a crown of thorns and set it on the head of the Lord. ⁴And others standing about would spit in his eyes, and others slapped his face, while others poked him with a rod. Some kept flogging him as they said, "Let's pay proper respect to the son of God."

K66.2: Simon of Cyrene Carries the Cross

Mark 15:21	Matt 27:32	Luke 23:26–32
	2732a As they were going out,	2326a And as they were marching him away,
1521a And they conscript someone named Simon of Cyrene,	b they came across a Cyrenian named Simon.	b they grabbed someone named Simon, a Cyrenian,
b who was coming in from the country,		c as he was coming in from the country.
c the father of Alexander and Rufus,		
d to carry his cross.	c This fellow they conscripted to carry his cross.	d They loaded the cross on him,
		e to carry behind Jesus.
		27a A huge crowd of the people followed him,
		b including women who mourned
		c and lamented him.
		28a Jesus turned to them
		b and said,
		c "Daughters of Jerusalem, do not weep for me.
		d Weep instead for yourselves and for your children.
		29a Look, the time is coming
		b when they will say,
		c 'Congratulations to those who are sterile,
		d to the wombs that never gave birth,
		e to the breasts that never nursed an infant!'
		30a Then they will beg the mountains:
		b 'Fall on us';
		c and the hills:
		d 'Bury us.'
		31a If they behave this way
		b when the wood is green,
		c what will happen
		d when it dries out?"
		32a Two others, who were criminals,
		b were also taken away with him
		c to be executed.

K66.3: Soldiers Crucify Jesus

Mark 15:22–32	Matt 27:33–44	Luke 23:33–43
1522a And they bring him to the place Golgotha	2733a And when they reached the place known as Golgotha	2333a And when they reached the place
b (which means "Place of the Skull").	b (which means "Place of the Skull"),	b called "The Skull,"
23a And they tried to give him wine mixed with myrrh,	34a they gave him a drink of wine mixed with something bitter,	
	b once he tasted it,	
b but he didn't take it.	c he didn't want to drink it.	
24a And they crucify him,	35a After crucifying him,	c they crucified him there along with the criminals,
		d one on his right and the other on his left.

K66.3: Soldiers Crucify Jesus

† John 19:17–24

[17]. . . who carried the cross for himself, out to the place called Skull (known in Hebrew as *Golgotha*). [18]There they crucified him, and with him two others—one on each side, with Jesus in the middle.

[19]Pilate also had a notice written and posted it on the cross; it read: "Jesus the Nazarene, the King of the Judeans." [20]Many of the Judeans saw the notice, since Jesus was crucified near the city and it was written in Hebrew, Latin, and Greek. [21]The ranking Judean priests tried protesting to Pilate: "Don't write, 'The King of the Judeans,' but instead, 'This man said, "I am King of the Judeans."'"

[22]Pilate answered them, "What I have written stays written."

[23]When the soldiers had crucified Jesus, they took his clothes and divided them into four shares, one share for each soldier. But his shirt was woven continuously without seam. [24]So they said to each other, "Let's not tear it, but toss to see who gets it."

(This happened so that the scripture would come true that says, "They divided my garments among them, and for my clothes they cast lots.")

Ps 68:22 (LXX; MT 69:22) ◊ Mark 15:23

[22]They gave me something bitter for food, and to quench my thirst they gave me vinegar to drink.

Mark	Matt	Luke
1524 b and they divide up his garments,	**27**35 b they divided up his garments	**23**34 a They divided up his garments
c casting lots to see who would get what.	c by casting lots.	b after they cast lots.
	36 a And they sat down there	35 a And the people stood around
	b and kept guard over him.	b looking on.
25 It was 9 o'clock in the morning when they crucified him.		
26 a And the inscription, which identified his crime,	37 a And over his head they put an inscription	38 **a** There was also this sign over him,
b read,	b that identified his crime:	
c 'The King of the Judeans.'	c 'This is Jesus the King of the Judeans.'	**b** 'This is the King of the Judeans.'
27 a And with him they crucify two rebels,	38 a Then they crucified two rebels with him,	
b one on his right	b one on his right	
c and one on his left.	c and one on his left.	
29 a Those passing by kept taunting him,	39 a Those passing by kept taunting him,	
b wagging their heads,	b wagging their heads,	
c and saying,	c and saying,	
d "Ha! You who would destroy the temple	40 a "You who would destroy the temple	
e and rebuild it in three days,	b and rebuild it in three days,	
30 a save yourself	c save yourself;	
	d if you're God's son,	
b and come down from the cross!"	e come down from the cross!"	
31 a Likewise the ranking priests had made fun of him to one another,	41 a Likewise the ranking priests made fun of him	35 c And the rulers kept sneering at him,
b along with the scholars;	b along with the scholars and elders;	
c they would say,	c they would say,	d saying,
d "He saved others,	42 a "He saved others,	e "He saved others;
e but he can't save himself!	b but he can't even save himself!	f he should save himself
		g if he is God's Anointed,
		h the Chosen One!"
32 a 'The Anointed,' 'the King of Israel,'	c He's the King of Israel;	
b should come down from the cross here and now,	d he should come down from the cross here and now	
c so that we can see and trust for ourselves!"	e and we'll trust him.	
	43 a He trusted God,	
	b so God should rescue him now	
	c if he holds him dear.	
	d After all, he said,	
	e 'I'm God's son.'"	
		36 a The soldiers also made fun of him;
		b they would come up
		c and offer him sour wine,
		37 a and they would say,
		b "If you're the King of the Judeans,
		c why not save yourself?"
		38 a There was also this sign over him:
		b 'This is the King of the Judeans.'

15:28 V. 28 is lacking in: ℵ A B C D X Ψ *pc*; insert, *And the scripture was fulfilled which says, "He was counted with the criminals"* (cf. Luke 22:37, Isa 53:12): K L P (Δ) Θ Π *f¹ f¹³* 28 33 *pm.*

† GPet 4:1–5

[1]And they brought two criminals and crucified the Lord between them. But he himself remained silent, as if in no pain. [2]And when they set up the cross, they put an inscription on it, "This is the king of Israel." [3]And they piled his clothing in front of him; then they divided it among themselves, and gambled for it. [4]But one of those criminals reproached them and said, "We're suffering for the evil that we've done, but this fellow, who has become a savior of humanity, what wrong has he done to you?" [5]And they got angry at him and ordered that his legs not be broken so he would die in agony.

☆ John 2:19 ◊ Mark 15:29–30

[19]Jesus replied, "Destroy this temple and I'll resurrect it in three days."

☆ Thom 71 ◊ Mark 15:29–30

Jesus said, "I will destroy [this] house, and no one will be able to build it [. . .]."

Ps 21:19 (LXX; MT 22:18) ◊ Mark 15:24

[19]They divided my clothes among themselves,
and they cast lots for my garment.

Ps 21:8 (LXX; MT 22:8) ◊ Mark 15:29

[9]Everyone who saw me mocked me,
they spoke with their lips,
they wagged their heads.

Mark	Matt	Luke
1532d Even those being crucified along with him would abuse him.	2744 In the same way the rebels who were crucified with him would abuse him.	2339a One of the criminals hanging there
		b kept cursing and taunting him:
		c "Aren't you supposed to be the Anointed?
		d Save yourself and us!"
		40a But the other ⟨criminal⟩ rebuked the first:
		b "Don't you even fear God,
		c since you are under the same sentence?
		41a We are getting justice,
		b since we are getting what we deserve.
		c But this man has done nothing improper."
		42a And he implored,
		b "Jesus, remember me
		c when you come into your domain."
		43a And ⟨Jesus⟩ said to him,
		b "I swear to you,
		c today you'll be with me in paradise."

K66.4: Jesus Breathes His Last

Mark 15:33–41	Matt 27:45–56	Luke 23:44–49
1533a And when noon came,	2745a Beginning at noon	2344a It was already about noon,
b darkness blanketed the whole land	b darkness blanketed the entire land	b and darkness blanketed the whole land
c until mid-afternoon.	c until mid-afternoon.	c until mid-afternoon,
		45a during an eclipse of the sun.
34a And at 3 o'clock in the afternoon Jesus shouted at the top of his voice,	46a And about 3 o'clock in the afternoon Jesus shouted out at the top of his voice,	
b "*Eloi, Eloi, lema sabachthani*"	b "*Eli, Eli, lema sabachthani*"	
c (which means "My God, my God, why did you abandon me?").	c (which means, "My God, my God, why did you abandon me?")	
35a And when some of those standing nearby heard,	47a When some of those standing there heard,	
b they would say,	b they would say,	
c "Listen, he's calling Elijah!"	c "This fellow's calling Elijah!"	
36a And someone ran	48a And immediately one of them ran	
b and filled a sponge with sour wine,	b and took a sponge filled with sour wine	
c stuck it on a pole,	c and stuck it on a pole	
d and offered him a drink,	d and offered him a drink.	
e saying,	49a But the rest would say,	
f "Let's see if Elijah comes to rescue him!"	b "Wait, let's see if Elijah comes to rescue him."	

15:34b This cry is a transliteration of Hebrew/Aramaic: אֱלָהִי אֱלָהִי לְמָה שְׁבַקְתַּנִי.

K66.4: Jesus Breathes His Last

† John 19:25–37

25. . . Jesus' mother, his mother's sister, Mary the wife of Clopas, and Mary of Magdala stood by his cross. 26When Jesus saw his mother, and standing nearby the disciple he loved most, he says to his mother, "Woman, here is your son." 27Then he says to the disciple, "Here is your mother." And from that moment the disciple considered her part of his own family.

28Then, since Jesus knew the course of events had come to an end, so the scripture would come true, he says, "I'm thirsty."

29A bowl of sour wine was sitting there, and so they filled a sponge with wine, stuck it on some hyssop, and held it to his mouth. 30When Jesus had taken some wine, he said, "It's all over."

His head sank, and he breathed his last.

31Since it was the day of preparation, the Judeans asked Pilate to have the legs of the three broken and the bodies taken away. Otherwise their bodies would remain on the cross during the sabbath day. (That sabbath was a high holy day.)

32The soldiers came and broke the legs of the first man, and then of the other who had been crucified with him. 33But when they came to Jesus, they could see that he was already dead, so they didn't break his legs. 34Instead, one of the soldiers jabbed

him in the side with his spear, and right away blood and water came pouring out. (35The one who observed this has given this testimony and his testimony is true. He knows he is telling the truth, so you too will believe.) 36This happened so the scripture that says, "No bone of his shall be broken," would come true, 37as well as another scripture that says, "They shall look at the one they have pierced."

† GPet 5:1–6

1It was midday and darkness covered the whole of Judea. They were confused and anxious for fear the sun had set since he was still alive. ⟨For⟩ it is written that, "The sun must not set upon one who has been executed." 2And one of them said, "Give him vinegar mixed with something bitter to drink." And they mixed it and gave it to him to drink. 3And they fulfilled all things and brought to completion the sins on their head. 4Now many went about with lamps, and, thinking that it was night, they laid down. 5And the Lord cried out, saying, "My power, ⟨my⟩ power, you have abandoned me." When he said this, he was taken up. 6And at that moment, the veil of the Jerusalem temple was torn in two.

† Luke 23:36 ◊ Mark 15:36

36The soldiers also made fun of him: they would come up and offer him sour wine, . . .

Amos 8:9 (LXX) ◊ Mark 15:33

9"And it will happen on that day," says the Lord God, "that the sun will set at midday, and light will fail on the earth during the day."

Ps 22:1a (MT) ◊ Mark 15:34

My God, My God, why did you abandon me?

Ps 68:22 ◊ Mark 15:36

22They gave me something bitter for food, and to quench my thirst they gave me vinegar to drink.

Mark	Matt	Luke
15 37 a But Jesus let out a great shout	**27** 50 a Jesus again shouted at the top of his voice	**23** 46 a Then Jesus cried out at the top of his voice,
		b "Father, into your hands I entrust my spirit!"
		c Having said this
b and breathed his last.	b and stopped breathing.	d he breathed his last.
38 And the curtain of the temple was torn in two from top to bottom!	51 a And suddenly the curtain of the temple was torn in two from top to bottom,	45 b The curtain of the temple was torn down the middle.
	b and the earth quaked,	
	c rocks were split apart,	
	52 a and the tombs were opened	
	b and many bodies of sleeping saints came back to life.	
	53 a And they came out of the tombs after his resurrection	
	b and went into the holy city,	
	c where they appeared to many.	
39 a When the Roman officer standing opposite him saw that he had died like this,	54 a The Roman officer and those keeping watch over Jesus with him witnessed the sign	47 a Now when the Roman officer saw what happened,
	b and what had happened,	
	c and were terrified,	
		b he praised God
b he said,	d and said,	c and said,
c "This man really was God's son!"	e "This man really was God's son."	d "This man was completely innocent!"
		48 a And when the throng of people
		b that had gathered for this spectacle
		c observed what had transpired,
		d they all returned home beating their chests.
		49 a And all his acquaintances
40 a Now some women	55 a Many women were there	b and the women who had followed him from Galilee
b were observing this	b observing this	d watching these events.
c from a distance,	c from a distance	c were standing off at a distance
d among whom were Mary of Magdala,	56 a among whom were Mary of Magdala,	
e and Mary the mother of James the younger and Joses,	b and Mary the mother of James and Joseph,	
f and Salome.	c and the mother of the sons of Zebedee.	
41 a ⟨These women⟩ had regularly followed	55 d —those who had followed Jesus from Galilee to assist him,	*cf. Luke 23:49b*
b and assisted him when he was in Galilee,		
c along with many other women who had come up to Jerusalem in his company.		

15:40b *Mary of Magdala* rather than *Magdalene* to avoid misunderstanding the second term as a proper name and to indicate that *Magdala* is a place name.

GNaz 10a, 10b ◊ Mark 15:38

In the gospel that is written in the Hebrew alphabet we read not that the curtain of the temple was torn, but that the lintel of the temple, which was huge, collapsed.

Jerome, *Epistulae* 120.8

In the gospel that we have often mentioned we read that the lintel of the temple, which was immense, was fractured and broken up.

Jerome, *Comm. in Mattheum* 4

☆ Luke 8:1–3 ◊ Mark 15:40–41

¹And it so happened soon afterward that he traveled through towns and villages, preaching and announcing the good news of God's imperial rule. The twelve were with him, ²and also some women whom he had cured of evil spirits and diseases: Mary, the one from Magdala, from whom seven demons had taken their leave, ³and Joanna, the wife of Chuza, Herod's steward, and Susanna, and many others, who provided for them out of their resources.

☆ Luke 23:55 ◊ Mark 15:40–41

⁵⁵The women who had come with him from Galilee tagged along. They kept an eye on the tomb, to see how his body was laid to rest.

Ps 37:12 (LXX) ◊ Mark 15:40–41

¹²My friends and neighbors come close and stand opposite;
  my next of kin stand far away.

K67: Joseph of Arimathea Buries Jesus

Mark 15:42–47	Matt 27:57–61	Luke 23:50–56
15 42 a And when it had already grown dark,	27 57 a When it had grown dark,	
b since it was preparation day		23 54 a It was the day of preparation,
c (the day before the sabbath),		
		b and the sabbath was about to begin.
43 a Joseph of Arimathea,	b a rich man from Arimathea,	50 a There was a man named Joseph,
	c by the name of Joseph,	
b a respected Council member,		b a Council member,
		c a decent and upright man,
		51 a who had not endorsed their decision or gone along with their action.
		b He was from the town of Arimathea in Judea,
c who himself was anticipating God's imperial rule,		c and he lived in anticipation of God's imperial rule.
	d who himself was a follower of Jesus,	
d appeared on the scene,	e appeared on the scene,	
e and dared to go to Pilate	58 a and went to Pilate	52 a This man went to Pilate
f to request the body of Jesus.	b and requested the body of Jesus.	b and requested the body of Jesus.
44 a And Pilate was surprised that he had died so soon.		
b He summoned the Roman officer		
c and asked him whether he had been dead for long.		
45 a And when he had been briefed by the Roman officer,		
b he granted the body to Joseph.	c Then Pilate ordered it to be turned over ⟨to him⟩.	
46 a And he bought a shroud	59 a And taking the body,	53 a Then he took it down
b and took him down	b Joseph wrapped it in a clean linen shroud	
c and wrapped him in the shroud,		b and wrapped it in a shroud,
d and placed him in a tomb	60 a and put it in his new tomb,	c and laid him in a tomb
e that had been hewn out of rock,	b which had been cut in the rock.	d cut from the rock,
		e where no one had ever been buried.
f and rolled a stone up against the opening of the tomb.	c He rolled a huge stone in the opening of the tomb	
	d and went away.	
		55 a The women
		b who had come with him from Galilee
		c tagged along.
		d They kept an eye on the tomb,
47 a And Mary of Magdala and Mary the mother of Joses noted	61 a But Mary of Magdala	e to see how his body was laid to rest.
b where he had been laid to rest.	b and the other Mary stayed there,	
	c sitting opposite the tomb.	
		56 a Then they went home
		b to prepare spices and ointments.
		c On the sabbath day they rested in accordance with the commandment.

K67: Joseph of Arimathea Buries Jesus

† John 19:38–42

[38]After all this, Joseph of Arimathea—a disciple of Jesus, but only secretly because he was afraid of the Judeans—asked Pilate's permission to take Jesus' body down. Pilate agreed, so ⟨Joseph⟩ came and took his body down. [39]Nicodemus—the one who had first gone to him at night—came too, bringing about a mixture of myrrh and aloes weighing about seventy-five pounds. [40]So they took Jesus' body, and wound it up in strips of burial cloth along with the spices, as the Judeans customarily do to bury their dead. [41]Now there was a garden in the place where he had been crucified, and a new tomb in the garden where no one had yet been laid to rest. [42]Since this tomb was handy and because of the Jewish day of preparation, it was here that they laid Jesus.

† GPet 2:1–3a

[1]Joseph stood there, the friend of Pilate and the Lord, and when he realized that they were about to crucify him, he went to Pilate and asked for the body of the Lord for burial. [2]And Pilate sent to Herod and asked for his body. [3]And Herod replied, "Brother Pilate, even if no one had asked for him, we would have buried him, since the sabbath is drawing near. For it is written in the Law, 'The sun must not set upon one who has been executed.'" And he turned him over to the people on the day before the Unleavened Bread, their feast.

† GPet 6:1–4

[1]And then they pulled the nails from the Lord's hands and set him on the ground. And the whole earth shook and there was great fear. [2]Then the sun came out and it was found to be the ninth hour. [3]Now the Judeans rejoiced and gave his body to Joseph so that he might bury it, since ⟨Joseph⟩ had observed how much good he had done. [4]⟨Joseph⟩ took the Lord, washed ⟨his body⟩ and wound a linen ⟨shroud⟩ around him, and brought him to his own tomb, called "Joseph's Garden."

☆ Deut 21:22–23 (LXX)

[22]If anyone commits a crime the penalty for which is death and he is put to death and you hang him on a tree, [23]his body is not to be on the tree overnight. Rather, you are to bury him that same day. For anyone hanging on a tree is accursed by God. You must not defile the land which the Lord your God gives for an inheritance.

Josh 10:18 (LXX) ◊ Mark 15:46

[18]Joshua said, "Roll stones against the mouth of the cave and appoint men to guard them."

Josh 10:27 (LXX) ◊ Mark 15:46

[27]And when the sun had set, Joshua gave the orders and they took them down from the trees and threw them into the cave where they had run hiding. And they rolled stones up against the cave ⟨which remain⟩ until this day.

K68: The Two Marys at the Tomb

Mark 16:1–8	**Matt 28:1–8**	**Luke 24:1–12**
16 1 a And when the sabbath day was over,	**28** 1 a After the sabbath day,	
	b at first light on Sunday,	*cf. Luke 24:1a*
b Mary of Magdala	c Mary of Magdala	*cf. Luke 24:10a*
c and Mary the mother of James	d and the other Mary	*cf. Luke 24:10c*
d and Salome		
e bought spices		**24** 1 c bringing the spices they had prepared.
f so they could go		
g and embalm him.		
	e came to inspect the tomb.	a On Sunday, at daybreak
2 a And very early on Sunday		b they made their way to the tomb,
b they got to the tomb just as the sun was coming up.	*cf. Matt 28:1b*	
3 a And they had been asking themselves,		
b "Who will help us roll the stone away from the opening of the tomb?"		
4 a Then they look up		
b and discover that the stone has been rolled away!		2 They found the stone rolled away from the tomb,
c (For in fact the stone was very large.)		
	2 a And just then there was a strong earthquake.	
	b You see, a messenger of the Lord had come down from the sky,	
	c arrived ⟨at the tomb⟩,	
	d rolled away the stone,	
	e and was sitting on it.	
5 a And when they went into the tomb,		3 a but when they went inside
		b they did not find the body of the Lord Jesus.
b they saw a young man sitting on the right,		
	3 a The messenger gave off a dazzling light	
c wearing a white robe,	b and wore clothes as white as snow.	
		4 a And so,
		b while they were still uncertain about what to do,
		c two figures in dazzling clothing suddenly appeared
		d and stood beside them.
d and they grew apprehensive.	4 a Now those who kept watch were paralyzed with fear	5 a Out of sheer fright
	b and looked like corpses themselves.	
		b they prostrated themselves on the ground;
6 a He says to them,	5 a In response the messenger said to the women,	c the men said to them,
b "Don't be alarmed!	b "Don't be frightened!	

K68: The Two Marys at the Tomb

† John 20:1–18

[1]On Sunday, by the half-light of the early morning, Mary of Magdala comes to the tomb—and sees that the stone has been moved away. [2]So she runs and comes to Simon Peter and the other disciple—the one that Jesus loved most—and tells them, "They've taken the Master from the tomb, and we don't know where they've put him."

[3]So Peter and the other disciple went out, and they make their way to the tomb. [4]The two of them were running along together, but the other disciple ran faster than Peter and was the first to reach the tomb. [5]Stooping down, he could see the strips of burial cloth lying there; but he didn't go in. [6]Then Simon Peter comes along behind him, and went in. He too sees the strips of burial cloth there, [7]and also the cloth they had used to cover his head, lying not with the strips of burial cloth but rolled up by itself. [8]Then the other disciple, who had been the first to reach the tomb, came in. He saw all this, and he believed. [9]But since neither of them yet understood the prophecy that he was destined to rise from the dead, [10]these disciples went back home.

[11]Mary, however, stood crying outside, and in her tears she stooped to look into the tomb, [12]and she sees two heavenly messengers in white seated where Jesus' body had lain, one at the head and the other at the feet.

[13]"Woman, why are you crying?" they ask her.

"They've taken my Master away," she tells them, "and I don't know where they've put him."

[14]No sooner had she said this than she turned around and sees Jesus standing there—but she didn't know that it was Jesus.

[15]"Woman," Jesus says to her, "why are you crying? Who is it you're looking for?"

She could only suppose that it was the gardener, and so she says to him, "Please, mister, if you've moved him, tell me where you have put him, so I can take him away."

[16]"Mary," says Jesus. She turns around and exclaims in Hebrew, "Rabbi!" (which means "Teacher"). [17]"Don't touch me," Jesus tells her, "because I have not yet gone back to the Father. But go to my brothers and tell them this: 'I'm going back to my Father and your Father—to my God and your God.'"

[18]Mary of Magdala goes and reports to the disciples, "I have seen the Master," and relates everything he had told her.

† GPet 9:1–13:3

[1]Early, at first light on the sabbath, a crowd came from Jerusalem and the surrounding countryside to see the sealed tomb. [2]But during the night before the Lord's day dawned, while the soldiers were on guard, two by two during each watch, a loud noise came from the sky, [3]and they saw the skies open up and two men come down from there in a burst of light and approach the tomb. [4]The stone that had been pushed against the entrance began to roll by itself and moved away to one side; then the tomb opened up and both young men went inside.

10 [1]Now when these soldiers saw this, they roused the centurion from his sleep, along with the elders. (Remember, they were also there keeping watch.) [2]While they were explaining what they had seen, again they see three men leaving the tomb, two supporting the third, and a cross was following them. [3]The heads of the two reached up to the sky, while the head of the third, whom they led by the hand, reached beyond the skies. [4]And they heard a voice from the skies that said, "Have you preached to those who sleep?" [5]And an answer was heard from the cross: "Yes!"

11 [1]These men then consulted with one another about going and reporting these things to Pilate. [2]While they were still thinking about it, again the skies appeared to open and some sort of human being came down and entered the tomb. [3]When those in the centurion's company saw this, they rushed out into the night to Pilate, having left the tomb which they were supposed to be guarding. And as they were recounting everything they had seen, they became deeply disturbed and cried, "He really was God's son!" [4]Pilate responded by saying, "I am clean of the blood of the son of God; this was all your doing." [5]Then they all crowded around ⟨Pilate⟩ and began to beg and urge him to order the centurion and his soldiers to tell no one what they saw. [6]"You see," they said, "it is better for us to be guilty of the greatest sin before God than to fall into the hands of the Judean people and be stoned." [7]Pilate then ordered the centurion and the soldiers to say nothing.

12 [1]Early on the Lord's day, Mary of Magdala, a disciple of the Lord, was fearful on account of the Judeans and, since they were enflamed with rage, she did not perform at the tomb of the Lord what women are accustomed to do for loved ones who die. [2]Nevertheless, she took her friends with her and went to the tomb where he had been laid. [3]And they were afraid that the Judeans might see them and were saying, "Although on the day he was crucified we could not weep and beat our breasts, we should now perform these rites at his tomb. [4]But who will roll away the stone for us, the one placed at the entrance of the tomb, so that we may enter and sit beside him and do what ought to be done?" [5](Remember, it was a huge stone.) "We fear that someone might see us. And if we are unable ⟨to roll the stone away⟩ we should, at least, place at the entrance the memorial we brought for him, and we should weep and beat our breasts until we go home."

13 [1]And they went and found the tomb open. They went up to it, stooped down, and saw a young man sitting there ⟨in⟩ the middle of the tomb; he was handsome and wore a splendid robe. He said to them, [2]"Why have you come? Who are you looking for? Surely not the one who was crucified? He is risen and gone. If you don't believe it, stoop down and take a look at the place where he lay, for he is not there. You see, he is risen and has gone back to the place he was sent from." [3]Then the women fled in fear.

Mark	Matt	Luke

Mark

16 6c You are looking for Jesus the
Nazarene

d who was crucified.
e He was raised,
f he is not here!

g Look at the spot where they put him!
7a But go
b and tell his disciples, including
'Rock,'

c 'He is going ahead of you to Galilee!

d There you will see him,
e just as he told you.'"
8a And once they got outside,
b they ran away from the tomb,

c because great fear and excitement
got the better of them.
d And they didn't breathe a word of it
to anyone: talk about terrified . . .

Matt

28 5c I know you are looking for Jesus

d who was crucified.
6b You see, he was raised,
a He is not here!
c just as he said.

d Come,
e look at the spot where he was lying.
7a And run,
b tell his disciples

c that he has been raised from the
dead.
d Don't forget, he is going ahead of
you to Galilee.
e There you will see him.
f Now I have told you so."

8a And they hurried away from the
tomb,
b full of apprehension and an
overpowering joy,

c and ran to tell his disciples.

Luke

24 5d "Why are you looking for the living
among the dead?

6b —he was raised.
a He is not here
c Remember what he told you
d while he was still in Galilee:
7a 'The son of Adam is destined to be
turned over to heathen,
b to be crucified,
c and on the third day to rise.'"
8 Then they recalled what he had said.

9a And returning from the tomb,

b they related everything to the eleven
c and to everybody else.
10a The group included Mary of
·   Magdala
b and Joanna
c and Mary the mother of James,
d and the rest of the women
companions.
e They related their story to the
apostles;
11a but their story seemed nonsense to
them,
b so they refused to believe the
women.
12a But Peter got up
b and ran to the tomb.
c He peeped in
d and saw only the linen wrappings,
e and returned home,
f marveling at what had happened.

16:8d The Gospel of Mark ends with v. 8 in: א
B 304 syrˢ cop (in part), arm (in part) geo (in
part) Clement Origen Eusebius Jerome *pc*. The
so-called shorter ending of Mark, *They related
briefly to Peter and his companions everything
they had been told. Later Jesus himself, through*

*them, dispatched the sacred and imperishable
gospel of eternal salvation from east to west,* is
found in itᵏ; L Ψ *pc* combine the shorter and the
longer endings.
Luke 16:12 Only D it omit v. 12. However, v.
12 may have been created on the basis of John
20:3–10.

MAP OF JERUSALEM

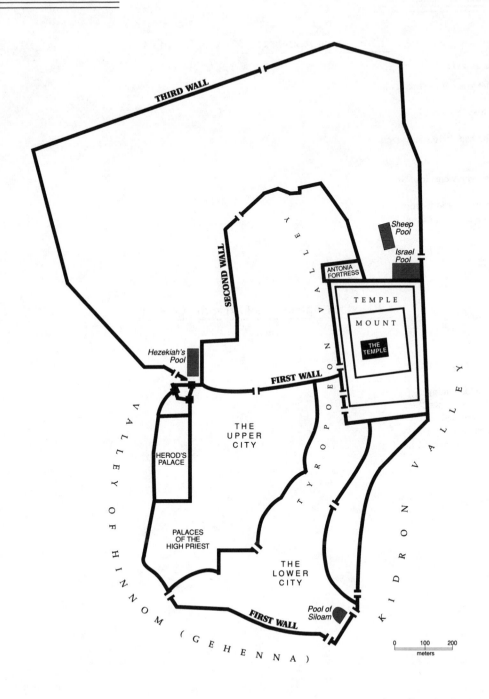

THIRD WALL

SECOND WALL

Hezekiah's Pool

FIRST WALL

Sheep Pool

Israel Pool

ANTONIA FORTRESS

TEMPLE MOUNT

THE TEMPLE

V A L L E Y

T Y R O P O E O N   V A L L E Y

HEROD'S PALACE

THE UPPER CITY

PALACES OF THE HIGH PRIEST

THE LOWER CITY

Pool of Siloam

FIRST WALL

V A L L E Y   O F   H I N N O M   (G E H E N N A)

K I D R O N   V A L L E Y

0   100   200
meters

THE LONGER ENDING

K69: Jesus Appears to Mary of Magdala

Mark 16:9–11	**Matt**	**Luke**
16 9a [[Now after he arose at daybreak on Sunday,		
b he appeared first to Mary of Magdala,		
c from whom he had driven out seven demons.		
10a She went		
b and told those who were close to him,		
c who were mourning and weeping.		
11a But when those folks heard that he was alive		
b and had been seen by her,		
c they did not believe it.		

K70: Jesus Appears to Two in the Country

Mark 16:12–13	**Matt**	**Luke**
16 12a A little later		
b he appeared to two of them in a different guise		
c as they were walking along,		
d on their way to the country.		
13a And these two returned		
b and told the others.		
c They did not believe them either.		

16:11c See the textual note on Mark 16:20.
16:13c See the textual note on Mark 16:20.

K69: Jesus Appears to Mary of Magdala

K70: Jesus Appears to Two in the Country

† Luke 24:13–27 ◊ Mark 16:9–13

¹³Now, that same day two of them were traveling to a village named Emmaus, about seven miles from Jerusalem. ¹⁴They were engaged in conversation about all that had taken place. ¹⁵And it so happened, during the course of their discussion, that Jesus himself approached and began to walk along with them. ¹⁶But they couldn't recognize him.

¹⁷He said to them, "What were you discussing as you walked along?"

Then they paused, looking depressed. ¹⁸One of them, named Cleopas, said to him in reply, "Are you the only visitor to Jerusalem who doesn't know what's happened there these last few days?"

¹⁹And he said to them, "What are you talking about?"

And they said to him, "About Jesus of Nazareth, who was a prophet powerful in word and deed in the eyes of God and all the people, ²⁰and about how our ranking priests and rulers turned him in to be sentenced to death, and crucified him. ²¹We were hoping that he would be the one who was going to ransom Israel. And as this weren't enough, it's been three days now since all this happened. ²²Meanwhile, some women from our group gave us quite a shock. They were at the tomb early this morning ²³and didn't find his body. They came back claiming even to have seen a vision of heavenly messengers, who said that he was alive. ²⁴Some of those with us went to the tomb and found it exactly as the women had described; but nobody saw him."

²⁵And he said to them, "You people are so slow-witted, so reluctant to trust everything the prophets have said! ²⁶Wasn't the Anointed One destined to undergo these things and enter into his glory?" ²⁷Then, starting with Moses and all the prophets, he interpreted for them every passage of scripture that referred to himself.

☆ Luke 8:1–3 ◊ Mark 16:9

¹And it so happened soon afterward that he traveled through towns and villages, preaching and announcing the good news of God's imperial rule. The twelve were with him, ²and also some women whom he had cured of evil spirits and diseases: Mary, the one from Magdala, from whom seven demons had taken their leave, ³and Joanna, the wife of Chuza, Herod's steward, and Susanna, and many others, who provided for them out of their resources.

† Luke 24:28–33 ◊ Mark 16:12–13

²⁸They had gotten close to the village to which they were going, and he acted as if he were going on. ²⁹But they entreated him, saying, "Stay with us; it's almost evening, the day is practically over." So he went in to stay with them.

³⁰And so, as soon as he took his place at table with them, he took a loaf, and gave a blessing, broke it, and started passing it out to them. ³¹Then their eyes were opened and they recognized him; and he vanished from their sight. ³²They said to each other, "Weren't our hearts burning within us while he was talking to us on the road, and explaining the scriptures to us?" ³³And they got up at once and returned to Jerusalem.

† John 20:11–18 ◊ Mark 16:9–11

¹¹Mary, however, stood crying outside, and in her tears she stooped to look into the tomb, ¹²and she sees two heavenly messengers in white seated where Jesus' body had lain, one at the head and the other at the feet.

¹³"Woman, why are you crying?" they ask her.

"They've taken my Master away," she tells them, "and I don't know where they've put him."

¹⁴No sooner had she said this than she turned around and sees Jesus standing there—but she didn't know that it was Jesus.

¹⁵"Woman," Jesus says to her, "why are you crying? Who is it you're looking for?"

She could only suppose that it was the gardener, and so she says to him, "Please, mister, if you've moved him, tell me where you've put him, so I can take him away."

¹⁶"Mary," says Jesus.

She turns around and exclaims in Hebrew, "Rabbi!" (which means "Teacher").

¹⁷"Don't touch me," Jesus tells her, "because I have not yet gone back to the Father. But go to my brothers and tell them this: 'I am going back to my Father and your Father—to my God and your God.'"

¹⁸Mary of Magdala goes and reports to the disciples, "I have seen the Master" and relates everything he had told her.

K71: Jesus Appears to the Eleven

Mark 16:14–18	**Matt**	**Luke**

1614a Later

    b he appeared to the eleven as they were reclining ⟨at a meal⟩.

    c He reproached them for their lack of trust

    d and obstinacy,

    e because they did not believe those who had seen him after he had been raised.

  15a And he said to them:

    b "Go out into the whole world

    c and announce the good news to every creature.

  16a Whoever trusts

    b and is baptized

    c will be saved.

    d The one who lacks trust

    e will be condemned.

  17a These are the signs that will accompany those who have trust:

    b they will drive out demons in my name;

    c they will speak in new tongues;

  18a they will pick up snakes with their hands;

    b and even if they swallow poison,

    c it certainly won't harm them;

    d they will lay their hands on those who are sick,

    e and they will get well."

K72: Jesus Is Taken up into the Sky

Mark 16:19–20	**Matt**	**Luke**

1619a The Lord Jesus,

    b after he said these things,

    c was taken up into the sky

    d and sat down at the right hand of God.

  20a Those ⟨to whom he had spoken⟩ went out

    b and made their announcement everywhere,

    c and the Lord worked with them

    d and certified what they said by means of accompanying signs.]]

16:18e See the textual note on Mark 16:20.

16:19a Greek (κύριος): The reference here is clearly christological.

16:20d The following witnesses contain the longer ending of the Gospel of Mark (16:9–20): A C D K (W) X Δ Θ Π *f*¹³ 28 33 *pm.*

K71: Jesus Appears to the Eleven

† Matt 28:16–20 ◊ Mark 16:14–16

[16]The eleven disciples went to to the mountain in Galilee where Jesus had told them to go. [17]And when they saw him, they gave him homage; but some were dubious.

[18]And Jesus approached them and spoke these words: "All authority has been given to me in heaven and on earth. [19]You are to go and make followers of all peoples. You are to baptize them in the name of the Father and the son and the holy spirit. [20]Teach them to observe everything I've commanded. I'll be with you day in and day out, as you'll see, so long as this world continues its course."

† John 20:19–23 ◊ Mark 16:14

[19]That Sunday evening, the disciples had locked the doors for fear of the Judeans, but Jesus came and stood in front of them and he greets them: "Peace."

[20]Then he showed them his hands and his side. The disciples were delighted to see the Master. [21]Jesus greets them again: "Peace," he says. "Just as the Father sent me, so now I'm sending you."

[22]And at this he breathed over them and says, "Here's some holy spirit. Take it. [23]If you forgive anyone their sins, they are forgiven; if you do not release them from their sins, they are not released."

Freer Logion ◊ Mark 16:14

And they would apologize and say, "This lawless and faithless age is under the control of Satan, who by using filthy spirits doesn't allow the real power of God to be appreciated. So," they would say to the Anointed, "let your justice become evident now."

And the Anointed would respond to them, "The time when Satan is in power has run its course, but other terrible things are just around the corner. I was put to death for the sake of those who sinned, so they might return to the truth and stop sinning, and thus inherit the spiritual and indestructible righteous glory that is in heaven." (Manuscript W contains the longer ending to Mark—vv. 9–20—expanded by the Freer logion given here.)

K72: Jesus Is Taken up into the Sky

† Luke 24:50–53 ◊ Mark 16:19

[50]Then he led them out as far as Bethany, and lifting up his hands he blessed them. [51]And while he was blessing them, it so happened that he parted from them and was carried up into the sky. [52]And they paid homage to him and returned to Jerusalem full of joy, [53]and were continually in the temple blessing God.

TABLE OF PARALLELS

	Mark	Matt	Luke	John	Thom	Other	OT
K1: Title	1:1		†1:1–4	✩15:27	Title	†Acts 1:1–5 InThom Title, 1:1	
K2: A Voice in the Wilderness	1:1–8	3:1–12, **11:10**	3:1–20, 7:27	△1:15 †1:19–28 1:31–32		✩Acts 1:5 ✩Acts 11:16 Acts 13:24–25 △Acts 19:1–7 GEbi 1a GEbi 3 Justin, *Dial.* 88.7	2 Kgs 1:8 Isa 40:3 Mal 3:1a
K3: John Baptizes Jesus	1:9–11 ✩9:7	3:13–17 ✩17:5	3:21–22 ✩9:34–35	†1:29–34 1:32 12:28–30		GEbi 4 GNaz 2 GHeb 3	Ps 2:7 Isa 42:1 Isa 44:2
K4: Jesus Is Put to the Test	1:12–13	4:1–11	4:1–13	✩1:51		✩InJas 1:9–11	
K5: Jesus Proclaims the Good News	1:14–15 6:17	4:12–17 14:3 3:1–2	3:19–20, 23a †4:14–15 †4:16–30	✩1:43 ✩4:1–3 ✩4:43			
K6: Simon and Andrew Become Followers **K7**: James and John Become Followers	1:16–18 1:19–20	4:18–20 4:21–22	†5:1–3 †5:4–11	†1:35–42 †1:43–51 †21:1–14		GEbi 2 GPet 14:1–3	
K8: Jesus Gives Orders to an Unclean Spirit	1:21–28 ✩11:18	7:28–29 ✩13:54 ✩22:33	4:31–37	✩6:69 ✩7:15 ✩7:46		✩InThom 19:2–5	
K9: Jesus Heals Simon's Mother-in-law	1:29–31 ✩13:3	8:14–15	4:38–39				
K10: Sick and Demon-Possessed Come to Jesus	1:32–34 ✩3:7–12 ✩6:55	8:16–17 ✩12:16	4:40–41				
K11: Jesus Steals Away	1:35–39	4:23–25	4:42–44				
K12: Jesus Cures a Leper	1:40–45	8:1–4	5:12–16			GEger 2:1–4	
K13: Jesus Cures a Paralytic	2:1–12	9:1–8	5:17–26	✩5:8–9a			
K14.1: Jesus Teaches by the Sea	2:13						
K14.2: Levi Becomes a Follower	2:14	9:9	5:27–28			GEbi 2	

† a primary parallel lacking substantial verbal or narrative agreement, yet which serves the same narrative function

‡ a parallel exhibiting some agreement, but which serves a different narrative function

• a doublet: the repetition in the same gospel of a narrative segment or sayings cluster

△ a similar narrative incident that appears in a different context

✩ a parallel with a comparable theme or motif

	Mark	Matt	Luke	John	Thom	Other	OT
K14.3: Jesus Dines with Toll Collectors	**2:15–17**	**9:10–13**	**5:29–32** ☆15:1–2			POxy1224 5:1–2 Justin, *Apol.* 1.15.8	
K15: Why Don't Your Disciples Fast?	**2:18–22**	**9:14–17** 11:18–19	**5:33–39** ☆7:33–34 ☆18:12	☆3:29–30	**47:1–5** ☆27:1–2 ☆104:1–3	☆Did 8:1	
K16: What Is Permitted on the Sabbath?	**2:23–28**	**12:1–8**	**6:1–5**		☆27:1–2	☆InThom 2:1–7	Exod 20:10 Lev 24:5–9 Deut 5:14 Deut 23:25 1Sam 21:2–7
K17: Jesus Heals on the Sabbath Day	**3:1–6**	**12:9–14**	**6:6–11** ☆14:1–6	☆11:53		☆InThom 2:1–7 GNaz 4	
K18: Jesus Withdraws to the Sea	**3:7–12** ☆6:56	**12:15–21** ☆4:25 ☆14:36	**6:17–19** ☆4:41				
K19: Jesus Forms the Twelve	**3:13–19** 6:7	**10:1–4**	**6:12–16** 9:1–2	1:42 ☆6:70–71		△Acts 1:12–14 △GEbi 2	
K20.1: Jesus' Relatives Come to Get Him	**3:20–21**	**12:22–23**	**11:14**	☆7:20 ☆8:48 ☆8:52 ☆10:20			
K20.2: Scholars Accuse Jesus	**3:22–30**	**12:24–32** 9:32–34	**11:15–23** **12:10**		35:1–2 △21:1–10	☆Did 11:7	
K20.3: True Relatives	**3:31–35**	**12:46–50**	**8:19–21**	☆15:14	99:1–3	GEbi 5 2 Clem 9:11	
K21.1: Jesus Teaches from a Boat	**4:1**	**13:1–2**	**8:4a–b** ☆5:1–3				
K21.2: Parable of the Sower, Seeds, Soils	**4:2–9**	**13:3–9**	**8:4c–8**		**9:1–5**	☆InThom 12:1–4 ☆SecJas 8:1–4	
K21.3: Secret of God's Imperial Rule	**4:10–12**	**13:10–17**	**8:9–10**	9:39	☆62:1	SecJas 6:5–6	Isa 6:9–10 Jer 5:21 Ezek 12:2
K21.4: Understanding the Sower	**4:13–20**	**13:18–23**	**8:11–15**			☆SecJas 6:16–18	
K21.5: Placing the Lamp	**4:21–23**	**5:15,** **10:26**	**8:16–17** **11:33, 12:2**		**33:2–3** 5:2, 6:5–6	**POxy654 5:2–3, 6:5**	
K21.6: The Same Standard	**4:24–25**	**7:2** **13:12** **25:29**	**8:18** **19:26** 6:37–38		**41:1–2**	1 Clem 13:2 PolPhil 2:3	
K21.7: Seed and Harvest	**4:26–29**	☆13:24–30			△21:1–10	☆SecJas 8:1–4	Joel 4:13

	Mark	Matt	Luke	John	Thom	Other	OT
K21.8: Parable of the Mustard Seed	**4:30–32**	**13:31–33**	**13:18–21**		**20:1–4**		Dan 4:20–22 Dan 4:12
K21.9: Only in Parables	**4:33–34**	**13:34–35**					
K22: Jesus Rebukes the Wind and the Sea	**4:35–41**	**8:18, 23–27**	**8:22–25**				Jonah 1:4, 5b
K23: The Demon of Gerasene	**5:1–20** ✩1:24 ✩1:34 ✩3:11	**8:28–34**	**8:26–39**	✩2:4			
K24.1: Jairus Begs for Jesus' Help	**5:21–24a**	**9:18–19c**	**8:40–42b**				
K24.2: Jesus Cures a Woman with a Vaginal Flow	**5:24b–34** ✩6:56 ✩10:52	**9:20–22** ✩14:36	**8:42c–48** ✩6:19 ✩7:50 ✩17:19 ✩18:42				
K24.3: Jesus Cures Jairus' Daughter	**5:35–43**	**9:23–26**	**8:49–55**				
K25: No Respect at Home	**6:1–6**	**13:53–58** ✩9:35	‡4:16–30	4:44 ✩7:15	31:1–2	POxy1 31:1–2	
K26: Jesus Sends the Twelve Out in Pairs	**6:7–13** ✩3:14–15	**10:1, 5–15**	**9:1–6** △10:1–16 ✩22:35			✩Did 11:4–6	
K27: King Herod Beheads John	**6:14–29** ✩8:28	**14:1–12** ✩16:14	**9:7–9** ✩9:19 3:19–20	✩1:19–21			Esth 5:3 Esth 7:2
K28: The Twelve Report	**6:30–34**	**14:13–14** 9:36	**9:10–11** 10:17				Num 27:15–17 1 Kgs 22:17
K29: Loaves and Fish for Five Thousand	**6:35–44** •8:1–9 ✩14:22	**14:15–21** •15:32–39 ✩26:26	**9:12–17** ✩22:19 ✩24:30	6:1–15		✩Acts 27:35	2 Kgs 4:42–44
K30: Jesus and His Disciples Depart	**6:45–46** 8:10	**14:22–23** 15:39		6:15			
K31: Jesus Walks on the Sea	**6:47–52** ✩8:17	**14:24–33**	✩24:37	6:16–21			
K32: Many Sick Are Brought to Jesus	**6:53–56** ✩5:27–33	**14:34–36** ✩9:20–21	✩8:43–47	△6:22–24			
K33: Unwashed Hands	**7:1–13**	**15:1–9**				△POxy840 2:1–9 GEger 3:1–6	Exod 20:12 Exod 21:16 Lev 20:9 Deut 5:16 Isa 29:13

	Mark	Matt	Luke	John	Thom	Other	OT
K34: What Comes Out Defiles	**7:14–23**	**15:10–20**			14:1–5		
K35: Greek Woman's Daughter	**7:24–30**	**15:21–28**					
K36: Jesus Cures a Deaf-Mute	**7:31–37**	**15:29–31**					
K37: Loaves and Fish for Four Thousand	**8:1–10** • 6:35–45 14:22	**15:32–39** 9:36 • 14:15–22 ☆26:26	△9:12–17 ☆22:19 ☆24:30	△6:1–15		☆Acts 27:35	2 Kgs 4:42–44
K38: The Pharisees Demand a Sign	**8:10–13**	**15:39b, 16:1–4** △12:38–42	☆11:16 △11:29–32 ☆12:54–56	☆6:30			
K39: Bread and Leaven	**8:14–21**	**16:5–12**	12:1	☆6:32–35			Jer 5:21 Ezek 12:2
K40: Jesus Cures a Blind Man	**8:22–26**			△9:1–7			
K41: Who Do People Say I Am?	**8:27–30**	**16:13–20**	**9:18–21**	☆1:49 ☆6:68–69 ☆11:27	△13:1–8		
K42: Son of Adam Must Suffer	**8:31–33** 9:30–32 10:32–34	**16:21–23** 17:22–23 20:17–19	**9:22** 9:43b–45 18:31–34			△SecJas 4:10–5:6	
K43: Saving One's Life	**8:34–9:1**	**16:24–28** 10:33 10:38–39	**9:23–27** 12:9 14:27 17:33	12:25	55:1–2 101:1–3		
K44.1: Jesus Transformed	**9:2–8** ☆1:10–11	**17:1–8** ☆3:16–17	**9:28–36** ☆3:22				Ps 2:7 Isa 42:1
K44.2: Elijah Must Come	**9:9–13**	**17:9–13**			☆51:1–2		1 Kgs 19:1–3, 9–10 Mal 4:5–6
K45: The Man with the Mute Spirit	**9:14–29**	**17:14–20**	**9:37–43**				
K46: Son of Adam Will Die and Rise	**9:30–32** 8:31–33 10:32–34	**17:22–23** 16:21–23 20:17–19	**9:43–45** 9:18–22 18:31–34	7:1			
K47: Number One Is Last	**9:33–37** • 10:13–16 • 10:41–45	**18:1–5** • 10:40 △20:24–28 ☆23:11–12	**9:46–48** • 10:16 18:15–17 △22:24–30	☆12:44–45 13:20	☆12:1–2		

	Mark	Matt	Luke	John	Thom	Other	OT
K48: For and Against	**9:38–41**	**12:30, 10:42**	**9:49–50** • 11:23			POxy1224 6:1–2	
K49: Hand, Foot and Eye	**9:42–50**	**18:6–10, 5:13** **5:29–30**	**17:1–2, 14:34–35**				Lev 2:13 Isa 66:24
K50: Jesus Goes to Judea	**10:1**	**19:1–2**					
K51.1: Is Divorce Permitted?	**10:2–9**	**19:3–8** **5:31**				☆1 Cor 7:10–11	Gen 1:27 Gen 2:24 Deut 24:1–4
K51.2: The Disciples Question Jesus	**10:10–12**	**19:9** **5:32**	**16:18**				
K52: Let the Children Come	**10:13–16**	**19:13–15** ☆18:3	**18:15–17**	☆3:3–5	☆22:1–7		
K53.1: The Man with Money	**10:17–22**	**19:16–22**	**18:18–23**			GNaz 6	Exod 20:12–16 Deut 5:16–20
K53.2: The Needle's Eye	**10:23–31**	**19:23–30** **20:16**	**18:24–30** **13:30**		**4:2–3** ☆81:1–2	POxy654 4:2–3 ☆SecJas 4:1–3	
K54: Son of Adam Will Die and Rise	**10:32–34** **8:31–33** **9:30–32**	**20:17–19** **16:21–23** **17:22–23**	**18:31–34** **9:18–22** **9:43b–45**			SecMk 1:1–13	
K55.1: Jesus' Cup and Baptism	**10:35–40**	**20:20–23**	☆12:49–53				
K55.2: Number One Is Slave	**10:41–45** • 9:33–37	**20:24–28** △18:1–4 △23:11	**22:24–27** △9:46–50				
K56: Jesus Cures Blind Bartimaeus	**10:46–52**	**20:29–34** ‡9:27–31	**18:35–43**	△9:1–7		SecMk 2:1–2	
K57: Jesus Enters Jerusalem	**11:1–11**	**21:1–11**	**19:28–40**	12:12–19			Ps 117:26 Zech 9:9
K58.1: The Fig Tree Without Figs	**11:12–14**	**21:18–22**	‡13:6–9			☆InThom 3:1–4 ☆InThom 4:1–4	
K58.2: The Temple as Hideout	**11:15–19** ☆12:12 ☆14:1–2	**21:12–17**	**19:45–48**	‡2:13–22			Isa 56:7 Jer 7:11
K59.1: Mountains Into the Sea	**11:20–25** ☆9:28–29	**21:20–22** ☆6:14 • 17:19–20 ☆18:19	‡13:6–9 17:5–6	☆14:13–14 ☆15:7 ☆16:23	• 48 • 106:1–2		
K59.2: Who Gave You the Authority?	**11:27–33**	**21:23–27**	**20:1–8**	☆2:18		☆POxy840 2:1–9	

	Mark	Matt	Luke	John	Thom	Other	OT
K59.3: Parable of the Leased Vineyard	12:1–12	21:33–46	20:9–19		65–66		Ps 118:22–23 Isa 5:1–2
K59.4: Is It Permissible to Pay the Tax?	12:13–17	22:15–22	20:19–26	3:2	100:1–4	‡GEger 3:1–6	
K59.5: Whose Wife Will She Be?	12:18–27	22:23–33	20:27–40				Gen 38:8 Exod 3:6 Deut 25:5–6
K59.6: Which Commandment?	12:28–34	22:34–40	‡10:25–29 ☆20:39 ☆20:40		☆25:1–2 ☆82:1–2	‡Did 1:2 △Barn 19:5 ☆InThom 15:7	Lev 19:18 Deut 6:4–5 1 Sam 15:22
K59.7: Whose Son Is the Anointed?	12:35–37	22:41–46	20:41–44	☆7:40–44		☆1 Cor 15:20–28	Ps 109:1
K59.8: Scholars in Long Robes	12:38–40	23:6	20:45–47 ‡11:37–44 ☆14:7–11				
K59.9: The Widow's Pittance	12:41–44		21:1–4				
K60.1: What Wonderful Buildings!	13:1–2	24:1–2	21:5–6 ☆19:44b				
K60.2: Signs of the Final Agonies	13:3–13 ☆13:21–23	24:3–9, 13–14 10:17–22 10:35–36 ☆24:23–26	21:5–19 ☆17:23 12:11–12	☆14:26 ☆15:18–21 ☆16:2			2 Chr 15:6 Dan 2:28
K60.3: Days of Distress	13:14–23	24:15–28	21:20–24 17:31		☆79:1–3 113:1–4		Deut 13:2–4 Dan 9:27 Dan 11:31 Dan 12:1 Dan 12:11 1 Macc 1:54
K60.4: Son of Adam Comes on Clouds	13:24–31 ☆9:1 ☆14:62	24:29–35 ☆16:28	21:25–33 ☆9:27			☆1 Thess 4:15–16 ☆Rev 1:7 4 Ezra 13:1–3 1 Enoch 46:1–5	Deut 30:3–4 Isa 13:10 Isa 34:4 Dan 7:13–14 Zech 2:10
K60.5: No One Knows the Day or Hour	13:32–37	24:36, 42 ☆25:13 †24:37–51	△12:35–40 †21:34–36			☆Did 16:1	
K61.1: Some Way to Kill Jesus	14:1–2 ☆11:18 ☆12:12	26:1–5 ☆21:45	22:1–2 ☆19:47–48 ☆20:19	†11:45–53 †11:54 †11:55–57			
K61.2: A Woman Anoints Jesus	14:3–9	26:6–13	†7:36–50	†12:1–8			
K61.3: Priests Promise to Pay Judas	14:10–11	26:14–16	22:3–6				

	Mark	Matt	Luke	John	Thom	Other	OT
K62: Jesus Celebrates Passover	**14:12–26**	**26:17–30**	**22:7–23** †22:39	☆6:48–58 †13:21–30 †18:1		☆1 Cor 11:23–25 GEbi 7 ☆Did 9:1–5 ☆Justin, *Apol.* 1.66.3	Exod 24:8 Ps 40:10 Jer 38:31 Zech 9:11
K63.1: Peter Takes an Oath	**14:27–31**	**26:31–35**	**22:31–34**	☆11:16 †13:36–38 ☆16:32		Fayyum Fragment	Zech 13:7
K63.2: Jesus Prays in Gethsemane	**14:32–42**	**26:36–46**	**22:39–46**	†12:27 †18:1 ☆18:11 †14:31			
K63.3: Judas Turns Jesus In	**14:43–52**	**26:47–56**	**22:47–54**	†18:1–11 †18:20			
K64.1: Trial Before the Council	**14:53–65** ☆13:26	**26:57–68** ☆24:30	**22:54–55, 63–71**	☆2:19 †18:13–14 †18:19–24	☆71	†GPet 3:4 4 Ezra 13:1–3 1 Enoch 46:1–5	Lev 24:16 Ps 109:1 Dan 7:13–14
K64.2: Peter Swears and a Rooster Crows	**14:66–72**	**26:69–75**	**22:56–62**	†18:15–18 †18:25–27			
K65: Trial Before Pilate	**15:1–15**	**27:1–2, 11–26**	**23:1–16, 18–25**	†18:28–19:16 †18:39 †18:40		☆GNaz 9	
K66.1: Soldiers Make Fun of Jesus	**15:16–20**	**27:27–31**		†19:1–3		†GPet 2:3–3:4	
K66.2: Simon of Cyrene Carries the Cross	**15:21**	**27:32**	**23:26–32**				
K66.3: Soldiers Crucify Jesus	**15:22–32**	**27:33–44**	**23:33–43**	☆2:19 †19:17–24	☆71	†GPet 4:1–5	Ps 68:22 Ps 21:8 Ps 21:19
K66.4: Jesus Breathes His Last	**15:33–41**	**27:45–56**	**23:44–49** ☆8:1–3 ☆23:55 †23:36	†19:25–37		GNaz 10a, 10b †GPet 5:1–6	Ps 22:1a Ps 37:12 Ps 68:22 Amos 8:9
K67: Joseph of Arimathea Buries Jesus	**15:42–47**	**27:57–61**	**23:50–56**	†19:38–42		†GPet 2:1–3a †GPet 6:1–4	☆Deut 21:22–23 Josh 10:18 Josh 10:27
K68: The Two Marys at the Tomb	**16:1–8**	**28:1–8**	**24:1–12**	†20:1–18		†GPet 9:1—13:3	
K69: Jesus Appears to Mary of Magdala **K70**: Jesus Appears to Two in the Country	**16:9–11** **16:12–13**		☆8:1–3 †24:13–27 †24:28–33	†20:11–18			
K71: Jesus Appears to the Eleven	**16:14–18**	†28:16–20		†20:19–23		Freer Logion	
K72: Jesus Is Taken up into the Sky	**16:19–20**		†24:50–53				

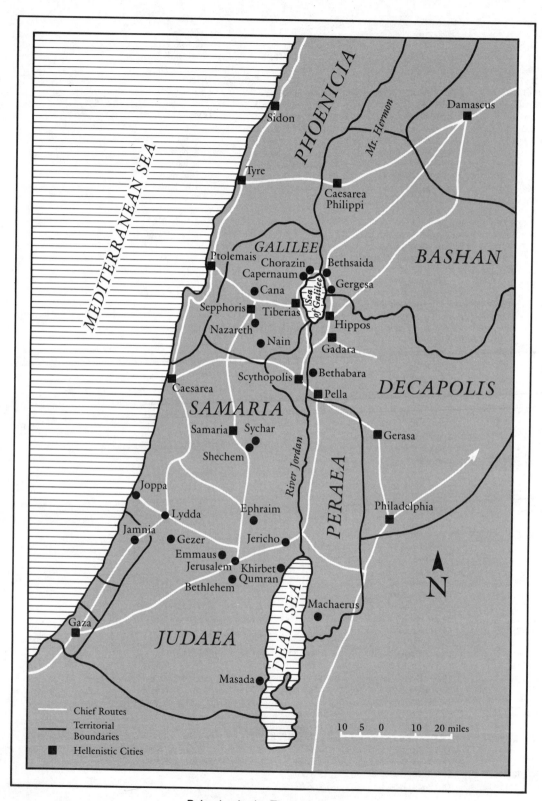

Palestine in the Time of Jesus